Shipwrecks of the Ulster Coast

Schooner 'LILY' in an evening setting, Portstewart, 1931.

Wreck of the *Ulrica*, Copeland Islands, January 1897

Ian Wilson

Shipwrecks of the Ulster Coast

From Carlingford Lough to Inishowen Head.

DESIGNED, PRINTED AND PUBLISHED BY IMPACT PRINTING (OF COLERAINE) LIMITED

1979

2nd EDITION — 1985

3rd EDITION — 1997

4th EDITION — 2000

ISBN 0 948154 99 3

CONTENTS

List of Illustrations

List of Maps

Acknowledgments

Introduction

Bibliography

Index of Ships' Names

LIST OF ILLUSTRATIONS

LIST OF MAPS

or the forbidding cliffs of Rathlin Island.

The sheer number of wrecks prevents treatment of anything like the complete list, but I have tried to include all that involved large vessels, and all that included fatalities. A rough distance limit of two miles has been set for offshore casualties, but in cases of specially interesting vessels, or those with direct Ulster connections, this rule has been waived. Another limit, again broken on occasions, excludes inshore fishing craft and pleasure boats. One famous loss that some may feel should have been included is the Larne – Stranraer ferry *Princess Victoria*, which foundered five or six miles northeast of Mew Island in 1953. However, her story, to be done justice, would need many pages. The definitive account appears in 'The Short Sea Route', by Fraser G. MacHaffie (T. Stephenson and Sons, Prescot, 1975). For sailing vessels, I have tried to keep to net registered tonnage, and for steamers, gross tonnage – respectively, the most common measurements in my sources. A sailing vessel's gross tonnage was usually only a little more than net.

Many people have helped in the compilation of this book, from crew members of the ships to divers descending on the remains, and elsewhere I acknowledge my thanks to all, but I must record a special debt to two people – Tom Clarke, for invaluable assistance with the maps, and Robert Anderson, for constant help with all aspects of this book's subject and preparation.

IAN WILSON

Bangor, Co. Down.

July 1979.

Author's Note to Fourth Edition

It certainly seems a long time since I wrote the above introduction! I simply thought, as I gathered more and more material, that here was a story worth telling. "Cornish Shipwrecks" (in three volumes!) by Clive Carter and Richard Larn was an inspiration. Moreover, walking the clifftops around Pendeen and St. Just in the knowledgable and enthusiastic company of Clive Carter made me feel the coast itself, the inhabitants and history, had to be part of the story. So things develop. No-one was to know how successful the book would be or that demand since would result in fresh editions. But tales of shipwrecks have an irresistible lure. Unlike other disasters, the sea usually offers a chance of escape, through luck, daring or even selfishness. There is often hope. Shipwrecks are laden with metaphors for life!

Maritime archaeology gathers strength all the time. The reader will find I refer to this, and to the continuing flow of new material that is still coming to light, in an addendum to this fourth edition of 'Shipwrecks of the Ulster Coast'.

Ian Wilson,   September 2000

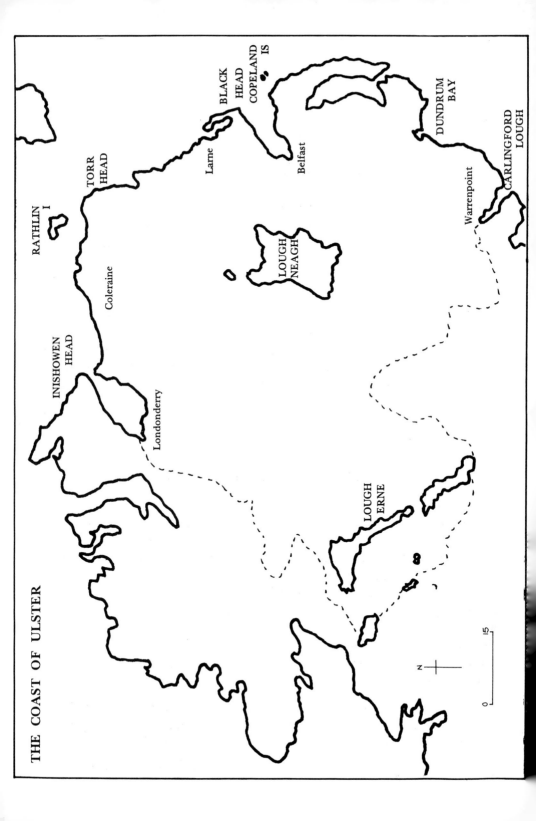

THE COAST OF ULSTER

RATHLIN I

TORR HEAD

BLACK HEAD

COPELAND IS

DUNDRUM BAY

CARLINGFORD LOUGH

Larne

Belfast

Warrenpoint

INISHOWEN HEAD

Coleraine

LOUGH NEAGH

Londonderry

LOUGH ERNE

N

0 15

ACKNOWLEDGEMENTS
(for fourth edition)

The number of people who have helped with information has swelled with the second and third editions, and to all I wish to record my sincere thanks:- Robert Anderson, Edwin Beat, Martin Benn, Jim Blaney, Michael Booth, Colin Breen, Margaret Butler, Dr H.C. Calwell, Tommy Cecil, Francis Cox, David Donnan, Ian Duffin, J.S. Fowler, W. Glass, Captain J.B. Gordon, Jimmy Irvine, Les Jones, Michael McCaughan, Jack McCoy, John McCullough, Bert McGinty, Hugh McGrattan, Margaret McKee, Alex McKillop, Harry McMullan, Tom Martin, Alec Niblock, Emma O'Hanlon, Don Patterson, Dr E.M. Patterson, Dan Rainey, Dr Crosbie Smith, Patric Stevenson, Dr A.T.Q. Stewart, Tom Wilks, Brian Williams, George Williams, W.J. Williams, Tom Wilson.

Also to the custodians of: Naval Historical Branch, Ministry of Defence; Central Record of Shipping Information, World Ship Society; Rescue Records, Royal National Lifeboat Institution.

Front Cover: Wreck of the brig *Lion* of Strangford at the entrance to Strangford Lough, 1857, (from a painting by Les Jones in the collection of Down County Museum, Downpatrick.)

Back Cover: Barque ashore near Annalong, Co. Down, almost certainly the Norwegian *Ascalon*, 1907. Profits from the salvage are said to have enabled the Tedford family to build a fine villa on Millisle Road, Donaghadee! (Author's Collection)

INTRODUCTION

This book is the result of ten years research, which began with a slow realisation that an immense subject lay untouched. Apart from a few newspaper articles and scattered references in books and journals, nothing has ever been set down on the story of wreck and rescue around the Ulster coast, a story on which statistics do not lie. At a conservative estimate, 1200 ships were totally lost on the coast between Carlingford Lough and Inishowen Head in the nineteenth century; for the five years 1877 — 1881 inclusive, eighty-one vessels were wrecked, an astonishing fifty-two of them on the Co. Down coast alone. Just a few of this host of casualties have been widely remembered, such as the *Enterprise* near Carnlough in 1827, the emigrant ship *Wild Deer* off Cloughey, 1883, and the *Connemara* and *Retriever* at Carlingford bar in 1916, but there are innumerable other vivid tales of disaster and salvation, involving nearly every headland, reef or bay around our shores.

I have tried throughout to place the ships in the context of their times. Again, the wider subject of Irish maritime history has been largely neglected over the years, though happily there are definite signs of an upsurge of interest. To observe the shipping scene a century ago would be to see a totally different world. Most obviously, there were simply far more vessels at sea. Harbours now long closed to commercial traffic were scenes of constant activity. At Annalong and Kilkeel, granite from the Mournes was being shipped to pave Liverpool streets, the local schooners hoisting sail under the command of a Gordon, Chambers or McKibbin; a dozen or more coasters of all types of rig would slip out of Strangford Lough on the ebb tide, away from Kircubbin, Castle Espie or Ballydorn, where now weeds grow on the quays; at Ballywalter and Donaghadee apple-bowed Cumberland brigs discharged coal; at Glenarm and Carnlough, limestone or ore was daily toppled into the holds of smacks, schooners or Scottish steam 'puffers'. Out at sea, too, was a constant procession of shipping — smart square-riggers with British manufactured goods for the Colonies, tall-funnelled tramp steamers with Spanish ore for the Clyde, the barques and full-rigged ships of the great Belfast fleets inward with Canadian timber or off to load under the Cardiff coal tips.

Such craft have disappeared from the seas, and the coming of the motor lorry largely killed the trade of the minor ports, but the places themseyes are often little changed. Mostly unspoilt, too, is the Ulster coastlne, the same today as when these ships were passing and attempting to give a wide berth to the sands of Dundrum Bay, the shallow, treacherous Ards Peninsula,

Gerard Boate, writing in the mid-seventeenth century, crystallized the advantages, and crucial disadvantages, of Carlingford Lough as a natural harbour:

'This haven is some three or four miles long, and nigh of the same breadth, being everywhere very deep, so as the biggest ships may come there to anchor; and so inviren'd with high land and mountains on all sides, that the ships do lye defended off all winds; so that this would be one of the best havens of the world, if it were not for the difficulty and danger of the entrance, the mouth being full of rocks, both blind ones and others, betwixt which the passages are very narrow: whereby it cometh that this harbour is very little frequented by any great ships.'

While describing Carlingford Lough as potentially one of the best harbours in the world may be a rather lofty claim, it is the only natural sheltered harbour on the east coast of Ireland, and 200 years later Boate's praises were to be echoed by the Royal Commission on Harbours of Refuge, which, after a careful study, recommended that extensive dredging work be carried out on the bar to facilitate access by vessels experiencing bad weather in the Irish Sea. Almost all the wrecks of the Carlingford Lough area occurred on this surf-pounded bar, enclosed by Cranfield Point to the north and Ballagan Point to the south, for, once it has been safely crossed, ships, as Boate said, lay 'defended off all winds'.

Carlingford Lough, as its derivation, the Danish *Cairlinn's Fiord,* would suggest, is a typical fiord formed by ice action, a steep-sided divide between the Mourne mountains to the north and the County Louth mountains to the south. The mouth is studded with low islands, the sea bed between them, the troublesome bar, being composed mostly of clay and boulders scoured from the mountains and deposited by the melting ice. Most of the shipping using the Lough over the past few centuries has been bound to and from Newry, Warrenpoint and Greenore, notably the former. A canal from Newry to Lough Neagh was completed in 1742 to aid the export of coal to Dublin, the erroneous belief being that there were large workable deposits in mid-Ulster, while the first canal between Newry and the deeper water at the head of the Lough proper was completed in 1756. A new canal was opened in 1850 and closed in 1974 on the transfer of Newry's trade to the expanding modern port of Warrenpoint. Although Newry and Warrenpoint both had cross-channel passenger links in the last century, Greenore, near the Lough entrance on the southern side, developed into the leading passenger terminal, having a service to Holyhead from 1873 to 1926 operated by the steamers of the L.N.W.R. These included the ill-fated *Connemara*, sunk, as we shall see, in a disastrous collision shortly after leaving Greenore one never-to-be-forgotten night in 1916. Rostrevor, a little resort nestling in the warm shelter of the Mournes, received cargoes at its stone quay, while Carlingford town, first raised to prominence by the Normans, is also by-passed by coastal vessels nowadays.

The story of wreck and rescue in Carlingford Lough and its approaches centres around the hazards of the entrance. The first danger vessels nearing the Lough have to face is the Hellyhunter, a rocky shoal lying just over a mile south-east of Cranfield Point, but only a few total losses are recorded here. On 4th June 1878, the brig *Jason* of Workington, a vessel of 83 net tons, was on passage from her home port to Dundalk with railway iron. Despite the bell buoy warning ships, she struck the Hellyhunter and subsequently went to pieces. Her master, Captain Wilson, and his crew of three, however, escaped unscathed. Although casualties on the Hellyhunter itself were rare, two serious accidents nearby three years after the wreck of the *Jason* gave rise to suggestions of replacing the bell buoy by a lightship. The *Eleanor*, an iron paddle steamer on the Holyhead to Greenore route, failed to make the Lough in fog and went ashore about six miles to the north, at Leestone Point, on 27 January 1881. Although her crew and eight passengers were landed safely at Kilkeel, the *Eleanor*, which had been built on the Tyne in 1873 specifically for the new Greenore route, became a total loss, and her replacement, the *Telegraph*, also ran aground in dense fog when entering the Lough on her first crossing! She was freed, but these worrying incidents prompted proposals to place a lightship off the entrance to Carlingford Lough. Commenting on the subject, the *Belfast News Letter* asserted ' . . . the bell on Hellyhunter Rock is comparatively useless in a fog, and the proposed lightship is an absolute necessity for the safety of steamers entering the Lough'. No action was taken, and the fact that vessels generally had little difficulty in entering and leaving the Lough after the dredging of the bar in the 1860s suggests that the existing lights on the Haulbowline Rock and at Greenore were in fact adequate. However, when the situation before then is examined, we find a very different story.

According to legend, as the night wind blew around their cottages, the children of the Cranfield area used to pray, 'God bless mammy and daddy, and send a big ship ashore in the morning.' They must have rendered thanks for pickings wrecks offered on many occasions, for there is a long list of strandings of vessels large and small. Cranfield lighthouse was built in 1803

Chapter One

CARLINGFORD LOUGH
AND THE MOURNE COAST

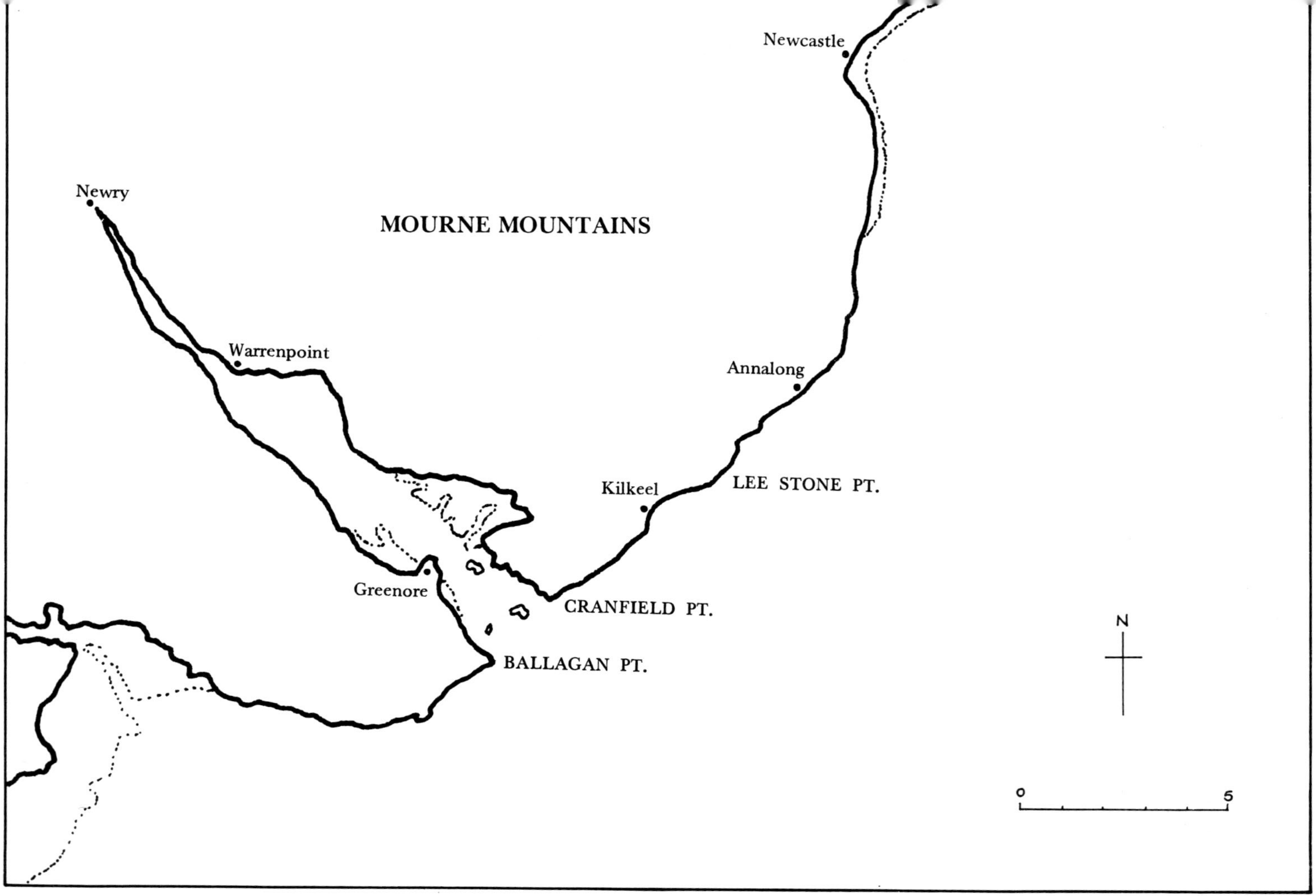

MOURNE MOUNTAINS

Newcastle

Annalong

LEE STONE PT.

Kilkeel

CRANFIELD PT.

BALLAGAN PT.

Greenore

Warrenpoint

Newry

N

5

0

MAP 2

in an attempt to lessen the dangers of the passage into the Lough, but as the granite tower became unsafe it was replaced by Haulbowline light, in the middle of the bar, in 1823. Casualties still occurred almost every year, however, for example the sloop *Barbara and Janette*, which on 18 February 1824, as *Lloyd's List* tersely reported, 'struck on Newry bar and sank, the crew all being drowned'. Until mid-Victorian times accidents like this, occurring daily around the British Isles, seem to have been taken completely for granted, and recorded in that spirit. Another light was erected at Greenore in 1830, but the strandings continued: in 1838 the brig *Mary Stewart* and the schooner *Elizabeth*, in 1841 the schooner *Clytie*, a total wreck on Ballagan Point, in 1842 the brig *Tagus*, with a valuable timber cargo from New Brunswick. On 3 March 1845, the barque *Orissa*, caught in a fierce easterly gale when outward bound from Liverpool to Bombay with general cargo worth £20,000, attempted to enter Carlingford Lough for shelter. Striking heavily on the bar, she unshipped her massive rudder and was helplessly blown on to the sands at Cranfield. When the storm subsided, the cargo was unloaded from the leaking barque and removed to Warrenpoint for safe keeping — well away from the local people, it is tempting to suggest! In fairness, it must be said that wrecks were certainly welcome to seaside dwellers all round the British coast, but for every tale there is of plunder, one of selfless attempts to rescue endangered mariners exists to balance it. The *Orissa* was repaired and the cargo re-stowed when she was ready to resume her voyage to India. It was exactly this kind of incident that led the Royal Commission on Harbours of Refuge to recommend improvements to Carlingford Lough entrance. Things were to get worse before they got better, however.

The early 1850s saw several serious wrecks. The Newry schooner *Favourite* came to grief on the bar in October 1850, and the following year the *Ebenezer,* a sailing coaster belonging to Preston, Fletcher, master, capsized and sank in a squall off the Lough, taking with her the three-man crew. On 31 January 1852 the brigantine *Glencaple,* 115 net tons and owned by J. Edgar of Dumfries, arrived off Carlingford Lough with a cargo of corn from the Black Sea port of Ibrail, destined for Newry. The normal procedure was for vessels requiring a pilot to signal for one to put out from Cranfield, but the skipper of the *Glencaple,* Captain Rodick, preferred to avoid hiring a pilot. He sailed on in himself, but only succeeded in putting his ship aground at Cranfield. The *Glencaple* was refloated, but later that year, on 7 November, another vessel on the same voyage with the same cargo became a total loss at almost the same spot! She was the *Louisa C.,* an Austrian brig registered in Trieste. The *Louisa C.* missed stays twice while attempting to enter the Lough in an easterly gale and struck Cranfield Point.

Captain Soich and his crew of nine were saved as was the cargo, although a portion of the corn was damaged by sea water. Carlingford Lough is exposed to easterly weather and this particular spell of gales and snow also accounted for the *John and Charles* of Maryport, the *Lito* and the smack *Three Brothers* of Carnarvon which disintegrated near Haulbowline lighthouse at the height of the blizzard, her crew not having a chance of survival.

In April 1858 there occurred another severe easterly gale, which, although not sending any vessels to their doom in or off Carlingford Lough itself, resulted in three wrecks nearby with the loss of fifteen lives. The barque *Sylvia* ran ashore in Dundrum Bay, nine men lost, the Spanish brig *Triton,* Liverpool for Barcelona with railway iron, at Ballymartin near Kilkeel, three men drowned, and a Welsh sloop to the south, also with three dead. Captain Richard Hoskyn, at the time in charge of a survey of Carlingford Lough, wrote to the secretary of the Royal Commission of Harbours of Refuge saying that these disasters 'forcibly illustrate the benefit that would be conferred by making Lough Carlingford more easily accessible'. The mid-Victorians were extremely concerned about the enormous toll of ships and men that occurred annually around the coasts. The average loss of life between 1852 and 1857 was 780 per annum, 1549 being lost in 1854, and the annual loss of property averaged £1½ million. In 1853, 421 vessels were total losses, and it was common for twenty ships to strand on the Co. Down coast alone in a year. The value of the great harbours of Kingstown, Portland and Holyhead, where the huge breakwater was still under construction, had been proved, and the Royal Commission on Harbours of Refuge was appointed in 1858 to examine more sites in which ships could shelter in adverse weather conditions. Hoskyn's letter commenting on the wrecks of April 1858 may well have influenced the Commission in their conclusions on Carlingford Lough: 'It is very desirable that the natural harbour be made available for refuge'. It was proposed to dredge a channel 650 yards long and 200 yards wide through the bar, the least depth being increased from the existing 12 feet to 21 feet. No great difficulty was anticipated, because the bed consisted mostly of clay and stones and the anticipated expenditure was £50,000. Work on the project was carried out in the 1860s, and in 1868 it was reported that a cut through the bar had been accomplished, although the intended width and depth had not yet been reached. In fact, a least depth of 21 feet never seems to have been accomplished, 17 feet being ultimately arrived at.

While these improvements were an obvious boon to vessels trading to Newry, Warrenpoint and the smaller quays, the Lough was never widely used as a place of refuge. The entrance was still narrow and islet-strewn, and sailing vessels experiencing bad weather usually preferred to stand out to sea rather than risk entering such a haven. Certainly, the number of ships wrecked to the north, like the *Sylvia* and the *Triton,* showed no decrease after the dredging operations.

Those ships carrying the area's imports and exports could now enter and leave the Lough much more easily, and casualties on the bar show a downward trend beginning in the 1860s. However, in 1866 there occurred a tragedy that was particularly keenly felt in the locality. One blustery Sunday afternoon in February of that year, a vessel hove-to off Cranfield flying signals for a pilot. The small steam tug *Sally* put out with Henry Coffey, a Lough pilot who owned the vessel, and a crew of six other local men. Off Cranfield coastguard station a sudden gust capsized the *Sally*; the coastguards, seeing the accident, at once launched their boat to go to the rescue. Two survivors were spotted clinging desperately to the upturned keel of the tug, but before the oarsmen could pull through the waves to reach them, they were washed off and lost to sight. Two years later, further loss of life occurred off Cranfield when the schooner *Margaret and Ann* of Aberystwith was wrecked on rocks adjacent to Haulbowline lighthouse, while inward bound to Newry with coal from Cardiff. One of her complement was drowned, three others, including Captain Davies, escaping.

Relatively few wrecks took place in the Carlingford area during the latter decades of the last century, there being on average one every three years in the 1870s, 1880s and 1890s, a small figure indeed when one considers that in this period there was an average of seven total losses every year on the Down coast as a whole. Two vessels were lost inside the Lough, the smack *Newry*, Cardiff for Newry with coal, ashore near Warrenpoint in February 1872, and, more seriously, the schooner *Margaret Anne* of Preston which foundered off Killowen Point, between Cranfield and Rostrevor, on 21 January 1873. Of 63 net tons, built at Tarleton, Lancashire, in 1858 and owned by J. Whiteside of Hesketh Bank in the same county, the schooner entered the Lough safely in a severe easterly gale, but was then seen to sink suddenly, the three crew members drowning. Carlingford Lough would appear to have had a fatal attraction for similarly-named sailing coasters, for another Lancashire-owned *Margaret Anne*, this one an iron dandy-rigged craft belonging to J. Butterfield of Ulverstone, was lost at the bar in 1892. Three years previously the schooner *Martha Ann* of Liverpool was driven ashore at Cranfield Point, while in 1909 another *Martha Ann*, a Newry schooner laden with granite from Annalong for Liverpool, went to pieces on the Hellyhunter!

The sole steamship casualty of this late nineteenth century period was the collier *Strathesk*, Glasgow for Newry, which piled up on rocks below Haulbowline lighthouse on 21 November 1889, later slipping off and sinking. Bound from Carnarvon to Irvine with slates, the little smack *Frances* of Carnarvon was wrecked off Greenore in September 1902. There then followed a long uneventful period in the story of Carlingford Lough wrecks, but the next incident was a disaster of such magnitude that it dwarfs anything before or since in the area, and, indeed, on the entire Down coast in modern times.

The evening of Friday, 3 November 1916, was a threatening one. A southerly gale, with some west in it, sent heavy clouds scudding low overhead. Only now and again did the clouds part and the moon inch through. Peter Morgan, a pilot, was in his house near Cranfield Point, when, shortly after eight-thirty, he was surprised to hear two explosions. Recognising these as the detonations the Haulbowline lighthouse keepers let off during fog, and knowing there was no fog that night, he realised that something must be amiss. Together with neighbouring farmers William Hanna and Hugh Doyle, he hurried the short distance to the shore where large quantities of wreckage could dimly be seen in the heavy seas, among it the bobbing heads of cattle frantically trying to make the land. As the three friends struggled to comprehend what could have happened, they spotted a figure in the surf close to the water's edge. Hanna rushed into the waves and dragged the man the final few yards to safety. It was James Boyle, a twenty-one year-old seaman from Warrenpoint, and he was the only survivor of a collision that had claimed the lives of ninety-three men, women and children.

Boyle was a member of the eight-man crew of the *Retriever*, a steamer of 459 gross tons, built at Troon in 1906 for the Clanrye Steamship Co. Ltd. of Newry, and commanded by Captain Patrick O'Neill. The *Retriever* left Garston at 4.25 a.m. on Friday the 3rd on one of her regular crossings from the Mersey to Newry with coal. Although the weather was bad, it was nothing exceptional for the ship and her crew, who were used to a hard trade across the Irish Sea. Boyle recalled that as they approached the cut into Carlingford Lough, the *Retriever* had a slight list to port owing to the cargo having shifted, but he was adamant that she was completely manageable. As the *Retriever* neared Cranfield Point, against the ebb tide, Boyle saw a steamer about half a mile distant approaching them, and this he took to be the *Connemara*. He then went below to attend to the stove in the master's cabin, but a few minutes later he heard the collier's steam whistle sound;

rushing on deck he heard and felt a tremendous impact. The *Retriever* had struck the *Connemara* amidships, penetrating her almost to the funnel.

The *Connemara* was a passenger and cargo steamer of 1197 gross tons, which had been completed by Wm. Denny and Bros. Ltd. of Dumbarton in 1897 for the London and North Western Railway Company, by whom she had been employed on the Holyhead to Greenore route all her career. On this her last voyage she left Greenore at 8.5 p.m. under the command of Captain G. H. Doeg, and carrying fifty-one passengers, in addition to thirty crew, nearly all Welshmen, three cattlemen and a luggage guard. Among her passengers were seventeen young Irish women on their way to Liverpool, thence Canada where they intended entering domestic service or undertaking farm work, and several members of the British forces who were returning to their units having been on leave. The passengers scarcely had time to settle on board when the *Retriever* smashed into the *Connemara*, which sank in seven or eight minutes, by Boyle's reckoning. He had stood by to launch the starboard lifeboat, but when the collier took a sudden list to starboard, he cut the boat's ropes and jumped in. Boyle's boat overturned in the rough seas and, exhausted, he found himself tossed among surf until willing hands hauled him to safety. Thus this young seaman was the only person who could tell the tale of Carlingford Lough's darkest hour. His shipmates on the *Retriever* had all been local men. Captain O'Neill was a native of Kilkeel, but was now residing at Merchant's Quay, Newry; with him aboard were his son Joseph, the second mate, and brother-in-law Joseph Donnan, an A.B., while the others were from Newry, Warrenpoint or Kilkeel. It was thought that some other survivors might have reached the shore alive but been dashed against the rocks or expired on the sand. Strangely, a few cattle from the *Connemara* did manage to struggle to safety and had to be rounded up by the local people.

At low tide the next morning a melancholy spectacle unveiled itself — the wrecks of both vessels, lying about fifty yards apart, just outside the cut on the Co. Down side. Gradually, day by day, bodies were washed ashore until almost all the victims had been identified. As many of those lost were in poor circumstances, a fund for dependants was opened, the distribution of the sum raised being entrusted to the National Disasters Relief Council. On learning of the calamity, King George V and Queen Mary sent a telegram of sympathy to Sir Gilbert Claughton, chairman of L.N.W.R., whose worst marine disaster this was.

The official Board of Trade inquiry was held in Belfast in March and April 1917. The primary task was to determine the cause of the accident, but in the course of the hearing several other issues were thoroughly examined. If Boyle came ashore alive, could not others have done likewise? Why were they not found and assisted to safety? Why were ninety-four lives lost a mere 700 yards from land? A mixture of inefficiency and an almost total lack of co-ordination in the local life-saving services were exposed and heavily criticised.

A key witness was Assistant Keeper John Gillespie, who had been on duty that night in Haulbowline lighthouse, and had, with two colleagues, stood on the balcony and watched the *Connemara* pass just before 8.30 p.m. Gillespie recalled that the steamer appeared to slow as usual on entering the cut, and when he first saw the *Retriever* he thought she was a sailing vessel as she was not burning a masthead light. The collier was yawing from side to side, "but that was nothing out of the ordinary in heavily laden vessels at that point", as Gillespie commented, and both ships appeared to be keeping their proper courses — that is, they would pass port side to port side. However, the bows of the approaching collier suddenly swung away to port and she rammed the *Connemara*.

The responsibility for alerting the coastguards and the lifeboat at Greenore obviously fell to the lighthouse men, but they appear to have been uncertain as to what measures to take, for no clear procedure seems to have existed. The lighthouse could not communicate with land after dark, but was equipped with twelve sky rockets, a gun and detonators, the latter being exploded until about 9.15 p.m. The rockets were not fired, probably because the keepers felt that these may have been interpreted as a sign they themselves needed aid. The Greenore lifeboat was not launched — although admittedly it could probably have done little by the time it was rowed to the scene — and neither were the coastguards on either side of the Lough made aware that anything was amiss. For example, the station at Greencastle, just two miles from where Boyle came ashore, did not hear the detonations and knew nothing for four hours. So for several crucial hours after the collision, no professional or systematic search of the coast was mounted as debris and bodies were washed in with every wave. As part of the judgement of the inquiry stated, 'The Court considers it probable that more lives would have been saved in the region of Cranfield Point had any sort of organised effort been made to pick up and then assist some of those who were washed ashore . . . '

For some reason, the erroneous belief seems to have arisen and been repeated in print that the *Retriever* caused the collision by not showing the requisite lights. However, this is quite at variance with the findings of the inquiry. The core of the matter it found to be the collier's behaviour as she steamed through the cut against the ebb tide, which can run at up to four knots here. Gillespie's first-hand account of the sudden swinging of the collier's bows to port and the subsequent impact 'about the bridge somewhere', as he thought, was verified by the evidence of a diver who had examined the wrecks. The verdict of the inquiry was as follows:

' . . . that the collision and the resultant large loss of life was primarily due to the s.s. *Retriever* not complying with Article 23 of the regulations for preventing collisions at sea. On such a stormy night, with a heavy sea running, she should have avoided meeting another vessel in a narrow and dangerous channel. The court is of the opinion that the collision was caused by the s.s. *Retriever* not being able, on account of the severe weather conditions and the strong ebb tide on her starboard bow, to comply with the regulations to avoid the collision'.

There exist one or two noteworthy stories connected with the *Retriever* and *Connemara* disaster. Both vessels had been involved in accidents before. Only the previous August the *Retriever* had struck and sunk the Spanish steamer *Lista* at Garston, owing to the sudden death on the bridge of the collier's master, Captain Barry, who was navigating the ship out of dock. The *Connemara* had survived two collisions. On 23 June 1900, while rounding Holyhead breakwater bound for Greenore, she was run into by another L.N.W.R. steamer, the second *Eleanor,* and suffered damage which necessitated her return to Holyhead. Ten years later, in the early hours of 20 March 1910, the *Connemara* collided with and sank the Liverpool steamer *Marquis of Bute* about three miles north of Holyhead, though fortunately without loss of life. As so often is the case with disasters, whether at sea or elsewhere, the loss of the *Retriever* and *Connemara* engendered uncanny stories. A Mrs. Small of Birkenhead, who had been on a visit to Armagh with her daughter, was due to return on the *Connemara* on 3 November. However, the previous night, as she told reporters, she had a vivid nightmare in which she saw herself as a passenger on a steamer which sank in a gale shortly after leaving port. She was sufficiently affected by her dream to decide against travelling back to Holyhead the next evening. A further cold touch of the supernormal is provided by the reported appearance of the 'ghost ship of Carlingford Lough' to relatives of James Boyle on the afternoon prior to the disaster. This is supposedly the phantom of the *Lord Blayney*, a passenger steamer wrecked with all on board near Prestatyn in 1833, when on passage from Newry to Liverpool. The legend warns that when she appears on the Lough a local vessel is invariably lost soon afterwards. In his book 'Legendary Stories of the Carlingford Lough District', first published in 1913, Michael George Crawford gives an astonishing, eerie description of the spectral ship which he claims to have seen a few days before the stranding of the *Robert Brown*, a schooner built and owned in Warrenpoint and driven aground in Dublin Bay in October 1880 with the loss of three lives.

Unhappily, the accident involving the *Retriever* and the *Connemara* was not the last serious collision in Carlingford Lough, and the 1930s, in fact, saw a spate. Three collisions, including one that brought back unwelcome memories of 1916, all involved steamers of Joseph Fisher and Sons Ltd., Newry, Co. Down's leading shipowners over the last century. On 21 November 1936, during a strong north-easterly gale, the *Pine*, on a voyage from Garston to Dundalk with coal, put into the Lough for shelter. While at anchor, she was rammed by another Fisher steamer, the *Olive*, and sank in ten minutes. Her master, Captain McKee, and the crew were picked up by the *Olive*, which had been bound to Kilkeel to load potatoes, under the command of Captain George Campbell. Salvage of the *Pine* was undertaken by Samuel Gray, the well-known Belfast stevedore, shipowner and salvage contractor, and the coaster eventually returned to service in 1939 under the ownership of Isaac Stewart of Belfast.

The same day as the *Pine* and *Olive* collided, a third unit of the Fisher fleet, the *Rowan*, was also in trouble, colliding with a Welsh auxiliary coaster, the *Florette*, at Narrow Water, near the entrance to the Newry ship canal, though with merely superficial damage to both vessels. In the early hours of the following morning, the *Lady Cavan*, a steamer belonging to the British and Irish Steam Packet Company Ltd., of Dublin, who maintained a general cargo service between Newry and Liverpool, grounded at Killowen Point but managed to refloat herself after a couple of hours. Thus accidents in this spell of dirty weather had involved five ships; a few months later two of them were to make the headlines again, under more tragic circumstances.

At 4 a.m. on 4 April 1937, Fishers' steamer *Alder* groped her way into the Lough in dense fog, steam whistle sounding sonorously. Unwilling to proceed through Narrow Water, Captain George Campbell, the same man who had skippered the *Olive*, dropped anchor off Greencastle. Scarcely ten minutes later, the *Lady Cavan* loomed out of the murk and struck the *Alder* amidships. There was not thought to be any immediate danger, although coal could be seen pouring through a rent in the plates, but suddenly the *Alder* heeled over and sank, all on board going down with her. The *Lady Cavan*, which had also been bound for Newry, picked up three survivors who had surfaced and clung to wreckage, but despite searching until daylight, no sign was there of Captain Campbell, his wife, who had only at the last minute decided to accompany him on the voyage, or the other four crew members. As in the case of the *Retriever*, most of those lost were locals, for Campbell and his wife lived in Kilkeel, while three of the others were natives of Newry, the fourth being a Belfast man. The *Alder* was a serious hazard to navigation, and was raised and beached at Greenore in March 1938. Unlike the *Pine* she never sailed again.

Since this unusual series of mishaps in the mid-1930s, little of note has happened in the area. The steam coaster *Falavee*, owned by Howdens Ltd., Larne, became a total loss after going aground on 14 January 1942, but most of the strandings in recent years have been harmless, just the occasional coaster taking the ground while passing through Narrow Water. The development of Warrenpoint harbour has meant renewed dredging at the bar, and, although ships no longer visit the Victoria Basin in Newry, the two remaining ports in Carlingford Lough, Warrenpoint and Greenore, now handle a greater tonnage of shipping than ever before.

Moving north-east from Carlingford Lough, the coast is low-lying and rocky as far as a mile or two north of Annalong, where it takes on a spectacular character. Here, in the immortal words of Percy French's song, 'the mountains of Mourne sweep down to the sea'. For about six miles, until Newcastle is reached, the Mournes tower over the water and the coast road, and a measure of the precipitous nature of the land is the fact that the peak of Slieve Donard, at 2,796 feet the highest in the range, lies only two miles from the sea. Kilkeel and Annalong have always been the chief harbours of the region, the former now being Ulster's leading fishing port, but Annalong, handicapped by the difficulty of its entrance, has seen little trade over the past thirty years, since the cessation of the export of Mourne granite.

The first pier at Newcastle was built early in the last century in an attempt to provide refuge for vessels embayed in Dundrum Bay, and to assist efforts to check smuggling, a feature of life in the Mourne parts in the eighteenth and early nineteenth centuries. This section of the Down coast was frequented by smugglers, who appreciated the lonely beaches and the proximity of the mountain wastes. In October 1820 the revenue cutter *Hardwick* was wrecked in Dundrum Bay while pursuing a vessel that had landed contraband goods at Glasdrumman, two miles north of Annalong. The coastguards in the Mourne area were stationed there more with a view to combating smugglers than saving life from shipwreck, for wrecks were relatively infrequent on the Mourne coast. Of course, before transfer to the Admiralty in 1856, Britain's coastguards were employed by the Customs Department. The sands to the north, in Dundrum Bay, are the real graveyard of ships in this part of the Ulster coast. Shipping, apart from small coasters trading to Kilkeel, Annalong and Newcastle, had no occasion to pass close to the Mourne coast.

Two of the more serious nineteenth century strandings, the *Triton* and the *Eleanor,* have already been mentioned in connection with the Carlingford Lough story, but in terms of loss of life the worst casualty among merchant vessels during this era was the full-rigged ship *John Stamp.* Nearing the end of a long voyage from Bombay to Liverpool, the *John Stamp* was driven aground on 17 February 1839 at Leestone Point, seven of her crew perishing. Her valuable cargo, consisting principally of cotton, was recovered in a damaged condition and forwarded to Liverpool.

One member of the crew of the barque *Bee* died when his vessel ended her days on the Mourne coast near Annalong on 6 December 1848, while bound from Liverpool to Charleston, South Carolina, but more seamen were lost from local fishing vessels than died in the wrecks of cargo ships. In 1814 there had been loss of life involving local boats, but a worse disaster occurred on 13 January 1843. On the morning of that day ten yawls left Newcastle, and six Annalong, to fish a few miles off the coast. Suddenly, the wind shifted from the south to the north-west and a blanket of snow engulfed the little fleet of open boats. Although sources vary as to how many boats were lost, the official number of men drowned is an appalling seventy-three, including twelve from an Annalong boat that put out into the blizzard in a rescue bid. The effect of such a decimation on the small, tightly-knit seafaring communities of Newcastle and Annalong can be imagined, and to this day the visitor to Newcastle can see, above the road to Annalong, a group of houses, the Widows' Row, built for families bereaved in the calamity. The town was given a grim reminder of 1843 in April 1914, when a local skiff, the *Morning Star,* was lost with the five persons aboard, including Edward Murphy, a member of the local lifeboat crew, and his son Michael John.

Apart from the *John Stamp,* the *Triton* and the *Bee,* the actual coast-line has been remarkably free of shipwrecks occasioning loss of life. The 1850s, however, witnessed three wrecks from which the respective crews were lucky to escape. The men of the schooner *Perseverance* of Westport, Co. Mayo, managed to run her ashore at Kilkeel on 10 May 1850 after a fire had begun while they were five miles offshore, bound for Glasgow with a load of flour from Cork. Two years later, in the spell of bad weather that wrecked the *Louisa C.* and the others at Carlingford bar, the former Mersey pilot cutter *Irlam* was cast ashore on Leestone Point in a howling gale and hammered to fragments, while on her first voyage for a new owner. The loss of the *Water Lily* was an episode long remembered in the neighbourhood. A brig belonging to Dublin, she went aground near Glasdrumman on 9 December 1859, and Henry Boyd, a local fisherman, at the third attempt rescued the entire crew of eight and ferried them safely to land in his boat. For his gallantry Boyd was awarded the silver medal of the Royal National Lifeboat Institution. Among other total losses in the nineteenth century were the schooner *Maria Lowther,* north of Bloody Bridge, 2 October 1878, the brigantine *Sally and Ann* at Annalong, 17 March 1880, and the schooner *Albion,* Annalong 3 March 1881.

On 14 January 1905, the Glasgow tramp steamer *Beechgrove,* 1,221 gross tons, was off Holyhead, making her slow way south in heavy seas from Ardrossan to the coal tips in Penarth docks where she was to load for La Rochelle. Without warning, the cover of the high-pressure cylinder blew up, leaving the *Beechgrove* wallowing helplessly and drifting north before the wind. Captain Woodall ordered signals for assistance to be flown, but ship after ship passed them without acknowledgement, until eventually a steam trawler, the *Mermaid,* came to stand by. All that day and the ensuing night the crippled *Beechgrove* was blown northwards, until the Co. Down coast was sighted. Nearer and nearer the tramp drifted until the anchors had to be let go off Glasdrumman. However, early on the morning of the 15th the south-easterly wind increased in force, the starboard cable parted and the *Beechgrove* crashed on to the rocks at Dunmore, between Newcastle and Annalong. The Newcastle lifeboat *Farnley* was launched into the teeth of the gale, but after breaking several oars had to put back; using borrowed horses, the *Farnley* was then towed by road to a point to windward of the stranded steamer, but again attempts to reach the *Beechgrove* were thwarted by damage sustained in launching. Eventually, Captain Woodall and his cosmopolitan crew of ten Britons, two Swiss, two Swedes and a Spaniard were brought ashore safely safely by the coastguards' rocket apparatus. For seven of the men it was their second experience of shipwreck in little over a fortnight, for on 31 December 1904, they had been in the steamer *Kathleen* when she was sunk off Greenock in a collision with the *Stromboli.* The *Beechgrove* quickly began to break up, and the weather's work was continued by the McCausland family, the salvage experts of Ballyhenry, Portaferry, to whom the wreck was sold for scrap by the owners, Alexander and Arthur.

Two Norwegian sailing ships were wrecked near Annalong in 1907. On 7 February, the barque *Ascalon* sprang a serious leak on her voyage from the Mersey to Drobakk on Oslofjord. With the hands unable to stem the copious inflow of water as they pumped frantically, Captain Sivertsen made for the Co. Down shore. Finally, with six feet of water in the hold, the *Ascalon* drove aground off Murphy's Point. Sivertsen and his crew of twelve were landed by breeches buoy, and the coastguards had to press their rocket equipment into service again the following Boxing Day, to rescue the complement of the barquentine *Vamos,* ashore a little to the south of Murphy's Point. The story of the *Vamos* is rather similar to that of the *Beechgrove,* for she had run before a south-easterly gale that caught her off Holyhead, when seven days out from Oporto for Garston in ballast. Captain Lars Larsen was trying to make Belfast Lough for shelter, but his vessel had no chance of clawing her way off the Mourne coast, a deadly lee shore in such conditions, with the wind reaching force nine.

Since that day, no large vessel has become a total loss on this stretch of coast. Two of the once-large Annalong trading fleet, the ketch *Christina Ferguson* and the schooner *Phillis* ended their careers after going aground while trying to enter the harbour on 17 January 1908 and 25 May 1917 respectively, while more recently the small coaster *Celt,* a steamer of 147 gross tons, testified to the difficulty of the narrow entrance at Annalong when she grounded on 1 April 1960, with a load of coal from Glasgow. Pumps had to be brought from Portadown, fifty miles away, to aid the lengthy refloating operations.

Chapter Two

NEWCASTLE
TO ST. JOHN'S POINT

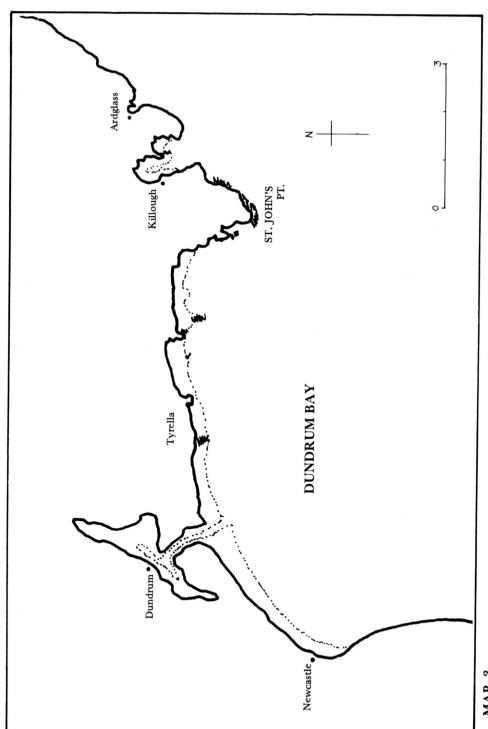

Ardglass

Killough

ST. JOHN'S
PT.

Tyrella

DUNDRUM BAY

Dundrum

Newcastle

N

0   3

MAP 3

A line drawn from Newcastle to St. John's Point encloses Dundrum Bay, a part of the Ulster coastline which has probably seen more heroic rescues than any other. From Newcastle the coast makes a long curve to the eastward, there being fifteen miles of golden sand interspersed with a few low reefs and only broken once, by the narrow entrance to Dundrum Inner Bay, an inlet which dries almost completely at low water, and on which is situated the quiet village of Dundrum, dominated by its Norman castle. The quays here are reached by crossing a nasty sand-bar over which the tide runs at up to four knots, and although trade was once much brisker, coal and Baltic timber are still imported by coasters of up to 500 tons. Summer visitors who flock to the strand at Tyrella and admire the glorious view across the water to the Mournes see only the friendly side of Dundrum Bay; in winter the beaches are grim, bleak places, especially in gales from the south or south-east, to which the bay is completely exposed. Dundrum Bay is the sudden beginning of an easterly trend in the coastline of Ireland which sets much of Co. Down out into the path of shipping in the Irish Sea. Almost all the major wrecks in Dundrum Bay involved sailing vessels; if a ship failed to weather St. John's Point and became embayed, she had very little hope of escape. The danger of embayment was accentuated by the fact that about five miles south-east of St. John's Point there is an area of still water where the two tides from the Atlantic meet, one coming around the north of Ireland, the other from the south. Thus sailing vessels being forced towards Dundrum Bay in an easterly or south-easterly wind 'have no tide to help them out', as Walter Harris, who never failed to spare a thought for mariners braving the perils of the Down coast, wrote in 'The Ancient and Present State of the County of Down', published in 1744. Harris' century. and the first half of the following one, saw the toll of ships and men in Dundrum Bay at its highest, but records, albeit scanty, exist of wrecks here in earlier times.

It seems that the Norse, who plundered so far and wide in the British Isles, discovered that Co. Down was a land worth settling rather than just pillaging, as there is strong evidence of a Norse settlement being established in Strangford Lough, or in Irish *Loch Cuan*, in the ninth century. The presence of the foreigners, and perhaps the example of King Alfred's new English fleet, stimulated Irish ship-building activity, and the Norse also had to be on guard against attacks by their enemies the Danes. About 923 — 925 however, their ranks were thinned, for, according to the Ulster Annals, 'A great new fleet of the foreigners of *Loch Cuan* was drowned at *Fertas Rudhraighe* [Dundrum bar] where 900 persons or more were lost'. If this

figure is in any way accurate, the wreck of the Norse fleet is easily the worst
Co. Down shipping casualty on record.

George Hamilton was a notable resident of Tyrella in the late
eighteenth century. The Collector of Customs for the Strangford district,
he won public praise for his efforts to save life and property from wrecks
over a long span of time. About the year 1796, Hamilton, pulling down
some old buildings at Tyrella, was surprised to find that the beams and
lintels were made of cedar. On enquiry, a local tradition came to light:
a cedar-built ship had been wrecked in the bay a great many years
previously, while laden with slaves, ivory and gold dust from the coast of
Guinea. The sands of Tyrella had swallowed up the wreck, but locals
informed Hamilton that at very low tides, two weed-covered pieces of wood
could be seen marking the spot. About 1815, an expedition was made to the
marks at low tide, and, after some digging, the upperworks of a ship were
discovered. Despite the soft, oozy nature of the sand, six elephant's tusks,
a silver goblet and the remains of chains were recovered, the latter seeming
to be the fetters of the unfortunate slaves. In a fascinating memorandum
submitted to the Royal Irish Academy, and published in the 'Proceedings' of
that body for 1845 — 7, George A. Hamilton M.P., probably Hamilton's
grandson, reveals how on 10 November 1829 he made a similar excavation.
After initial difficulty in finding the correct spot, as the marks had now
disappeared, Hamilton and his helpers uncovered a rich haul:

‘ . . . in one tide I obtained sixteen elephants' tusks, a large quantity
of cedar, four cannons, the remains of a number of swords, muskets and
chains, a number of small shells, some coral, a piece of metal, nearly in the
shape of a horse-shoe, which, at the time, we supposed to be the handle of
a trunk, and several pieces of a heavy metallic substance.'

Experts examined Hamilton's find, and pronounced the shells to be
of the type the natives of the Guinea coast, west Africa, used for money, the
piece of metal a bracelet used by visiting merchants for bartering purposes,
and the 'heavy metallic substance' of volcanic origin. It is tantalising indeed
to think that the wreck of the unknown slave ship still lies under the sands
at Tyrella, and that, were the position known, modern excavation techniques
could be employed in the hope of discovering more remains and artifacts.

Statistics published in the Parliamentary Sessional Papers for 1837
bear vivid witness to the dangers of Dundrum Bay. Between 1783 and
1835, no fewer than fifty-eight vessels had been lost here, their value and
that of their cargoes totalling £209,050. Most of these ships must remain

just statistics, however, as there are few detailed records of losses before about 1820. The brigantine *Isabella* of Drogheda was driven aground on 26 February 1785, while bound from Cowes to Belfast with wheat, and in a bad gale on 2 January 1788, the *New Loyalty* of Belfast, Liverpool for Belfast with sugar and woollen goods, came ashore near Tyrella. The aforementioned George Hamilton was responsible for saving most of the cargo, his 'extraordinary exertions' being praised by the *Belfast News Letter*, who added that he ' . . . has for many years been in the habit of affording every possible succour to such vessels as met with any disaster on the coast'. The *New Loyalty*, finished her days in another storm in Dundrum Bay in December 1797. In 1818 a vessel named *Ruby* was forced far to the north on a voyage from Liverpool to Newry, and met her end in the bay. There was no lifeboat in the area until 1825, the Royal National Lifeboat Institution having just been founded the previous year, but in view of the frequency of wrecks, it seems incredible that there was no light either in Dundrum Bay until as late as 1844, when St. John's Point lighthouse was built. The wooden spire of Killough parish church was a favourite landmark for mariners — until the famous 'Big Wind' of 6 January 1839 demolished it — but of course it was of no use at night.

The first lifeboat was stationed at Rossglass, in the north-east corner of the bay, in 1825, largely owing to the efforts of William Ogilvie, the remarkable Scot who did so much to enlarge and improve nearby Ardglass. The boat was propelled by eight oars and was only 18½ feet long. Her first recorded service was on 6 March 1826, when the barque *Richard Pope* was driven ashore in a fierce south-south-easterly gale. At least two boats put out to the stricken barque, but the tremendous surf beat them back. The *Richard Pope* carried a crew of fifteen, and realising the difficulties of their would-be rescuers, they decided to try to save themselves. Five men clambered into a ship's boat and attempted to make the shore, but the boat capsized in the breakers. Seeing what had happened, Alexander Douglas, an onlooker, swam through the surf in an effort to save life, but four of the men drowned. The remainder of the crew wisely stayed put, and eventually two boats reached them and brought them to safety. For his part in this prolonged and hazardous rescue Captain J. R. Morris R.N., a local coastguard, was awarded the silver medal of the R.N.L.I. Rescue escapades in Dundrum Bay in this period resulted in several more awards. The Rossglass boat saved six of the eleven men aboard the *Usk*, wrecked at Rossglass on 15 November 1826, a service for which the lifeboat master, Thomas Foy, received the silver medal, while in 1830 similar decorations were awarded to John Philip and Michael Casey for their part in saving fifteen men from the ship *Sir James Kempt*.

Every year in the 1830s saw its toll of ships in Dundrum Bay. Between November 1834 and November 1835, for instance, no fewer than five vessels came to grief here, the *Aid* of Stromness, the *Diligence*, the *Charlotte* of Drogheda, and two larger craft, the barque *Bellona* and the ship *Heroine* of Liverpool, both of which were later got off with difficulty. Dundrum Bay has the only long stretch of sand on the Co. Down coastline, and many more vessels have been refloated after going aground here than have survived encountering the rockier parts. The *Coeur de Lion*, a full-rigged ship, was successfully refloated having featured in the worst incident of the 1830s. Outward bound from Liverpool, her home port, to Montreal with a valuable general cargo, she was driven on to the sands inside St. John's Point on 11 September 1837. The Rossglass station had been moved to St. John's Point on the suggestion of Captain P. R. Browne of Janeville, on the point, in 1835, and it was from here that a boat put out to the stranded *Coeur de Lion*. Unfortunately, it capsized in the high seas and two lifeboatmen, Patrick Goolaghan and George Starkey, lost their lives. Five of the crew of the *Coeur de Lion* also perished, but twenty-five others were brought ashore safely, after wonderful efforts by the chief officer of the local coastguard, a Mr. Strains, Captain Browne, and Messrs Hogg, Adair and Adam, all five of whom later received the silver medal of the R.N.L.I. The Committee of Management of this body also granted £10 to the widow of Goolaghan and £5 to relatives of Starkey. The cargo of the *Coeur de Lion* was landed and sold, and the ship eventually towed back to Liverpool. Just over a year later the admirable Captain Browne distinguished himself further when the schooner *Bloom* was thrown on the rocks on the western side of St. John's Point. The date was 23 October 1838, a day which saw four vessels stranded in Dundrum Bay, the others being the schooners *Friendship* and *Rapid* and the brig *Stranger*. The *Bloom* was in the worst position, however, and despite heroic attempts that won Browne the gold medal and others monetary awards, only three of her six-man crew could be rescued.

The incidents of wreck, rescue and salvage in Dundrum Bay in the 1840s are dominated by one outstanding tale, the stranding and subsequent epic salvage of Brunel's *Great Britain*, undoubtedly the most famous of all the many ships that became casualties on the Co. Down coast. Until this accident in 1846, the decade had been a relatively quiet one for wrecks. The brig *Trevor*, Alicante for Belfast, was a total loss near Tyrella on 18 January 1840, and in 1845 two more brigs were lost, the *Active* and the *Frolic* of Liverpool, the sunken wreck of the latter on Dundrum bar later causing the sinking of the yawl *Victoria*, one of the very few, and according to one source the only, survivor of the fishing fleet disaster of 1843. Another decoration was won as a result of the *Frolic* wreck, incidentally, by James

Taylor for the rescue of the crew of six. Brigs, schooners, barques and full-rigged ships stranded on the sands were familiar sights to the people of the Dundrum Bay area, but when first light on 23 September 1846 revealed a steamer sitting on the beach at Tyrella, and not just any steamer, a colossal iron screw steamer, the world's largest, there was good cause for excitement.

Designed by Brunel and William Patterson, a Bristol shipwright, the *Great Britain* had been completed at Bristol in 1844. Her first four voyages for the Great Western Steamship Company were disappointing, but her fifth was disastrous for the owners. Under the command of Captain James Hosken, she left Liverpool for New York in fine weather at 11 a.m. on Tuesday 22 September 1846 with 180 passengers, her highest complement to date. During the afternoon the weather deteriorated, and when night fell visibility was poor. Shortly after 9 p.m. Hosken saw a revolving light to starboard. This was St. John's Point, but it confused him; he examined his chart, but could find no such light near the course he had plotted. At 9.30 p.m. the inevitable happened, as, with a resounding crash, the *Great Britain* drove ashore. When the passengers had been calmed and assured they would be taken off safely next morning, it was time to think why the ship had been a good twenty miles off course. Hosken declared that, if there was to be any blame, he would take it, but claimed that he had been misled by an outdated chart that should have shown St. John's Point light, first lit on 1 May 1844, but did not. More important, he admitted miscalculating the steamer's speed, which resulted in their being much further north than he had thought. Hosken left the merchant service for a post as harbour master and chief magistrate on Labuan, off Borneo, leaving behind the stranded giant, and the problem of refloating her. Captain Christopher Claxton, managing director of the owners, took charge of the salvage operations, which proved laborious, frustrating and extremely costly. The autumn gales began to damage the ship, until one especially bad one carried her up the beach and left her beyond the worst of the seas. Brunel himself visited the *Great Britain* and suggested erecting a massive breakwater of faggots to protect the ship from the coming winter onslaught. After enormous toil, this was completed, and was a crucial factor in the ship surviving her stranding largely intact. The owners were inundated with well-meaning but totally impracticable suggestions for refloating the *Great Britain*, and eventually hired a professional salvor, a Scot named Bremner, whose past successes, however, did not convince Brunel he could refloat the *Great Britain*. 'I do and have all along felt very anxious about old Bremner's proceedings', wrote the famous engineer on 7 July 1847. 'The *Great Britain* is bigger than anything he has had to deal with'. But Bremner did succeed in lifting the 2,936 gross ton vessel bodily out of the sand in which she was embedded, by levers on one side of the hull and boxes filled with 30 tons of sand suspended from the deck on the other side, and she was towed off on 27 August 1847 by the 600 hp engines of the steam frigate HMS *Birkenhead*. The total cost of salvage was about £22,000, and the owners had no alternative but to sell the *Great Britain*. The accident had, however, proved the strength of iron ships; the *Great Britain* was, of course, to survive many other vicissitudes before her triumphant return to Bristol, her birth-place, in July, 1970.

Had Captain Hosken identified St. John's Point lighthouse correctly, this whole worrying and expensive salvage project would never have been necessary. St. John's Point was the first dioptric lens light to be erected in Ireland, this being a lens system in which the rays of light — then from oil lamps — are concentrated by refraction on passing through glass prisms. Invented by Augustin Fresnel in 1822, the system was first introduced in Britain in 1835 at Inchkeith. St. John's Point light was important for the annually increasing number of steamers on the Irish Sea, but did nothing to prevent sailing vessels stranding in Dundrum Bay. In the ten years before the light was established, thirteen sailing ships went aground, while in the same period following, the bay saw sixteen sailing ships and the *Great Britain* become casualties. The vast majority of these occurred in southerly gales, and the only help St. John's Point light could be to vessels caught in such weather and being driven into Dundrum Bay was at least it told them where they were being wrecked — if that was any comfort. The late 1840s and the 1850s saw a number of bad wrecks, and matters were made worse by the fact that the lifeboat station at St. John's Point had lapsed. It was replaced in 1854 by a station at Newcastle, but for the boat to get to a wreck at Tyrella or Minerstown, where most tended to occur, meant rowing at least seven miles, a formidable task in a 28 foot boat in heavy weather. Wrecks before the new boat arrived included the *Ida*, 27 December 1847, crew drowned, the *Venus* of Maryport 18 August 1848, the *Welcome* of Newry, 20 November 1850, and the *Orford* of Workington, 30 September 1851. St. John's Point light was of no assistance to Captain Rowlands of the Beaumaris sloop *Juliana*, 37 net tons; he could see nothing in thick fog, and his calculation that they were in Dundalk Bay was effectively disproved when the *Juliana*, Carnarvon for Ayr with slates, ran aground some thirty miles to the north, on the west side of Dundrum Bar early on the morning of 12 February 1852. Rowlands refused coastguards' advice to lay out a kedge anchor and discharge some of his cargo, and paid the penalty when the sloop was subsequently washed further up the shore and severely damaged in the surf. The cargo was saved but the *Juliana* embedded herself in the sand. A larger and more typical Dundrum Bay casualty later that year was the barque *Chieftain* of Belfast. Built at Montreal in 1826, the *Chieftain* had long been a member of Belfast's deep-sea fleet, once under the ownership of Messrs Smith, and now of Mr. R. Corry. Her end came when, outward bound from Belfast to Savannah with salt, she was forced back by a force ten south-easterly gale and snow, and failed to weather St. John's Point, finally striking inside the headland at 1 a.m. on 25 November 1852. Happily, Captain McFarlane and his twelve-man crew escaped. Two days before Christmas that year, a Spanish brigantine, the *Nueva Carmen*, Havana for Hamburg with sugar and tobacco, came ashore in a south-westerly gale, but, although dismasted, she was refloated a month later and towed to Belfast for repair. It was the stranding of another Spanish brigantine almost a year later that probably finally prompted the establishment of Newcastle lifeboat. On 19 December 1853 the Irish coast was pounded by a fierce south-easterly storm, reaching force eleven on the Beaufort Scale. A total of twelve vessels went ashore, thirty-four lives being lost, eighteen of these in the wreck of the square-rigger *Chatham* at the mouth of the River Boyne. A casualty in Dundrum Bay was almost inevitable in such a hurricane, and the unlucky ship was the *Adolpho* of Corunna, 110 net tons, which was swept helplessly to the north of her voyage from Seville to Liverpool with corn, and blown ashore at Newcastle. Her crew of nine were saved by the coastguards' rocket apparatus, but, writing his comments on the rescue for the Admiralty Wreck Register, the Inspecting Commander of Coastguards for the district remarked, '. . . the rocket lines were bad, and broke repeatedly, and a lifeboat would have been of the greatest service in this case'. A lifeboat was essential, for, because of the shallow nature of Dundrum Bay, vessels tended to ground far from the shore, out of range of the coastguards' rockets.

A lifeboat, however, could hardly have done much to save the crew of the Cardiff schooner *Catherine O'Flanagan*, who left their vessel before she stranded on 21 January 1854, and were all drowned in the breakers, like the men from the *Richard Pope* in 1826. The schooner came ashore near Tyrella little damaged, and the coastguards asserted that the crew could have been rescued had they stayed on board.

Newcastle's first lifeboat was built by Messrs Forrest at Limehouse on the Thames, and arrived at the new station in late April 1854, a boathouse being built through the generosity of the Earl of Annesley. Fittingly enough, it was almost opposite the spot where the *Adolpho* had been wrecked. The R.N.L.I. records show that the lifeboat saved five lives between 1854 and 1859, when it was replaced, but in this period over twenty persons died in Dundrum Bay. One man from the Newry brig *Sea*

Bird was drowned when she went ashore near Rossglass on 11 June 1854, but the entire crew of the sloop *Atalanta* of Annalong perished in January 1855, when she foundered near the Cow and Calf rocks off Tyrella. A large casualty concerning which the records show discrepancy is the barque *Fortune*, aground on Dundrum bar on 19 May 1855. The *Fortune*, 571 net tons, belonged to James Baines' famous Black Ball Line, a Liverpool fleet of Australia traders that included the *Marco Polo*, skippered by the notorious 'Bully' Forbes, and the record-breaking clipper *Lightning*. Outward bound for Hobart with 233 emigrants, and a general cargo, the *Fortune* became embayed after failing to weather St. John's Point, and her master, Captain McCarthy, was apparently forced to beach her at Dundrum bar. According to the *Belfast News Letter* 'two persons died in the confusion which followed the shock', but the Board of Trade records state that only one life was lost; the Admiralty Wreck Register for 1855 curiously omits to mention the *Fortune*. Although the barque was sitting upright on the sand and was making only a little water, it was considered expedient to land the unfortunate emigrants, and they were housed in tents on the shore until the steam tug *Dreadnought*, which had made an early and unsuccessful attempt to refloat the *Great Britain* in 1846, arrived to return them to Liverpool which they had probably never thought to see again. The *Fortune* became a total loss, as did another Liverpool barque, the *Sylvia*, 174 net tons, aground near Dundrum bar in a wild south-easterly on 7 April 1858, while on passage from Liverpool to St. John's, Newfoundland, with salt. The crew of nine took refuge in the rigging, the traditional sanctuary, but all three masts soon fell and no-one survived. Captain Thomas Thompson, who in his time had saved many lives, was buried by the local masons at Maghera, near Dundrum. The final wreck in this particularly grim era in Dundrum Bay came on 4 December 1859, and was a case of history repeating itself. Like the men of the *Catherine O'Flanagan*, the crew of the Austrian brig *Tiky* abandoned ship when they found themselves being swept towards land in a south-westerly gale. All fifteen of them put off in the ship's boat, and tried to row for St. John's Point, but, as we have seen, this is no place for small boats, and six were lost when it capsized in the surf. A local man, attempting to save life, almost drowned too, when his boat was upset, but Captain Ridge, the Inspecting Commander of Coastguards, at great personal risk waded into the breakers and dragged him to safety. The *Tiky*, like the *Catherine O'Flanagan,* came ashore unharmed, but never seems to have been refloated.

Newcastle's second lifeboat was the *Reigate*, which between 1859 and 1881 was launched on twenty-four occasions and saved fifty-five lives. The number of wrecks in Dundrum Bay continued unabated during her period of service; it was not until the 1890s, with the general decline in the number of wrecks around Britain, that casualties in the area became fewer. Thus the 1860s and 1870s provide a story of continual wrecks and gallant rescues in southerly gales, mostly involving schooners and brigantines, but occasionally larger vessels, such as the barque *Colima* on New Year's Day, 1871, bound Liverpool for Guatemala, and, very rarely, a steamer, notably the London and New York Line's splendid *Iowa* in 1866, which was refloated and taken over by the Anchor Line, later becoming the *Macedonia*. Newcastle lifeboat was supplemented by a boat stationed at Tyrella, and there was a very marked diminution in the number of lives lost in Dundrum Bay. Four of the five crew of the schooner *Bellona*, Liverpool for Dundrum with coal, died on 18 January 1862, when she stranded crossing the bar, the other man being saved by the Tyrella boat, but twelve years were then to pass before further loss of life. The schooner *Rose* of Cork, on passage from Bridgwater to Dublin with tiles, came ashore near Newcastle in a south-easterly gale and overwhelming seas on 26 February 1874. The *Reigate* was launched and succeeded in saving all but one of the schooner's five-man crew, a rescue for which James Hill, the lifeboat coxswain, and Captain C. Gray Jones, R.N., Second Assistant Inspector of Lifeboats, were both awarded the R.N.L.I. silver medal. Among other distinguished rescues by the *Reigate* were of the crews of the *Swift* of Wexford, 20 December 1872, the *Trader* of Portaferry, 13 February 1876, and the *Margaretta* of Aberystwith, Boxing Day 1876. The Tyrella boat saved Captain Nulty and the three crew of the brigantine *Bransty* of Whitehaven, Newry for Bristol with oats, which was wrecked at Tyrella on 6 February 1881. The boat could do little, however, on 9 February 1884 when the schooner *Victoria* of Beaumaris had the misfortune to miss the long stretches of sand and strike Ringmore Point, a rocky promontory extending seawards from Minerstown, her four-man crew perishing one by one as they fell from the rigging.

Most Dundrum Bay wrecks occurred when sailing vessels were being driven helplessly north up the Irish Sea, but there seems no good reason for the loss of the big squarerigger *Flying Foam*, 1,279 net tons, on the evening of 4 April 1884. There was a strong breeze, but no more, from the south-west, not a direction that generally troubled ships in these parts, but the *Flying Foam* managed to become embayed, and not having anything like enough sea room to escape, she grounded about a mile south of Dundrum bar. On board were Captain Bryde, his wife, twenty-three crew, and four stowaways who had hidden on the ship at Liverpool, hoping to cross the Atlantic, for the *Flying Foam* was bound for Quebec with salt. Captain Bryde decided to abandon ship, and three of the crew, a stowaway —

doubtless wishing he had stayed at home — and Mrs. Bryde got into the smallest of the ship's boats. Five people, however, overloaded it and Mrs. Bryde was put into the second boat, an act which saved her life, because the first boat must have capsized, tipping the occupants into the sea and drowning them, a tragedy which did not become apparent until daybreak, when the empty boat drifted ashore. The *Farnley*, the lifeboat which had replaced the *Reigate* in 1881, stood by the *Flying Foam* all night; at 5.30 a.m. some of the crew made the shore safely in the ship's longboat, while the remainder, numbering eleven, preferred to go in the *Farnley*. Although the *Flying Foam* rested on a sandbank that dried at low water, and was little damaged, she was never refloated, and her hulk lay there for several years until the Commissioners of Irish Lights ordered its removal. Alexander Gracie, a labourer who had reported the vessel ashore, was rewarded with 7/= from the Mercantile Marine Fund.

Tyrella strand, that graveyard of sailing ships over the centuries, claimed its last victims in the 1880s, but happily no loss of life was sustained in the wrecks of the schooners *Helen*, Garston for Rostrevor, 21 February 1885, *Rambler*, Carlingford for Liverpool, 9 August 1885, and *Barclay*, London for Ayr, 27 February 1886, nor when the French barque *Esperance* ended her long voyage from Bangkok with teak for Belfast here on 24 February 1887. There then followed a remarkably long period when no serious casualties took place in Dundrum Bay. The occasional coaster would stick in the sand while attempting to cross the bar, the *Lady Arthur Hill*, a steamer locally owned by the East Downshire Steamship Company, being one such in April 1897, but the region shared in the marked lessening of shipping casualties on the Down coast as the nineteenth century closed. An average of eight total losses per annum on the coast in the 1880s dropped to three annually in the first decade of the present century. But when a major wreck next occurred it was a spectacular one, involving the largest sailing vessel ever to come to grief in Dundrum Bay. The *Cannebiere* was a fine steel barque of 1,759 net tons, built at Nantes in 1900 for the Soc Marseillaises de Volliers of Marseilles. She took her name from the main thoroughfare of the city, a famous, not to say notorious street, of which Conrad in *The Arrow of Gold* wrote ' . . . for me it has been a street leading into the unknown'. The *Cannebiere's* voyage from Glasgow to New Caledonia with coal soon developed into a journey into the unknown when, on 14 March 1905, she encountered a force ten gale between Holyhead and Dublin. The big barque, with her crew of twenty commanded by Captain Lefeuvre, careered northwards, sail after sail being whipped from the masts. She drifted into Dundrum Bay the following day, and finally took the ground just outside the bar, her hull soon being submerged. The paddle tug

Flying Irishman, which had been purchased the previous month by Mr. James McCausland of Ballyhenry, Portaferry, for salvage work on the *Beechgrove*, was lying in Newcastle harbour. Her skipper, John McCausland, put to sea and crossed the storm-tossed bay to the *Cannebiere*, as did the Newcastle lifeboat under her veteran coxswain James Foland. Between them the *Flying Irishman* and the *Farnley* plucked twenty men from their precarious refuge in the barque's rigging, although four were injured, and one, the cook, lost. For their gallantry McCausland and Foland and two of the tug's crew, Joseph McGuigan and Laurence Ivers, were presented with gold medals and diplomas by the French Government, who also rewarded Mr. Clarence Craig of Tyrella with a binocular case for assistance rendered. The barque's strong steel hull enabled her to survive the battering she received, and after refloating she continued to trade until sunk by a U-boat in the English Channel on 24 October 1916.

While the war at sea was exacting its grim toll of ships like the *Cannebiere*, two casualties by stress of weather, the seaman's perpetual enemy, occurred in the Newcastle area in late 1916. The steam coaster *Plasma*, 325 gross tons, was making her slow way southwards into a gale on 27 October 1916 when her main shaft broke about four miles south-east of St. John's Point, and she was relentlessly driven towards the lee shore in Dundrum Bay, her anchors dragging. The Newcastle lifeboat, since 1906 the *Marianne*, was launched with Mr. Robert Hastings J.P., a member of the local lifeboat committee, as volunteer bowman, and he was a hero of a difficult rescue of the eight men aboard the *Plasma*. The steamer eventually came ashore on the site of the present Newcastle swimming pool. This in fact was the *Plasma's* second mishap on the Co. Down coast, for in January 1901 she had gone aground in Knockinelder Bay, near the tip of the Ards peninsula, while carrying limestone. Once again she was refloated and traded until 1946, when, as the *Archella*, she was scrapped after grounding at North Sunderland. The southerly gale that had the *Plasma* in distress was repeated only a few weeks later, and once more Dundrum Bay was the scene of a wreck, this time of the Danish schooner *Fulvia*. The *Fulvia* was a wooden vessel of 149 net tons, built in 1902 and owned by J. J. Nielsen of Thuro. Outward bound from Liverpool for the French Biscayan port of Les Sables d'Olonne with pitch, she, like the *Cannebiere*, drifted northwards for eighty miles before running aground 400 yards from the shore, about a mile north of the Slieve Donard Hotel, at 10 a.m. on 18 November 1916. The *Marianne* several times attempted to make a connection with the *Fulvia*, but on each occasion was driven to leeward in the high wind. The schooner had stranded at low tide, and as the incoming tide rose over the hull, Captain Petersen and his five-man crew were obliged to climb into the rigging. There they clung all afternoon as a crowd on the beach watched with concern as the *Marianne* made abortive attempts to get a line on board the *Fulvia*. Finally, at 5.30 p.m. the numb and hungry seamen decided they would have to try to save themselves. Detaching a yard from the foremast, they dropped it into the sea, jumped in after it, and, hanging on desperately, were washed ashore where willing hands pulled them from the surf. Among the rescuers were Corporal William Thomas Watson and Corporal Henry Holmes of the Reserve Battalion, Royal Irish Rifles, who carried the schooner's mate, Jens Peter Jensen, to the Slieve Donard Hotel in their greatcoats. Jensen seemed the worst affected by his ordeal, and despite medical assistance, he died shortly afterwards, having uttered only one word: 'saved'. Jensen, from Svendborg, was buried at Newcastle, and the local people erected a headstone on his grave. Watson and Holmes, who had done their best for the unfortunate Dane, were later awarded bronze medals for gallantry by the Board of Trade. Among the other crew members of the *Fulvia* was an adventurous Dutch boy, Isaac Post, aged sixteen, who had lied his way into the Canadian infantry, and served for nine months before his true age was discovered and he was discharged. The remains of the *Fulvia* were visible on the sands until about 1960.

Since that stormy day in 1916 only one cargo vessel has become a total loss in Dundrum Bay, the steam coaster *Bellavale*, which grounded near Rossglass on 15 October 1940, while on passage in ballast from Dundalk to Ayr. A larger wartime casualty at Minerstown was the motor vessel *Hoperidge*, 3,133 gross tons. The *Hoperidge*, a new vessel built in 1939 for Stott, Mann and Co of Newcastle-on-Tyne, became separated from her convoy after leaving Liverpool for Melbourne, and ran aground in an easterly gale and blinding snowstorm early on the morning of 19 January 1941. Shortly afterwards her master, Captain Bennett, shot himself; his grave is in unconsecrated ground between Clough Presbyterian Church and the adjoining field. The *Hoperidge* was refloated by tugs on 4 February, continuing to serve her owners until 1963. On 1 August 1969, as the Liberian *Bethlehem*, she sank after a collision with a Japanese vessel near Singapore.

While accidents elsewhere in the bay have been rare, coasters have on numerous occasions grounded whilst attempting to cross the bar. Generally they have been refloated fairly promptly, but the steamer *Katherine* was an exception. Bringing coal from Maryport, the *Katherine*, 238 gross tons and built at Paisley in 1898, struck on the bar in heavy seas on 22 December 1924. The Newcastle lifeboat *John Cleland* was launched by the new method of pulling the boat to the water by a tractor instead of manpower, but Captain Patrick O'Keeffe of the *Katherine* declined assistance with thanks. Over the Christmas holiday period, large numbers of sight-seers walked along the sands to gaze at the *Katherine*, with that fascination that stranded ships always seem to induce. The steamer came off the bar on a very high tide on 28 December, but was carried half a mile to the east and deposited again on the beach, not being refloated from here until mid-1925. Her salvors were Messrs Cooper of Widnes, who had bought the ship from John S. Monks Ltd., Liverpool, and subsequently used her as a barge at Widnes. Among the other coasters to fall victim to the bar were the East Downshire Steamship Company's steamers *Dromaine*, 29 June 1946 and *Downshire*, 12 December 1954, and the motor vessels *Lady Sylvia*, September 1957, *Ben Vooar*, March 1962, and *Ben Varrey*, 9 April 1964. A much more serious incident occurred on the evening of 10 November 1955, when the fishing vessel *Georgina Hutton* was attempting to enter Dundrum Inner Bay in strong southerly winds and heavy seas. She struck wartime anti-invasion poles which ripped her bottom open, and within minutes the four crew members were clinging for their lives to the bow, the only part of their boat now above water. The Newcastle lifeboat *William and Laura*, coxswain Pat McClelland, made an extremely daring and hazardous rescue which involved manoeuvring close to the wreck in huge breakers and an ebbing tide, while at the same time avoiding the poles. Ropes were thrown to the frozen hands of the men perched on the wreck, and one by one they were hauled to safety; the lifeboat then went astern across shallow shoals into the main channel, and landed the exhausted survivors at Dundrum — a miraculous rescue and a fitting place to end the story of Dundrum Bay shipwrecks.

Her rudder sheared off, the 'DOWNSHIRE' lies aground on Dundrum Bar

The 'HOPERIDGE', aground for a fortnight in Dundrum Bay, 1941.

Dundrum Bay in a gale, seen from the stranded 'BEN VARREY' 1964.

Chapter Three

ST. JOHN'S POINT
TO STRANGFORD LOUGH

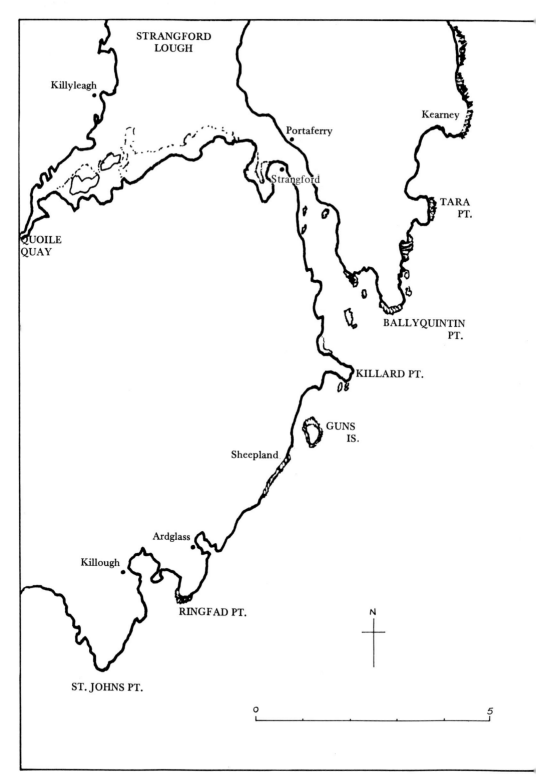

STRANGFORD
LOUGH

Killyleagh

Portaferry

Kearney

Strangford

TARA
PT.

QUOILE
QUAY

BALLYQUINTIN
PT.

KILLARD PT.

GUNS
IS.

Sheepland

Ardglass

Killough

N

RINGFAD PT.

ST. JOHNS PT.

0   5

MAP 4

St. John's Point marks the most southerly tip of a low-lying stretch of coastline roughly thirty-five miles in length, which is characterised by a succession of shallow, sandy bays and rocky headlands. Offshore lie many sunken reefs, small islands and half-tide rocks, which have claimed innumerable ships and mariners as long as men have sailed the Irish Sea. This rugged expanse of coast, so picturesque in fine weather, so forbidding in bad, continues as far as Belfast Lough, but is broken by the long, narrow entrance to Strangford Lough, that endlessly fascinating expanse of almost land-locked water. The part of the coast discussed in this chapter divides itself easily, from the point of view of the types of ship wrecked and the circumstances of their loss, into three sections: from St. John's Point to Strangford Lough entrance, the entrance, and the Lough itself. The list of vessels that came to grief between St. John's Point and the mouth of the Lough at Killard Point includes a wide variety of ships. Sailing coasters dominate, but there are also a number of deep-sea sailing ships of different flags, and in more recent times, a large freighter and an even larger troopship. In contrast, almost all the vessels wrecked at Strangford Lough entrance were small sailing coasters, the majority of them engaged in the trade of the Lough, a trade which thrived in the last century and well into the present, with Portaferry and Strangford the main harbours, and a dozen or more quays and open beaches handling cargoes. Thus these casualties, as well as being interesting for their own sake, give a valuable insight into the maritime history of Strangford Lough, and a vanished way of life. Wrecks in the Lough itself were rare, but the sheltered nature of the Lough shores has meant that a few hulks can still be seen — the only part of the Co. Down coast where this is possible.

St. John's Point is the *Isamnium* of Ptolemy, the second-century Egyptian geographer and astronomer; this name probably was derived from the Irish *isheal*, meaning "low". The point takes its modern name from the Church of St. John, one of the earliest ecclesiastical buildings in Co. Down, which was built nearby. Two miles north of St. John's Point is the village of Killough with its ruined harbour. Known as Port St. Anne in the eighteenth century, it shared a valuable export trade in grain with Ardglass then and in the first half of the nineteenth century. The two once-fine stone piers forming the harbour were built in the 1820s. The neighbouring town of Ardglass has a more distinguished history, being until the seventeenth century one of the busiest ports in the province of Ulster. Its later prosperity was based on the fishing industry and its position as a fashionable resort, and Ardglass is still an important fishing port, even though it no longer sees the vast fleets of boats that made the harbour their base for the herring fishing season every summer in the century prior to the last war.

Ardglass has seen many tumultuous events in its long history; it was burned in 1433 and taken by the insurgent Irish in the Great Rebellion of 1641. As the eighteenth century drew to its close, tension was again rising in Ulster. The radical United Irishmen, in part inspired by the ideals of the French Revolution, sought reform and plotted an uprising when the Dublin government proved intransigent. The United Irishmen's hopes of success were largely pinned on receiving aid from France, aid that was never fully forthcoming, but in 1797 the frigate *Amitie* of Brest was dispatched with guns. It would seem that these were to be delivered at some point on or off the Down coast, where the United Irishmen were particularly active, but no rendezvous was made, for the *Amitie* was wrecked in the vicinity of Sheepland harbour, to the north of Ardglass, in a south-easterly gale, all but one of the crew of 104 perishing.

Legend has it that the lone survivor was the helmsman, who arrived in the now-vanished village of Sheepland in the early hours of the morning. To prevent the Frenchman falling into the hands of authorities, the local people looked after him, and he lived in Sheepland for a long time. Day in, day out, though, he is said to have climbed the path to the clifftop and gazed reflectively over the scene of the wreck of his ship and the deaths of his colleagues. To this day the path is known as "The Steersman's Path". In the summer of 1963, members of Belfast Sub-Aqua club dived on the site of the *Amitie's* loss, and located a dozen cannon and some cannonballs.

The *Shamrock* of Belfast was on passage from Liverpool to her home port with cotton yarn, flour and other general cargo when she struck rocks near Ardglass at 5 a.m. on 24 February 1803. Her crew left her and scrambled to safety, but their skipper, Captain James McIlroy, could not be prevailed upon to leave his disintegrating vessel, and was shortly afterwards washed overboard and drowned. "A highly respected member of the Belfast seafaring community", as the *Belfast News Letter* described him, McIlroy's body was brought to Newtownbreda, then a village outside Belfast, for burial. A portion of the *Shamrock's* cargo was saved and lodged in stores provided by Lord Lecale. Records of wrecks as long ago as this are scanty, but a few can be traced, such as the *Hope*, aground near Killough with some loss of life in December 1796, the *Paroquet* in 1816, bound from Liverpool to the West Indies, and the *Brothers* in the winter of 1817 − 18, bound from Dublin to Glasgow; in neither of the last two instances can the exact location be determined but both vessels seem to have been lost to the south of Strangford bar. The mid − 1830s saw two bad casualties: the *Dale* of Maryport was lost with all on board near Killough in 1835, while on 16 December 1836, the schooner *Minapia* foundered off St. John's Point, also with all hands. Among only a few losses the following decade were the *Europe* of Dundee, Brodie, master, bound from Narva, in the Gulf of Finland, to Liverpool on 12 November 1844, and the *Garland*, Belfast for Venice, destroyed by fire near Killough on 19 December 1849.

The eastern side of St. John's Point has seen comparatively few wrecks, at least since the lighthouse was established in 1844. Between Killough and Ardglass lies Ringfad Point, the next headland to the north, and many more ships have been lost here. It was at Ringfad Point that the brig *Nova Providenza* of Genoa finished her days, when she sailed on to the rocks on the foggy morning of 2 July 1854, soon filling. Her wreck was sold by auction, most likely to provide firewood and fencing for the neighbourhood for months, Co. Down people not being ones to let anything go to waste! Later in 1854 came a particularly vicious spell of weather, in which no fewer than five large sailing vessels, all outward bound from Liverpool, met their ends on or off the Down coast. First to strike was the barque *Jupiter* of Dundee, for Vera Cruz with coal, at Tyrella on the morning of 28 October. It was a dreadful day to be at sea, blowing a near-hurricane from the south, and pouring with rain. Another barque, the *Sarah Ann*, for Matanzas, Cuba, with coal and railway chairs, had weathered St. John's Point and anchored off Ardglass, her master doubtless visualizing the rocks at Strangford bar or Ballyquintin Point waiting to claim his ship if they continued to be blown northwards. Of course, the anchorage was completely exposed, and the *Sarah Ann*, which was a new vessel only completed the previous June at Richibucto in Canada, dragged her anchors and crashed aground at Sheepland harbour. Her crew managed to get a line to the shore, and all but one of the fifteen men aboard reached safety through the heavy seas.

The year 1854 was certainly a black one for wrecks on this stretch of coast. The three crew and a passenger on board the *Johns*, owner Captain Brown of Portaferry, perished when the sloop was driven aground in a fierce south-easterly storm half a mile south of Killard Point on 15 November. In the same gale, the smack *John and William* of Carlingford broke adrift in Ardglass harbour and was dashed to pieces. "This is a small vessel, not seaworthy", recorded the local coastguards laconically.

The fate of the *Nautilus* on 5 April 1856 provides further indication of the hazards of life in the coasting trade in the last century. A smack of 33 net tons, built in 1836, and owned by Thomas Russell of Killough, the *Nautilus* was running across Dundrum Bay before a south-westerly gale, bound for her home port with oatmeal from Dundalk, when, almost within sight of her destination, her rotten tiller broke off in the helmsman's hand. Helpless, the little smack was carried on to the rocks, a few hundred yards north of St. John's Point. The three-man crew escaped and the only loss was a financial one for Russell; like most small coasters, the *Nautilus* had not been insured. Her value was about £200.

Bound in tow from Ardrossan to Dublin with coal, the elderly brig *Favourite*, dating from 1805, was wrecked at Ballyhornan on 12 October 1870, four men drowning. Another bad wreck on 29 November 1874 brought pleas in the correspondence columns of the *Down Recorder* for a harbour of refuge at Ardglass, of which, however, nothing came. The crew of the schooner *Lancashire Lass*, of Whitehaven, master and part owner Captain Christopher Holliday, sighted St. John's Point light in the early hours of that day having previously lost their reckoning in a south-easterly gale while on passage from Drogheda to Workington. The *Lancashire Lass* was put round, but was unable to fight her way off the land. Holliday then beached her at Ringfad Point; the mainmast fell and the next sea washed the three crew overboard as the schooner was knocked on to her beam ends. The only survivor was Patrick Woods, a seaman of Workington, who was cast up on the shore and sheltered in a nearby ditch until daylight.

The last sailing ship wreck in this area with fatal consequences was the brigantine *Beagle*. Bound from Maryport to Londonderry with coal, a southerly gale forced her ashore at Ballyhornan on 6 February 1883, her master, Captain McIlgorm, being swept overboard and drowned. After a long lull in casualties involving loss of life, two steamers were torpedoed in the closing weeks of World War I. The *Hunsdon*, 2,899 gross tons, which was sunk about three miles east of Ballyhornan on 18 October 1918, was a British prize, captured from the Germans at Duala, West Africa, in August 1914. One man, named McAleer, died, and the master, Captain Beedie, is said to have swum ashore as he had gone below when the ship was sinking and the crew had left without him. Captain Beedie, incidentally, had another encounter with the Down coast in October 1925 when his steamer *Oakgrove* grounded on the Skullmartin, but soon floated off again. Three days after the sinking of the *Hunsdon*, the *Saint Barchan*, 362 gross tons, owned by J. & A. Gardner Ltd., Glasgow, was torpedoed and sunk four miles off St. John's Point. Eight of her crew died, the last men of the merchant service to be lost in home waters, for the *Saint Barchan* was the final victim of U-boats operating around the British Isles. On 5 April 1918 she had been attacked by a U-boat in the Irish Sea, but the torpedo missed; had her luck lasted another three weeks the war would have been over.

As already stated, Ringfad Point has seen more than its share of wrecks. Anyone chancing to be there around dawn on 14 October 1874 would have witnessed a distasteful scene on board the brigantine *Posie*, which had just grounded. Bound from Ardrossan to Cuba with coal, the *Posie* was making for Strangford Lough, into which her master and part-owner, Captain John Curran of Portaferry, intended putting for stores. The subsequent Board of Trade inquiry heard how Curran, over-confident in his knowledge of the coast, had set the course before land could be seen, and had failed to take the bearing of St. John's Point light. When the *Posie* ran aground, the incensed Curran blamed the mate, whose watch it had been, and assaulted both him and a seaman. The crew abandoned ship, but Curran, remaining on board alone, went down with his ship when she slipped off the rocks and foundered, but was picked up by fishermen who had come to the wreck. Curran's inefficiency and subsequent misbehaviour probably warranted a stiffer sentence than the nine months' suspension of his master's certificate that the inquiry imposed, but the court declared that they did not want to cause excessive hardship to him, as he was the uninsured owner of half the shares of the *Posie*.

The early months of 1881 saw two total losses on Ringfad Point, the iron barque *Astarte* on 6 February and the schooner *Margaret Owen* on 3 March. The *Astarte*, 909 net tons, was bound in ballast from Dublin to Glasgow when she struck, while the *Margaret Owen*, 98 net tons, was loaded with bone manure from London for Londonderry. Other total losses on Ringfad Point in this era were the *Anne Eline*, a Danish schooner, on 4 January 1884, bound from Brake, Germany, to Belfast with empty bottles, the schooner *Native*, Aberdovey for Belfast with slates on 8 January 1886 and the steam coaster *Sunflower* on 16 April 1890.

The present century, if not notable for the number of wrecks on the coast between St. John's Point and Strangford Lough entrance, at least provides a number of interesting stories. Only three months of the new century had passed when the steamer *Kilbroney* was completed at Irvine for the Clanrye Steamship Co. Ltd., Newry. Classified Al at Lloyd's and having successfully completed trials, the *Kilbroney*, commanded by Captain M. F. Barry, set off on her maiden voyage from Ardrossan to Newry with coal on 14 April 1900. All went well until the ship took a list in heavy seas about three miles off Sheepland harbour, and refused to answer to the helm. Captain Barry gave the order to abandon ship, but, as the boat was being launched, he slipped and fell into the water. His crew, numbering eight, lowered the boat, but it took half an hour's exertions in very difficult conditions before they hauled their Captain on board and rowed for the shore, where the Ardglass coastguards, who had seen the *Kilbroney* sink, met them and hurried them to Ardglass. A doctor had to be called from Killough to attend to Captain Barry, but, despite his ordeal, he was able to travel home to Newry with the rest of the men.

The same spot on Ringfad Point has claimed two very different vessels in this century. On 18th July 1928 the auxiliary schooner *Lucy*, which had put into Killough Bay with engine trouble incurred on passage from Whitehaven to Dundalk, dragged her anchors and went ashore on the south-west side of the Point. A sharp contrast with the 70 — ton *Lucy* was the African Steamship Company's Hartlepool-built *Bereby*, 5,249 gross tons. Bound from Liverpool to Takoradi and Port Harcourt with general cargo that included military stores, she developed an engine defect on 23 September 1941, while on her way north to rendezvous with a convoy. The weather was very thick, and adding to this hazard was the fact that St. John's Point was unlit in wartime. The *Bereby* got under way again, but she had strayed miles off course, and about 1.30 a.m. the following morning she steamed right into Killough Bay past the coastguard station. The startled coastguards attempted to warn her off by foghorn, but, in turning, she grounded on Ringfad Point. A tug was hastily summoned, but refloating efforts failed, and the cargo, among which were lorries and aircraft packed in cases for reassembly, was eventually unloaded into two tank landing-craft and taken to Ardglass. In the spring of 1942 the Liverpool and Glasgow Salvage Association's vessel *Ranger* made a further attempt to refloat the *Bereby*. About a thousand tons of bunker coal were jettisonned and leaks in the hull patched with concrete, but just before the high tide on which it was hoped to free the ship, a gale sprang up and she broke her back. The hapless *Bereby*, launched in 1919 as the *War Raven*, was finally scrapped as she lay.

The dubious distinction of being the largest vessel wrecked on the Co. Down coast falls to the American troopship *Georgetown Victory;* her loss is also among the most inexplicable. Built in 1945, of 7,604 gross tons and registered at Baltimore, the ship left Fremantle for Glasgow on 27 March 1946 with 1,200 Royal Navy men and Marines due for demobilisation. Despite gales which delayed other vessels encountered on the voyage, the *Georgetown Victory* made a record passage for her class of ship to Land's End. The night of 30 April was a fine one, calm and clear, and as the service-men turned in, they were eagerly looking forward to arriving in Glasgow the next morning, thence to homes some had not seen since the outbreak of war. Shortly before midnight, casual watchers from the shore saw the lights of a ship passing close to St. John's Point, heading north; this they assumed to be a coaster making for Strangford Lough, but it was in fact the huge

Georgetown Victory, and she was, incredibly, about twelve miles west of her proper course for Glasgow. With a grinding and tearing of steel that was heard three miles away, she drove full tilt on to the rocks about a hundred yards south of Killard Point. The servicemen swarmed on deck in various states of undress, but, despite the general impression that they had struck a mine, order prevailed and preparations for disembarking the ship's complement were soon under way. The first priority was to convey the four occupants of the sick bay to a hospital, and they were lowered on to Newcastle lifeboat, which took them to Portaferry, from whence they were hurried by road to Newtownards. The rest of the men were ferried ashore by a fleet of small. boats, and had to trudge across the fields to Bishopscourt RAF station, cursing this delay to their long-awaited homecoming. At Bishopscourt they were fed, and then taken in lorries to Ardglass, thence Belfast by special trains. They finally arrived in Glasgow just a day late, but many had lost cherished war souvenirs, such as Japanese flags, for these were stored in the ship's holds, which were largely flooded when the *Georgetown Victory* broke her back within a few hours of stranding. She eventually split in two just forward of the bridge, and although most of the ship was cut up for scrap, remains still lie in the shallows off Killard Point. The inquiry was held *in camera*; its findings would make interesting reading.

Shipwrecks on the Down coast provide a wealth of dramatic tales, but the story of the Dutch motor coaster *Tide* is unique. The *Tide*, a well-known Irish Sea trader, was a vessel of 480 gross tons, built in 1952 and owned in Maastricht. At about 1 a.m. on Sunday 21 January 1973, she was some twenty miles south of the South Rock lightship, bound in ballast from Sligo to Par. Captain John Tooke had just gone off watch when a fire was discovered in the galley. All hands were alerted, but despite strenuous efforts, the blaze could not be controlled, and after sending out SOS signals, Captain Tooke, his eight-man crew and his young wife Lydia retreated to the foredeck. Here they huddled as the *Tide*, with no-one to steer or stop the engines, plunged out of control through heavy seas in winds gusting to force eight. But the Royal Navy was on hand. The distress messages had been received by the frigate *Berwick* and the minesweeper *Bronington*, both of which gave chase to the runaway through the stormy night. A helicopter from the *Berwick* tried to lift off the helpless crew, but was foiled because the men on the foredeck were unable to remove the stay above them between the bows and the mainmast. Daylight came, and the *Tide*, which had sailed herself close to the Down coast, was in imminent danger of grounding. Lieutenant Charles Freeman of the *Bronington*, who had first sighted the blazing coaster ten miles away, closed and despatched a dinghy, which at considerable risk took off the crew and Mrs. Tooke in two parties, the *Tide* in fact driving on to rocks south of Gun's Island before the second group were saved. 'There was nothing we could do except pray', said Captain Tooke on landing from the *Bronington* at Bangor. The *Tide* capsized and sank in the early hours of the next day, thus becoming the most recent total loss on the Down coast at the time of writing, but surely one whose story deserves to rank with past dramas of wreck and rescue.

The entrance to Strangford Lough is perhaps the most remarkable stretch of water in Ireland. The Norse bestowed on it the apt name *Strang Fiord*, the violent inlet, for the tide races at up to 7½ knots through some five miles of rock-littered narrows. In the middle of the channel, about a mile south of Strangford village, is a whirlpool, the Routen Wheel, into which Captain Beechey F.R.S. took his paddle surveying vessel in the last century, with spectacular results. The revolutions of the paddles dropped from 22 to 18 per minute, while the ship which had been making about nine knots, became stationary. The narrows open into the Irish Sea between Killard Point to the south-west and Ballyquintin Point to the north-east, and between these two headlands is Strangford bar, with the most dangerous rocks Angus Rock, Garter Rock and Pladdy Lug, all of which dry. Pladdy, a word of Norse origin meaning a flat rock, is frequently encountered on the Down coast. In 1846 a lighthouse to be built at Angus Rock was petitioned for; the 45 foot stone tower was complete in 1853, but never lit, for it appears that Belfast port authorities, apprehensive that making the Lough more easily navigable might threaten their trade, had the project dropped. The majority of wrecks in the area have occurred on the bar and its two enclosing promontories; conditions here can be appalling, especially with the wind against the tide, when a short, steep, confused sea is created.

The earliest recorded wreck at Strangford bar is also the worst. In October 1715, a vessel named *Eagle's Wing* met her end here with the loss of no fewer than seventy-six lives; it would thus appear likely that she was carrying passengers. Details of shipping losses were not systematically recorded until the 1850s, and there must have been many more casualties than those that can be traced, such as the *Gallant* in November 1818, the Strangford-built *Ann* in February 1823, and the *Helen*, Riga for Newry, in 1835. One stranding that left a tragic mark on the Portaferry community took place on 23 February 1826, when the *Three Brothers* of Workington struck a pladdy on the north side of the bar, while carrying coal to Belfast. Several boats went to her aid, but a freak wave swamped two of them and seven Portaferry men perished, including two pairs of father and son. Despite this calamity, the local men succeeded in righting the collier, which later got off and proceeded. Further loss of life occurred on 10 March 1839, when the sloop *United Friends* of Pembrey, Carmarthenshire, was wrecked on Killard Point in a south-westerly gale. She had been bound from Barmouth to Strangford with bark and iron, and it was not until the next day that her remains were discovered, and the bodies of the crew brought ashore for burial. The mate and three crew of the *Echo* of Dublin died when the schooner was wrecked at the Lough entrance on 27 November 1842.

Very few ocean-going vessels have ever come to grief on this part of the coast. The largest casualty is the *Anglia*, 6,538 gross tons, a cable steamer which sustained heavy damage after striking the western side of Ballyquintin Point on 15 December 1906. At the inquiry the lack of a light on Angus Rock was mentioned, and the fact that in the previous ten years four vessels had stranded in the vicinity, but the master of the *Anglia* was alone judged in default, and his certificate was suspended for three months.

It was on the opposite side of the Lough entrance, at Killard Point, that there occurred the only total loss of a deep-sea steamer. The *R. L. Alston*, a tramp owned by J. Brown of West Hartlepool, finished her days here while carrying iron ore from Bilbao to Glasgow on 25 January 1885. Captain H. F. Gray, who was later held to blame by the inquiry, and his crew escaped unharmed. By far the most serious accident to a deep-sea trader took place on Pladdy Lug one fearful January day in 1867. That year announced itself with a spell of easterly and south-easterly gales, and in its first five days no fewer than ten sailing ships were driven on to the Co. Down coast. On the night of 5 January, a corpse was washed ashore near Strangford, which was presumed to have come from a wreck on Pladdy Lug, for at low water a small portion of a ship's mast could be discerned here. However, there was no way of identifying the ill-fated vessel. Over the next few days, as the storms continued to rage, debris was left scattered along the shore by each tide, and on 9 January two more bodies were taken from the water at Portaferry. To the collection of wreckage that was carefully made was later added a ship's figurehead, yet by 15 January still no positive identification of the lost ship had been made. Suspicion was entertained that she was the *Gardella*, an Italian vessel that had sailed from Ardrossan for Genoa with pig iron. The Italian consul in Belfast believed that it was the *Gardella*, and although it was eventually accepted to have been her, the number of crew members who died was never ascertained; the Board of Trade records state tersely 'supposed eight'.

It was, of course, small coasting vessels that suffered most from the vagaries of Strangford Lough entrance, as they passed in and out in their hundreds, craft of every type of rig bringing coal from Ayrshire and

44

Cumberland, and exporting grain, potatoes and all manner of farm produce to the population centres on either side of the Irish Sea. Fog was a particular menace to vessels making their way through the narrows, and in 1856 it caused two wrecks in successive days. The *Harriet Matilda* of Belfast, a small schooner of 32 net tons, was carrying lime from Larne to Killyleagh when she hit rocks off Carrstown Point, to the north-east of Angus Rock, on 22 October. The crew rowed ashore in their boat, and were followed the next day by the men of the *Robert E. Ward*, another schooner which had stranded on Pladdy Lug on her way from Troon to Castle Espie quay with coal.

Another typical casualty of the mid-nineteenth century was the old brig *Lion* of Strangford, on 4 January 1857. Attempting to enter the Lough with a load of coal for her home port, the *Lion*, built in 1786, missed stays in an east-north-easterly gale. The anchor was let go, but the wind and the flood tide combined to carry her on to Angus Rock, where she became a total wreck although the five men on board escaped. Other total losses in this period included the Welsh smack *Providence* of Nevin, 16 June 1852, the schooner *Queensbury* of Annan, 15 January 1853, and the *Mary and Anne*, 12 March 1860, all at Strangford bar. Two staunch local men, James and John Maguire, saved the master and owner of the *Providence*, Jonathan Roberts, and his two companions, after their leaking craft had been driven from the Calf of Man at the mercy of a south-easterly gale, while on passage from Carnarvon to Largs with slates.

A Portaferry boatman named McDonnell was piloting his ferry across the narrows on 5 February 1861 when he was startled by a collision with a large portion of a ship's stern, which was being swept into Strangford Lough by the tide. This was the first intimation of the wreck of the brigantine *Manchester* on St. Patrick's Rocks, half a mile east of Killard Point. Laden with coal from Whitehaven for Dublin, the *Manchester*, 133 tons, had disintegrated with the loss of all five crew, the only survivor being the ship's dog, miserable but unscathed.

One man from the schooner *Lady Proby* drowned when his vessel stranded on the bar on 18 December 1862, later being refloated. After the *Gardella* disaster in 1867, twenty-five years were to pass before there was any further loss of life on this part of the Down coast, but the lull was rudely broken on 26 October 1892. Captain H. Evans and his crew of five all perished when the *Annie*, a schooner belonging to T. W. Tate of Liverpool, was wrecked on Killard Point when on a voyage from Port Dinorwic in North Wales to Dundee with slates. Some of the wrecks in the years between the *Gardella* and the *Annie* can briefly be recalled: the brigantine *Conflict* of Belfast, inside Ballyquintin Point, 2 March 1872, the brig *Cumbrian* of Whitehaven, Pladdy Lug, 3 July 1874, the schooner *Speedwell*, belonging to the Isle of Arran, Angus Rock, 16 November 1880, and the schooner *Leila* of Padstow, which sank beside Garter Rock on 23 February 1886, having a few hours earlier struck Angus Rock in fog, her crew walking into Portaferry to announce their plight! A total loss unique in the long list of Ulster shipwrecks was the small steamer *Sulby Glen*, which suffered a violent explosion of gas in the coal cargo she was carrying from Whitehaven to Quoile Quay, at the Lough entrance on 25 September 1897. With her leaks uncontrollable, she drifted aground at Killard Point.

As there was no railway on the Ards Peninsula, a very considerable seaborne trade was carried on between the villages and Belfast in the more leisurely days before the motor lorry became ubiquitous. In the twenty years prior to World War One, the bulk of Portaferry's business with Belfast was handled by two locally-owned ketches, the *Loch Long*, owners McMullan and Co., and the *Witch of the Wave*, belonging to Messrs. Elliott. The friendly rivals both sailed from Belfast on 9 February 1914, but when off the Ards coast dirty weather began to blow up from the south. Captain Adair of the *Witch of the Wave*, not relishing having to weather Ballyquintin Point and cross the bar into Strangford Lough, opted for an anchorage in Cloughey Bay, but Captain Polley of the *Loch Long* decided to press on. It was a fatal mistake. The ketch missed the tide for Portaferry and was forced to anchor off the bar, a most disagreeable spot in such conditions. During the night the mainmast and rudder were carried away and finally the anchor chain parted and she was battered to pieces on rocks at the bar. Polley, a native of Cloughey but resident in Belfast, and his crew of two other Cloughey men, David McCappin and Andrew McNamara, were drowned, all of them leaving wives and families.

With the increase in road transport and the attendant centralization of trade in larger ports, activity at the quays and harbours of Strangford Lough dwindled. The 1920s saw the end of the beautifully named ketches and smacks, the *Witch of the Wave* (broken up with difficulty for fencing posts), the *Passing Cloud* and other sturdy veterans, while even the steam and motor coasters which replaced them grew fewer gradually. However, centralization has an ugly tendency to turn into congestion, and the late 1960s saw a small but definite resurgence in the fortunes of the small ports here and elsewhere. In July 1967 the first container service between Northern Ireland and the Isle of Man was inaugurated by the Dutch coaster *Lireco*, trading between Strangford and Douglas. Dundrum was the Irish terminal in 1968, but the service returned to Strangford in 1969, operated by the motor coaster *Kingsgate* of Hull, 535 gross tons. However, the Lough entrance had not become any less hazardous since the days of sail, as the *Kingsgate* demonstrated on 10 March 1969. In the early hours of the morning, she struck heavily on Angus Rock while inward bound from Castletown. The flood tide freed her and she drifted through the narrows, taking water rapidly, and with the lifeboats from Newcastle and Portavogie standing by she was beached on Chapel Island, at the northern end of the narrows, subsequently being refloated, severely damaged, by the tug *Cultra*. Following the incident, there was some talk in the press of a campaign to have Angus Rock lit at long last, but nothing came of it.

From the widening of Strangford Lough above the narrows to the shallows at its head is some fourteen miles, while the width averages about four miles. The Lough shares the popular distinction of having 365 islands with other large expanses of water dotted with islands, such as Clew Bay, but in reality the number of named islands, rocks and pladdies is around 100 — still an enormous total, and the feature of the Lough which contributes most to its scenic charm. Interest is added by the number of disused quays such as Ballydorn, Castle Espie, once a very substantial structure, and Quoile Quay and Steamboat Quay serving Downpatrick. Here and there, too, the observant visitor can see the hulks of former Lough traders which have ended their careers rotting away ignominiously. At low tide in Kircubbin Bay lie exposed the charred remains of the Swedish-built *Dido C.*, a ketch which sat in Kircubbin harbour for about ten years until about 1964, when the locals, sick of the sight of her, set her ablaze and pushed her away from the quay. A few timbers and a massive rudder lying beside the small pier at Ringneill are all that is left of the once well-known schooner *Fanny Crossfield*, built by Rodgers of Carrickfergus in 1880. She ran ashore in the Lough in 1937, and lay idle until broken up a couple of years later. Amidst weeds and grass near the silted-up Quoile Quay are the bones of a sailing coaster, apparently the *Hilda*, while in Strangford Bay, below Castleward House, lie the scanty remains of what is said to be the smack *Amethyst*, owned in the 1920s by Captain John Drysdale of Cloughey. A favourite dive for sub-aqua enthusiasts is to the *Alisdair*, a large motor yacht lost by fire off Ringhaddy quay around the end of World War Two.

Only a very few ships have been wrecked inside Strangford Lough by stress of weather, and then it was usually a case of moorings being broken. The legendary 'Big Wind' of 6 January 1839, a westerly hurricane that devastated Ireland' — and is credited with blowing away all the fairies —

caused havoc among shipping in Strangford Lough, as elsewhere. The brig *Henry Hastings*, which had loaded a cargo of potatoes at Kircubbin, was hurled ashore there and badly damaged, while in Ballyhenry Bay, a favourite anchorage for vessels awaiting a suitable wind and tide to leave the Lough, several ships snapped their cables, including the *Helen* of Belfast. Three ships lying at Portaferry quay with every available rope restraining them were also cast adrift and damaged. On 9 February 1850, the Portaferry-owned schooner *Nimble* went on fire and foundered in Ballyhenry Bay, while another Portaferry schooner, the *Mary Ann*, owner H. Millar, was torn from her berth at the quay and blown before the wind onto rocks to the north of Strangford on 20 February 1877, becoming a total wreck.

The tiny smack *Nil Desperando*, 5 net tons, must be the smallest cargo-carrying vessel ever lost on the Ulster coast. Her owner and master, a Killyleagh man named McCleery, boldly ventured out from Kircubbin with a load of sand for Killyleagh in the east-north-east gale of 12 November 1901 that sank the steamer *Whiteabbey* in Belfast Lough, but she was wrecked in Killyleagh Bay, McCleery and a companion aboard being saved.

There have been two serious accidents in the present century involving the Portaferry to Strangford ferry. The two communities are well under a mile apart by sea, but some forty miles by road, and a ferry service has always been maintained. The *Lizzie*, an oar-propelled cutter, capsized off Strangford on 11 April 1913, drowning both her crew and one of the three passengers. The rowing boats were superseded by open motor boats, and shortly after World War Two came the first attempt to employ a vehicle ferry, the vessel used being an un-named converted landing craft. About 9 a.m. on 23 December 1947 she left Portaferry carrying a lorry, some cattle and five persons all told. The lorry shifted to the port side, and the strong ebb tide rolled the ferry over. Four of her complement managed to scramble onto the boat's upturned bottom, the exception being Robert Drysdale, a young Portaferry man, who was trapped below. No vehicle ferry operated again until 1969, when Down County Council introduced the powerful *Strangford Ferry,* specially built at Cobh for the testing crossing.

The Salvage Steamer 'JIM McCAUSLAND' belonged to the McCausland Family of Portaferry

Split in two, the troopship 'GEORGETOWN VICTORY' at Killard Point

The 'KINGSGATE', beached on Chapel Island in Strangford Lough.

Chapter Four

THE NORTH AND SOUTH ROCKS

'Beware of the South Rock on which many brave ships have perished; for it is overflowed every tide, and no Crew can save their lives (as it stands a full Mile from the Shore) if the winds blow high'.

This was sound advice that Walter Harris gave in 1744, for the South Rock and the neighbouring North Rock, two miles away, are the most deadly hazards of the whole dangerous Ards Peninsula. They are, in fact, rather more than the two single rocks, both really being collective names for islets and half-tide rocks. Between the South Rock and the mainland there is a depth of six fathoms, but Kirkistown Spit, in places scarcely covered at high water, extends out to the North Rock from the north of Cloughey Bay. Beyond the South Rock, stretching seawards for well over a mile, is the Ridge, a shoal of rocks and gravel over which the sea breaks menacingly in strong breezes. The entire area is, therefore, one to avoid, an ugly place with an evil reputation for wrecking ships and drowning their crews.

While the North Rock has seen its share of casualties, most notably the emigrant ship *Wild Deer* in 1883, the South Rock, the adjacent Cannon Rock and the Ridge, have always been more widely feared, and as early as 1683, in William Montgomery's description of the Ards, there were suggestions for a light on the rock. During the eighteenth century there was appalling loss of life and property on the North and South Rocks. Harris records that, about the year 1714, a ship was wrecked on the North Rock, the bodies of eighteen of her crew being brought ashore for interment, in the churchyard at Slanes, south of Cloughey. This old graveyard, situated on a hill commanding a panoramic view of the North and South Rocks, is certainly worth a visit by anyone interested in Co. Down shipwrecks. To the right of the entrance can be seen the grave of Joseph Erving, aged sixteen, who drowned with the rest of the crew of the *Mally* of Workington, lost on 24 March 1810 at the landward end of Kirkistown Spit.

As many of the ships wrecked had either belonged to, or being carrying goods for, Belfast, the merchants of the port were prompted to make a plea for a light on the South Rock in 1767. Nothing came of this, but in 1783 the newly-formed Belfast Chamber of Commerce drew up another petition which made the strongest of cases for a light:

' . . . it appears . . . that . . . from 1735 to 1768 no fewer than sixty-four vessels have been totally lost on these rocks and the coast adjoining, which vessels with their cargoes at a very moderate computation were worth nearly one hundred thousand pounds, and that the number of lives lost by those shipwrecks amounted at least to two hundred and fifty-three, besides which it is highly probable many shipwrecks have happened during that time which could not be recollected and many that were never heard of'.

The petition to the Dublin Parliament concluded 'That there is every reason to believe these misfortunes would not have happened had there been a light on the South Rock'. The history of death and destruction led the Irish Parliament to grant £1,400 for the erection of a lighthouse on the South Rock, but work did not commence until 1793. In the meantime, the *Belfast News Letter* had added its voice to the agitation for a light, declaring that it was 'a national disgrace' that the South Rock remained unlit. This comment followed the loss, on 2 January 1788, of a brig bound from Liverpool to Hull. Ten of the crew were drowned, the sole survivor being a boy who was picked up the next day by a boat from the shore.

The South Rock light first burned on 25 March 1797. Only two 'wave-washed' lighthouses, the Eddystone and the Bell Rock, had preceded it, and the problems of what was still a pioneering operation were intensified when plans for the supply of the granite blocks had to be altered. The original intention was to have them dressed at Wexford and carried to the rock by two sloops, but on the first trip a gale sank one sloop and drove the other to Penzance; thereafter Mourne granite was used! Eventually the squad of some twenty workers, employed by the Commissioners of Irish Lights, completed the conical tower, which had a base 30 feet in diameter and a height of 66 feet. It was named Kilwarlin Lighthouse in honour of Lord Kilwarlin, second Marquis of Downshire, whose influence had been vital in having the light built. The tower, unlit since 1877, still stands, as does a windmill known as Pat Keown's Mill, in Ballyherly to the north of Portaferry, which is said to have been built by the workmen on the South Rock project in the intervals of bad weather that suspended construction of the lighthouse!

It is impossible to ascertain the comparative figures for wrecks before and after the South Rock was lit, but there must have been a certain reduction. In fog, ships that might otherwise have stranded were warned off by a large bell that was tolled day and night. However, no lighthouse could help a sailing ship being driven before a gale under storm canvas or bare poles, and so, just as Dundrum Bay regularly claimed wrecks after St. John's Point was lit, vessels continued to be wrecked on the North and South Rocks. Lighthouses, furthermore, need to be identified correctly, and this is what the mate of the *Minerva* of Greenock failed to do when he saw the South Rock light in the early hours of 15 January 1805. Perhaps he can be forgiven, for the *Minerva* had experienced a harrowing voyage. Bound from Wilmington, Delaware to Liverpool with tar, turpentine, pitch and timber, she had met the North Atlantic in its vilest winter mood, and had laboured across through a succession of gales, the crew on short allowance. On 11 January, as the vessel neared the Irish coast, her master, Captain W. Smith, apparently driven insane, committed suicide by jumping overboard. The mate therefore had to assume responsibility for bringing the *Minerva* safely to the Mersey, but he mistook the South Rock light for the Copeland beacon, some 25 miles to the north, with the result that the ship drove aground on the North Rock, the crew and most of the cargo being saved, happily.

January 1805 also saw the demise of one of the most historically interesting vessels ever to perish on the Ulster coast, an end that came after some 130 years trading! The brigantine *Three Sisters*, commonly known as 'The Portaferry Frigate', was built in the 1670s and earned undying fame by her presence at the siege of Londonderry in 1689, when she is reputed to have supplied the garrison with provisions. This is mentioned in an article in the *Naval Chronicle* for July 1802, which goes on to state that the *Three Sisters* was the first vessel to enter the first dock built at Liverpool, opened in 1715, and was thereafter exempted from paying dues at the port! The astonishing career of 'this venerable piece of naval architecture . . . now viewed as a curiosity' ended, unfortunately, in the worst possible way when she was wrecked near the South Rock while on passage from Dublin to Portaferry, with the loss of Captain Donnan and two crew members.

Space obviously restricts a full treatment of the host of ships which became victims of the North and South Rocks in the early part of the last century. However, the sparse details contained in the casualty columns of 'Lloyd's List' for a sample year, 1821, can perhaps, be taken as typical of the toll exacted: the brig *Perseverance*, 29 January, bound Liverpool for Buenos Ayres, 'the crew were all saved, apart from a boy, with great difficulty by boats from the shore'; the brig *Emperor Alexander* of Sunderland, Liverpool for Bahia Blanca, 20 October, and the *Jean* of Ayr, 19 November. The *Jean* 'struck upon a rock near the South Light House . . . and almost immediately sank. The crew were rescued by the *Princess Royal* . . . and landed at Donaghadee the next morning.'

The chilling brevity of shipwreck reports in this period is well exemplified by the almost cursory reference in *Lloyd's List* to a brig, presumed to have been named *William Hobbs,* lost with her crew in the last days of 1823: 'a brig of about 100 tons has sunk between the South Light and Cannon Rock; a boat has been picked up with *William Hobbs* on her stern.'

The fate of the *Marquis of Normanby* is reminiscent of the story of the *Minerva.* A brig belonging to Sligo, the *Marquis of Normanby* left New York in February 1849 with a cargo of mahogany, hemp, tallow and logwood for Belfast. Early on the voyage, she sprang a leak and the crew had to pump half the Atlantic out of her as she slowly battled her way across. On 18 April 1849, no fewer than 61 days out from New York, and with the men on short rations and exhausted by their incessant pumping, the brig piled up in a storm near the South Rock lighthouse. Captain McFillin and the crew were all saved, doubtless thankful that the long nightmare was over. Earlier that year, on 18 January, another brig, the *Mantura* of Ardrossan, came ashore on the North Rock. The Cloughey coastguards and fishermen from Portavogie managed to bring all the crew to safety, including the master's two sons, but their father was left alone in a lifeboat that broke away from the side of the *Mantura* and drifted right up the coast as far as Millisle, where it was sighted by William Hunter, a Belfast Lough pilot, who rescued the frozen occupant.

Severe gales occur every winter around the British Isles, but once in a while will come a storm of exceptional ferocity, the 'Big Wind' of 6 January 1839 and the *Royal Charter* gale of 26 October 1859 being leading examples. Such a hurricane raged on 30 and 31 March 1850 with catastrophic results; some 70 vessels were driven aground on the shores of the British Isles, six of them on the Ulster coast. The storm, accompanied by rain, blew from the south-east, and it caught the galliot *Preston*, 98 net tons, on her way from Dundalk to Llannelly in ballast. The *Preston*, owned by Robert Wilson of Belfast, was borne northwards through the winter night and dashed to pieces on the Ridge, her identity only being established when the body of her master, Robert Mateer, drifted ashore. At first light on the 31st, the schooner *Peggy,* belonging to Port Gordon, Banffshire, Liverpool for Glasgow with salt, struck nearby in Cloughey Bay, but her crew escaped.

The major failing of the South Rock lighthouse was that it did not provide adequate warning of the Ridge. Vessels not keeping far enough to the eastward of the light, either through lack of knowledge of the coast or careless handling, were liable to strand here, especially at low water. The *Eagle* of Liverpool and the brig *Governor* of Limerick did just that in 1851, as did the schooner *Reynard* of Gloucester the next year, all refloating themselves with varying degrees of damage. Less fortunate was the Dutch barque *Ida Elizabeth*, Liverpool for Batavia with general cargo, which hit the Ridge on 29 October 1854, during the dreadful spell of weather that had wrecked the *Sarah Ann* and the *Jupiter* on the Down coast the previous day. The *Ida Elizabeth*, 442 net tons, grounded about a mile from the lighthouse in the early hours of the morning, and just a few hours later a fourth vessel outward bound from the Mersey was claimed by the Down rocks when the American square-rigger *Brother Jonathan*, disabled by colliding with and sinking the *William Penn* of Belfast, came ashore a little to the north of Ballyquintin Point.

Captain William Deans of the barque *Saxon King* of London was a tired man as his vessel made her way northwards for Glasgow early on the morning of 9 January 1859, at the end of a protracted voyage from Java. The previous day he had had an acrimonious dispute with his mate, the only other certificated crew member, which had resulted in the latter ceasing to do duty. Captain Deans had been on watch for over 24 hours when he saw the South Rock light, so when he misjudged the ship's distance from it and failed to heave the lead, he could plead mitigating circumstances. The *Saxon King* struck heavily on the Ridge, but after part of her cargo had been dumped over the side, she floated off again and proceeded for the Clyde. Gradually, however, the leaks she had incurred on stranding became uncontrollable and she sank at anchor off Corsewall Point, at the mouth of Loch Ryan. At the inquiry, held in Glasgow, Deans was found responsible for the loss of his ship, but the full circumstances of the incident were taken into consideration and his master's certificate was suspended for only three months.

The fate of the *Saxon King* again underlined the need for a new light situated well to the east of the South Rock itself. While the existing light was unsatisfactory for shipping, it seems to have been equally so for the light keepers. In 1859, the Commissioners of Irish Lights recorded that the structure shook greatly in heavy weather, when spray flew right over it. The under-keeper, Mr. Stapleton, complained that there was no lightning conductor and thus, 'lightning plays around the tower fearfully'. He also pointed out that the supply boat only put out from the shore once a week, so the keepers' food was often stale, that there was no medicine chest and that the library was changed only once yearly! However, it was 1877 before the lighthouse was abandoned and the South Rock light vessel put on station two miles east-north-east of the South Rock.

Following the loss of the *Preston*, the 1850s saw only one more ship-wreck involving loss of life, when the barque *Duke of York*, bound from her home port of Greenock to Madras with coal, lost her bearings in dense fog and stranded on the South Rock on 9 December 1854. Her fourteen-man crew took to the boats, one of which was lost with its six occupants.

The following decade opened angrily, with the ferocious snowstorm of 24 – 26 January 1860 that flung nine sailing coasters on to the Down coast between the Copelands and Strangford Bar, and accounted for fifteen sea-men. Four of them died when the old schooner *Barbara*, 73 net tons, was driven on to the South Rock, only her two masts being visible the next day. Dating from 1786, when she was built at Bo'ness, the *Barbara* was a well-known Co. Down trader; she had been owned for a number of years by Charles S. Trotter of Ballywalter, and at the time of her loss was the property of John Forsyth, a prominent Downpatrick merchant. It was to the Quoile Quay near Downpatrick that the schooner had been destined with a load of limestone from Whitehead, and the story goes that people living beside the Quoile River learned of the disaster when the wreckage of the *Barbara* found its way to the intended destination! Whether this is true or not, it is certain that the loss of the *Barbara* was felt keenly in Downpatrick, as her master, Captain McMullan, and mate Dougherty were both local men, while the two hands, Denvir and Smith, were natives of Portaferry.

The worst recorded wreck on this part of the coast occurred the next year. The *Coriolanus* was a full-rigged ship of 1,108 net tons, built at Quebec in 1850 and owned by J. and J. Wait of North Shields. Outward bound from Liverpool to Quebec under Captain David Kinnear, she became enveloped in fog on 14 August 1861 and strayed on to the Cannon Rock, where she stuck fast. On learning of the casualty, Lloyd's agents in Belfast, Sinclair and Boyd, despatched the tug *Wonder* to the aid of the stricken square-rigger, but in the meantime the weather was changing ominously. As squalls and rain set in, the crew of the *Coriolanus*, believed to number 28, abandoned her and were every one drowned. All that was found to bear witness to the toll of the sea was an empty boat picked up off Ballywalter by the brig *Betsey* of Maryport. The *Coriolanus* lay deserted for a few days and then slipped off the Cannon Rock and foundered at the seaward end of the North Rock, the locals asserting that it was as if she was anxious to join her crew in their watery grave.

The tale of the *Coriolanus* was strangely echoed twelve years later, when another full-rigged ship of almost exactly the same size fell victim to the Cannon Rock. She was the *Marseilles*, 1,104 net tons, built in 1855 and owned by Patton and Co. of London. Laden with Burmese teak from Moulmein for Glasgow, the *Marseilles* stranded on the Cannon Rock on 5 January 1873, and was soon abandoned by her crew of 24. A boat containing four of them was blown right across the North Channel by the south-westerly wind, the men eventually making a safe landfall on the Mull of Galloway, but six of their shipmates were drowned trying to reach the Down shore.

Further wrecks in the 1870s included the barque *Amoy* of Dundee, Pernambuco for Greenock with sugar, on the Ridge, 1 February 1877, the schooner *Friends*, Girvan for Killyleagh with coal, on the South Rock, Christmas Eve 1877, and the 110 year-old brig *William and Mary* of Workington, on the Ridge, 7 January 1897. The port of Greenock had a substantial export trade in coal, long since ceased, and two vessels bound from there to Demerara went aground on the North Rock in February 1879. The brigantine *Titania*, owned by C. T. Bowring of Liverpool, struck in a snowstorm on 2 February, an incident for which her skipper, Captain Pencarel, later had his certificate suspended for six months. The full rigged ship *Barbadian* followed the *Titania* on 20 February, but was successfully freed four days later.

In spite of the new lightship placed beyond the Ridge in 1877, wrecks continued to occur on the North and South Rocks usually owing to fog or stress of weather; what the lightship did do was to prevent most of the strandings on the Ridge in good weather, accidents such as that to the *Saxon King*. The North and South Rocks lay so close to shipping passing up and down the North Channel that it was really inevitable that casualties would still take place while sailing vessels, which needed so much sea room, continued in use. A considerable number of steamers ended their days here, too, but these were times before navigation aids on board, when all depended on the professional skills of the ships' officers, skills that were, alas, not always displayed.

There were eight total losses in the 1880s, and while the saga of the *Wild Deer* dominates by virtue of its engaging human interest, mention must be made of the brig *John Kendall*, both because she was the last wreck with fatalities in this area, and because of the heroic rescue of her survivors. The *John Kendall*, owned by R. T. James of Sithney, Cornwall, and registered at Penzance, was another coal-laden vessel from Greenock, her cargo being consigned to Barbados. In an easterly wind and high seas she stranded on the Ridge early on 27 February 1881. The crew lowered a boat but it was stove in by the waves; a second boat was then launched taking five men, including Captain Bowden, to a rock — probably the main portion of the South Rock — but the mate and two other crew members went down with the brig when she foundered. The survivors made signals of distress, which were seen in Cloughey, from whence eleven local men put out in a yawl owned by Thomas McMullan. For a full two hours they bobbed around plucking the wrecked mariners one by one from their bleak refuge. Among the rescuers were five men named Young, of the family several of whose later generations served with distinction in the Cloughey lifeboat. At the inquiry into the loss of the *John Kendall*, Captain Bowden was held to blame and his certificate suspended for three months, a punishment also meted out to Captain Corrigall of the tramp steamer *Craigrownie*. Owned by Walker, Donald and Co., Glasgow, she was lost on the North Rock on 13 December 1881 while bound from Bilbao to Troon with iron ore, the first of nine ore-carrying steamers totally wrecked on the Down coast between this date and 1916, and the sixteenth of a staggering seventeen total losses on the county's shore in 1881.

Until a few years ago a ship's figurehead, strikingly representing Diana, Goddess of Light, stood incongruously beside a petrol station on Ballyhalbert seafront. It was a slender yet tangible link with the days when so many sailing ships met violent ends on the Down coast, for this was the figurehead of the emigrant ship *Wild Deer*, wrecked on the North Rock on 11 January 1883. The *Wild Deer*, 1,016 net tons, was a full-rigged, composite-built ship with iron topsides, teak planking over the turn of the bilge and an elm bottom, completed in 1863 by C. Connell and Co. on the Clyde, being one of the first such composite vessels. She was a magnificent, fast clipper with turtle-back poop, painted ports and a counter covered with an intricate 'gingerbread' design. In her early days the *Wild Deer* was employed in the tea trade from China, first under the ownership of W. Walker of London and later the Albion Shipping Co., Glasgow, who appointed as her master Captain George Cobb. The master on her last voyage was a Captain Kerr, who had been the carpenter on the *Peter Denny*, a consort of the *Wild Deer*, years before. The *Wild Deer* left Glasgow for Otago on 10 January 1883 with 209 emigrants, 900 tons of general cargo insured in London for £14,000 and a crew of 40. For the passengers, the figurehead of Diana pointed to a fresh start in life far away in New Zealand, but hardly had they accustomed themselves to shipboard life when the *Wild Deer* was in trouble. On the evening of the 11th the sea began to rise as near gale force winds blew up out of the south-east. The only progress a sailing ship could make in such conditions was by zigzagging into the wind, so as full-riggers were not designed to tack — to go round head to wind — in heavy weather, it appears that Captain Kerr was wearing ship, that is turning away from the wind and running before it while the yards were hauled right round and the ship brought into the wind again, when a quiver running through the vessel indicated the *Wild Deer* had touched on a reef. It was the Cannon Rock, and everyone aboard must have known that they were at the mercy of wind and sea. Shortly before midnight, the *Wild Deer* crashed on to the North Rock; her mainmast toppled almost at once, and her complement cannot have been optimistic of their chances of seeing the dark night through. Distress rockets, flaring against the black sky, were answered by the Cloughey coastguards, who, under the command of Mr. Gammon, the station officer, arrived alongside at 3 a.m. after a strenuous row. There was little the coastguards could do beyond promising to muster boats for a rescue operation, so the passengers and crew of the *Wild Deer* were faced with a long, nervous wait, the ship under them groaning with each swell. However, there were no immediate signs that she was in danger of breaking up; local opinion afterwards was that had the *Wild Deer* become wedged on the Cannon Rock, instead of passing over it with the slightest of contact, she could not have survived long.

At first light an armada of small boats from Cloughey and the neighbouring coast gathered around the stranded ship, and the rescue of the hapless emigrants began. It was an extremely slow and difficult job, for owing to the swell and the height of the *Wild Deer* above the sea, no rope ladders could be used, and each individual had to submit to being tied to a rope, hoisted over the side, then lowered some twenty feet into a waiting boat. Unmarried women were given precedence in this hazardous operation, which took many hours to complete, with more than one unfortunate receiving a ducking in the icy water. At last, however, all 209 emigrants were landed safely. Hot meals were willingly provided by the local folk, and the problem of housing such a large and unexpected influx of people was solved by the Cloughey clergyman, Rev. E. W. Whitley, who opened the little Presbyterian church and let the crew and passengers of the *Wild Deer* sleep that night in the pews! The next day, they embarked in a convoy of carriages for Newtownards, thence Belfast by train, and, after a night at the Sailors' Home, all walked in procession to the Glasgow steamer. From Glasgow, the emigrants dispersed to the former homes which they had left only a few days previously never expecting to see again. Meanwhile, the *Wild Deer* was grinding and straining on the North Rock, until, on 17 January, she broke her back.

The inquiry into the loss of the *Wild Deer* was held at Glasgow on 5 February 1883, and Captain Kerr found guilty of careless navigation. This would, perhaps, seem to lend weight to his summary dismissal by Basil

Lubbock, the chronicler of clippers and their men: 'He was a very steady man, but no sailor'!

The year 1883 saw two more casualties in this area, the steamers *Emily* of Sunderland, Bilbao for Glasgow with iron ore, 22 September, and *Strathdon* of Glasgow, Abergele for the Clyde with limestone, 9 October. Knowles, the mate of the *Emily,* had made the grotesque mistake of taking the Mull of Galloway light to be the South Rock lightship, an error for which he had his certificate suspended for six months. The ship was refloated, but only five months later was wrecked in Belfast Lough. Iron ore was also the cargo of the tramp steamer *Eureka*, aground for a tide on the South Rock on 8 February 1886, while copper ore was in the holds of the *Wembdon*, another tramp owned by The 'Raleigh's Cross' Co. Ltd. of Cardiff. Sailing from the Spanish port of Huelva on 29 December 1886 bound for Troon, the *Wembdon* had a good passage until 8 p.m. on 4 January, when she was suddenly engulfed by heavy snow. Anxiously peering into the wintry night, Captain George tried to discern a light that would give him an inkling of his whereabouts, but in vain, for the sweeping snow reduced visibility to almost nil. The *Wembdon* blindly steamed inside the lightship and came to a shuddering halt on the Cannon Rock. Realising now where they were, and the peril of the position, Captain George immediately gave the order to abandon ship, and the fourteen Britons and one Spaniard who made up the crew launched the boats and rowed in the direction of the lightship. Five minutes after the *Wembdon* was abandoned, she broke in two, and dawn the next day revealed her as a complete wreck.

A surprising proportion of the casualties in this area is made up by just two types of ship — ore-laden tramp steamers and Norwegian barques. The *Amanda* of Sandefjord, Garston for Cronstadt with coal, which was lost on the North Rock on 26 June 1881, was the first of no fewer than six such Norwegians to end their careers littered around the North and South Rocks between this date and 1898. The *Urania*, Liverpool for Vyborg with salt, was lost on the North Rock on 9 June 1886, and within five years two more members of the great Norwegian fleet of world-wide traders were wrecked nearby. The *Kate*, 613 net tons, left the Mersey on 3 January 1888 with a cargo of Garston coal for Christiania. Off Great Orme's Head, she ran into a south-south-easterly gale that drove her inexorably northwards. The entire night of 4 — 5 January she spent trying to fight her way clear of the South Rock, but finally, at 7 a.m. on the 5th., the *Kate* drifted aground. By this time the gale had moderated somewhat so that Captain Hansen and his crew were able to row to the mainland in the ship's boats, returning later for their belongings, but the *Kate* soon became a total loss.

Her fate was closely paralleled by that of the *Grid* of Farsund, coal-laden from Liverpool for Buenos Ayres, except that this barque was beaten hither and thither in the Irish Sea for no fewer than six days before she smashed on to the Cannon Rock on the evening of 13 October 1891. The Cannon Rock also claimed the *Helen*, owned by S. C. Larsen of Brevik, which, in contrast to the *Kate* and the *Grid*, had been borne to the south on her voyage from Ardrossan to Christiania with coal. The date of her loss was 2 October 1895. The sixth and largest of the Norwegian barques was the *Beaconsfield*, 1,375 net tons, which belonged to the famous firm of sailing ship owners, Bruusgaard and Co. of Drammen. Having come all the way from Rangoon with teak for Greenock, the *Beaconsfield* ran aground on the North Rock on 9 April 1898.

So much iron ore has been deposited on the seabed around the North and South Rocks that rust can be seen on the shells of crabs and lobsters caught in the area! The year 1906 witnessed another several thousand tons spill from two wrecks, the steamers *Febo* and *Hazeldene*. The *Febo*, 2,289 gross tons, had been built in 1875 as the British *Naples* for Nelson, Donkin and Co., but since 1900 had been operated by Lagorara and Pittaluga of Genoa. Her ore was loaded at Almeria, but never reached its destination, Glasgow, for the *Febo* steamed on to the Cannon Rock in hazy weather at 1 a.m. on 6 February. Conditions were very much worse as the *Hazeldene*, Horndillo, Spain, for Glasgow, entered the North Channel on 26 December. In a south-easterly force eight gale and thick snow, Captain R. C. Begg mistook the South Rock lightship for the Mull of Galloway light, thus putting his ship on to the Cannon Rock, though he and his nineteen-man crew were all rescued. The *Hazeldene*, 2,204 gross tons, had been built on the Tyne in 1881 and was owned by I. Crocker of Cardiff.

Fog caused the loss of the Cornish schooner *Rippling Wave*, 1 March 1907, and the steam coaster *Glassford*, 30 September 1908, both on the South Rock. The *Rippling Wave*, a pretty vessel dating from 1869 and credited with the extremely fast passage of fourteen days from Fowey to Genoa in 1886, stranded on a trip from Par to Glasgow, her crew being picked up by the *Retriever* — a happier incident in this collier's ill-starred career. The *Glassford*, 311 gross tons, was bound from Neath to Belfast with coal, and her crew sought shelter in the tower of the old lighthouse, disturbing the hosts of seabirds which occupied it now. A mere six weeks later, there was another total loss only a matter of yards from the *Glassford*, involving the largest sailing ship ever to strand on the Down coast, and one of the largest barques ever to put to sea.

The *Croisset* was a steel three-masted vessel of 2,257 net tons, built in 1902 — at the end of the era of deepwater sail — and owned by the Societe Bretonne de Navigation of Rouen. Leaving New Caledonia in July 1908 with 3,500 tons of nickel ore for Glasgow, she had a long, arduous passage across the South Pacific, around Cape Horn and northwards up the full length of the Atlantic. With provisions running low, the *Croisset* laboured up the Irish Sea on 13 November 1908, the wind freshening. By that night it had increased to gale force, and with the sea running high she grated on to the South Rock shortly before midnight. Cloughey lifeboat, under coxswain Robert Young, splashed down the slip in answer to the rockets and flares that Captain Alphonse de Kervegan of the *Croisset* sent up, and after a taxing four hours the crew of over twenty were brought safely to the mainland. Next day, one of the powerful tugs belonging to McCauslands, the Portaferry salvage contractors, attempted in vain to free the big French barque, and the great vessel — whose shortest yard was longer than the longest on the clipper ship *Battle Abbey* — became a total loss.

The list of casualties on the North and South Rocks reveals a preponderance of large ships, in contrast to other parts of the Down coast, largely owing to the proximity of the rocks to the main shipping routes to the Mersey and the Clyde. The Blue Funnel liner *Agamemnon* spent a few days on the North Rock after stranding on 29 July 1910, while another iron ore steamer, the *Reading*, 2,043 gross tons, finished her days on the Cannon Rock on 5 November 1913, bound from Seville to Glasgow. It has been suggested that an obscure magnetic attraction in the vicinity of the South Rock or the neighbouring Ards coast could act on the compasses of ships laden with iron ore, which itself necessitates adjustment to the compass before sailing, but the author has never found any evidence for this hypothesis.

November 1916 was a grim month for wrecks around the Down shores: the *Retriever* and the *Connemara* collided, the *Fulvia* was wrecked near Newcastle, while the Russian barque *Frieda* became yet another victim of the South Rock. Twenty-eight days out from Mobile for Greenock with pitch pine, she, like the *Croisset* was assailed by a storm in the Irish Sea on the night of 6 — 7 November 1916. The deck cargo shifted, the heavy logs tumbling over the deck smashing fittings, and with the canvas being torn from her rigging, the *Frieda* hit the South Rock and stuck, firmly aground. The following morning, efforts to free her using a kedge anchor failed, and with the pine logs still rolling about dangerously as seas were shipped copiously, Captain Donner and his crew of twenty left the *Frieda* and rowed ashore at Kearney. Their barque had been built of iron as the full-rigged ship

County of Edinburgh for R. & J. Craig of Glasgow in 1885, passing in 1904 to German owners who renamed her. Before her final voyage could commence, incidentally, the *Frieda* had to be refloated and repaired after a hurricane had flung her ashore at Mobile.

The winter of 1916 also saw the last iron ore steamer becoming a total loss in the area, when, on 18 December, the *Benshaw*, 1,724 gross tons, stranded on the South Rock while on passage Bilbao to Ayr. The war years of course, brought the added menace of enemy U-boats; of the engagements off the Co. Down coast the worst British loss was sustained when the *Daybreak* was torpedoed a mile east of the South Rock lightship. A steamer of 3,238 gross tons, owned by the Scarisbrick Steamship Co. Ltd. of Cardiff, the *Daybreak* had been attacked by the guns of a surfaced submarine in the Arctic Sea on 1 November 1916. On that occasion she beat off her foe with her own defence gun, but had no chance with the torpedo that sank her on Christmas Eve, 1917, killing twenty-one crew members.

Bound from Sligo to Barry in ballast, the Tyneside-owned steamer *Scarpa*, 2,759 gross tons, was forced on to the North Rock by a gale on 18 November 1920. Captain Walner, whose wife was a passenger along with the wife and child of the steward, ordered distress rockets to be ignited and Cloughey lifeboat was launched to assist in a difficult rescue. The bo'sun of the *Scarpa* clambered over the side with a rope, which, with the aid of the lifeboatmen, he made secure to the rocks; one by one the twenty-six persons remaining on the *Scarpa* were hauled down on to the North Rock and thence taken aboard the lifeboat. Battered by high seas, the ship was abandoned to the insurance underwriters as a total loss by her owners, the Sutherland Steamship Co., but was refloated on 23 February 1921 — surprisingly, in view of the great slump that had followed the post-war trade boom. The *Scarpa* was towed to Belfast and after extensive repairs re-emerged a few months later as the Greek *Amazon*. She survived until New Year's Day, 1947, when as the *Caritas I*, her eighth name, she was sunk in a collision off Flushing.

The largest total loss in this area was the Dutch steamer *Alhena* — remembered locally as the 'Helena' — which stranded on the North Rock on 28 January 1941 while bound from Liverpool to Port Said with supplies for the Eighth Army. Her gross tonnage of 4,930 was surpassed by the Lamport and Holt cargo liner *Lassell*, 7,256 tons, which grounded at the same spot in the early hours of 9 August 1952, but the *Lassell* was eventually freed. The Liverpool and Glasgow Salvage Association were entrusted with refloating operations, a job which saw the last appearance in local waters of their famous salvage vessel *Ranger*, which had helped to refloat the *Agamemnon* here as far back as 1910. Built as a sloop for the Admiralty in 1880, the *Ranger,* a tremendously tough composite-built steamer, was a familiar sight at scenes of wrecks all round the British Isles for half a century until she was dismantled at Salthouse Dock, Liverpool, in March 1954.

At the time of writing, the most recent casualty on this part of the coast is the Dutch coaster *Wiebold Bohmer*, 500 gross tons. Having called at Dublin on her regular run between Continental ports and Ireland, the *Wiebold Bohmer* was proceeding to Belfast when she ran aground on the North Rock early on 10 December 1971, being left high and dry when the tide receded. The Holyhead tug *Afon Cefni* pulled her off on the evening of the following day, and towed her to Belfast with a fifteen degree list to port. So badly was the *Wiebold Bohmer* damaged, however, that it was not considered worthwhile to repair her and she was scrapped at Nieuw Lekkerland in Holland.

The 'WILD DEER', later the North Rock's most famous wreck.   Note Figurehead.

Chapter Five

THE ARDS PENINSULA

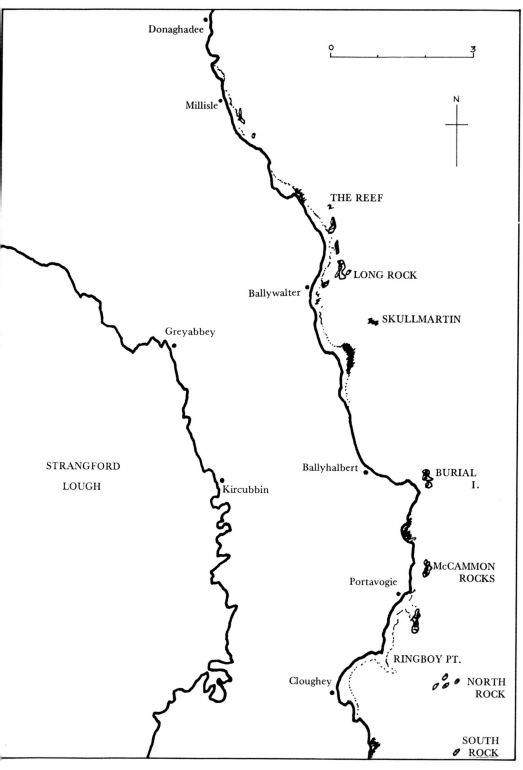

Donaghadee

Millisle

THE REEF

LONG ROCK

Ballywalter

SKULLMARTIN

Greyabbey

STRANGFORD
LOUGH

Ballyhalbert

BURIAL
I.

Kircubbin

McCAMMON
ROCKS

Portavogie

RINGBOY PT.

Cloughey

NORTH
ROCK

SOUTH
ROCK

N

0   3

MAP 5

Low-lying and gently undulating, the Ards Peninsula stretches from Orlock Point, at the entrance to Belfast Lough, to Ballyquintin Point, some thirty miles to the south, being bounded to the west by Strangford Lough and to the east by the Irish Sea. This western seaboard is, quite simply, vicious, a continuous succession of rocks, pladdies and reefs, some extending far out to sea, having claimed ships and men. The most feared parts have always been the North and South Rocks, off Cloughey, and such is the number of wrecks here that they have warranted a chapter to themselves. Almost every rock on the Ards coast, however, has victims to its name: Ballyferis Point, the Ship Rock, the Long Rock off Ballywalter, the Skullmartin, Burial Island and many others have seen ships of all types, sizes and flags meet their ends. The combination of the inherent dangers of the coast and the proximity of shipping in the North Channel has made the Ards Peninsula a veritable ships' graveyard; between 1875 and 1900, for instance, no fewer than seventy-five vessels were totally lost on the coast proper and the North and South Rocks, with the consequent deaths of twenty-nine men.

Only a very small number of the casualties in this area have involved ships bound to or from the local harbours, for only Donaghadee among them has seen much trade, Portavogie, Ballyhalbert and Ballywalter and the open beaches at Cloughey and Millisle being used just to import coal and other raw materials, and export farm produce. Donaghadee was the Irish terminal of the mail and passenger route to Portpatrick from the early seventeenth century until the Government withdrew the mail service in 1849. The splendid harbour was completed in 1834 for the passenger trade, and after the last sailings to Portpatrick, operated by private enterprise in 1873, the import of coal, much carried by the railway into central Down, became the mainstay of the port. Donaghadee, moreover, was the only harbour of refuge, albeit not a perfect one, on a coast devoid of shelter from all winds from north through east to south.

The present crew of the Donaghadee lifeboat are heirs to a long tradition of life-saving in the community. Reminded by the loss of William Smith in an attempt to assist the *Rose* of Maryport into Donaghadee in an easterly gale on 19 November 1791, the *Belfast News Letter* recorded, 'In February 1780 no less than eleven Donaghadee men were lost in helping the *Amazon* to Belfast'. On 25 February 1780, the privateer *Amazon* was wrecked near Bangor, so it would appear that the newspaper is referring to an abortive bid to aid the ship. In the same furious northerly that destroyed the privateer, a vessel named *Richard* was wrecked at the back of the old pier at Donaghadee, while two years later the *Junge Louisa*, from Danzig, stranded near the town.

Information on wrecks of this period is unfortunately scarce, but there must have been a very substantial number of casualties on the Ards coast. In the old graveyard on the grassy knoll at Slanes is a small stone, encrusted with lichen, which reads: 'Here lieth the body of John Auld, shipmaster of Irvine aged 49 years who was drove ashore in a hard gale upon the 15th of January 1789 at six in the morning when he and three more out of five in number perished'. November 1794 alone saw the losses of the brig *Jean* at Ballyquintin Point, four drowned, the full-rigged ship *Union* at Tara, two miles north of Ballyquintin, and a sloop alongside the *Union*, while an eighteenth century map of the area bears the tantalising inscription 'Here the *Wolf* was lost' printed beside Kearney Point. Another *Union* was wrecked on the Skullmartin on 23 February 1803, while bound from Workington to Dublin with coal and about the same time an American vessel, the *Delight*, 227 net tons, came ashore at Ringboy Point near Cloughey. Such disconnected references as survive from these times prior to the systematic tabulating of shipwrecks by Victorian civil servants give glimpses of a life at sea of perpetual danger, when the epitaph for a wrecked or missing ship was usually brief: 'A sloop, supposed to be the *Ann and Mary* . . . lately sank near Ballywalter and it is feared all the crew were drowned'. 'The *Sheffield*, from Irvine, is totally lost in Cloughey Bay and the crew and passengers all drowned'.

In February 1827 a widow, Mary Callaghan, embarked on the brig *Ocean* at Charleston, South Carolina, to return to her native Ireland, bringing with her the only surviving child of the six she had borne her late husband. The *Ocean*, a Belfast-owned vessel commanded by Captain John Thomson of the town, weathered the rigours of the Atlantic bound for her home port with cotton, but on 4 March was cast ashore on Ballyferis Point in a severe gale and thick snow. Happily, all on board were saved before the brig went to pieces, but Mrs. Callaghan lost all her savings, some £130, and most of her possessions. Her plight being acute, an appeal was organised by Captain Thomson and others, who called on the generosity of the Ulster people to assist the distressed widow and her child.

The dubious distinction of being the first steamship wrecked on the Down coast belongs, as far as can be ascertained, to the wooden paddler *Britannia*, a pioneer steamer built at Port Glasgow in 1815. Powered by two-cylinder beam engines, the *Britannia* carried passengers between Glasgow and

Londonderry from 1822 to 1829, before which she had operated summer excursions from the Clyde to the Giant's Causeway. It was on a voyage from Glasgow to Newry on 21 November 1829 that she got into difficulties, was driven into Donaghadee harbour and sank. At this time the new harbour was still being built by John Rennie, but on 6 January 1839 it was to its seven acres, now fully enclosed by the great limestone piers, that no fewer than twenty-four coasters ran as the 'Big Wind' raged. Amidst scenes of utter confusion, however, six of them sank in the harbour, including two Co. Down vessels, the *Eliza Jane*, belonging to Portaferry, and the *Belle Ann* of Annalong.

Burr Point, about a mile south-east of Ballyhalbert, is the most easterly point on the Irish mainland, and a few hundred yards offshore lies Burial Island, a grass-covered hump surrounded by jagged reefs. The name has a sinister ring, but is almost certainly a corruption of Burr Isle; it is marked on seventeenth-century maps as 'Bryalle' and was later variously referred to as 'Berry Island' and 'Burritt Rock'. It has been a constant source of danger to shipping, even in recent years, and throughout the last century the coast-guards stationed on Burr Point were frequently in action at scenes of shipwreck. Early in 1839, possibly in the 'Big Wind', the coal-laden brig *Shannon* of Whitehaven stranded here, her hull and equipment later being sold at an auction held on the mainland — a normal procedure in those days. The *Consbrook*, an ocean-going vessel of 423 net tons, which grounded on Burial Island on 12 February 1847, may have been refloated, but the *Canadienne* was certainly a total wreck on 15 January 1851. An American-built schooner registered in Fleetwood, she struck at 5.30 a.m. in a southerly gale and teeming rain, being apparently further disadvantaged by a defective compass, while bound from Runcorn to Galway with coal. The coastguards rescued Captain Rood and his crew of four, but when another schooner, the *Black Prince* of Carnarvon, struck below the watch-house on 19 December 1853, the crew's boat was upset in the surf and the mate lost.

Casualties on Burial Island have mostly involved small cargo ships, but a notable exception was the emigrant ship *Sapphire*. A full-rigged ship of 1,140 net tons, the *Sapphire* was feeling her way tentatively southward in thick fog when she ground to a standstill on Burial Island at midnight on Saturday, 4 November 1853. Outward bound from her home port of Glasgow, her destination Melbourne, the *Sapphire* had on board 113 emigrants and a general cargo worth £40,000, being manned by a crew of thirty-five under Captain William Bird. There being no immediate danger, the emigrants were not landed until daybreak, eventually being returned to

Glasgow via Belfast. The Parliamentary Sessional Papers for 1854 relating to emigration contain absorbing correspondence concerning the wreck of the *Sapphire*. A letter from Captain Charles Keele to the Colonial Office, dated at Glasgow Custom Office, 9 November, reports: 'This morning about fifty of the p :ngers met here in an hotel, and passed a resolution much in favour of the master and his officers. They have no complaints to make, except being plundered by t' .ountry people of their little property.'

Keele had concluded that Captain Bird was to blame, 'in hugging the Irish coast so much, particularly at night', while Lieutenant de Courcey, Government Emigration Officer for Ireland, had been in Belfast at the time of the wreck, but had felt bound to stay there owing to the crisis of the *Guiding Star* being in port with cholera on board and attributed no blame for the loss of the *Sapphire*. The coastguards' return to the Admiralty opines she was wrecked, 'by error in judgement, not making allowance for tide, hazy weather etc.' It appears, too, that the lead was not hove, which certainly seems remiss of the master if he thought he was near the Ards coast. As to the complaints of looting, it should be said that coastal communities everywhere felt they were exercising a natural right to appropriate anything and everything the sea, usually an enemy, might present to them!

Dense fog lured another passenger vessel on to Burial Island on 12 August 1857, a very different ship, the iron paddle steamer *Waterloo*, belonging to Langtry and Herdman of Belfast who employed her on their Liverpool service. Again, the lead line was not used to establish the depth before the paddler churned her way on to the rocks, but after lightening she was towed off. The next year, all three persons on board the yacht *Brandywine* perished when a north-westerly gale threw her on to Burial Island.

An enormous amount of coal was needed in the mid-Victorian age to satisfy the domestic and industrial demands of the rapidly growing city of Belfast, but a heavy price in human life was paid for the fuel. Although the 1860s saw a diversity of ships stranding in the Ards area, stories of wreck and rescue involving Belfast colliers dominate. The dreadful blizzard of 26 January 1860 claimed the *Joseph* and *Venilia*, dashed to pieces on Ballyferis Point with the loss of a total of ten men, while three other Belfast colliers the *Betseys*, *Pivot* and *Purchase* were also cast ashore nearby but later refloated. The crew of the *Betseys* had a particularly fortuitous escape, as she bumped over the reef where the *Venilia* was being pounded, into calmer water off the beach now popular with holidaymakers at the adjacent caravan site. Further loss of life occurred at Ballyferis Point on 8 February 1861, when the *Martha* of Belfast was lost with all hands.

This rugged stretch of coast with its black-fanged rocks witnessed exciting scenes on 17 January 1864, when, in a hard south-easterly gale, the Belfast schooner *Daniel Webster* was forced aground. Her crew clambered into the rigging, and, observing their plight, two boats set out from the shore, manned by Joseph Mountstephens and Frederick Gray, both coast-guards, and nine Ballywalter men. At great risk, the six crew of the schooner were taken off their disintegrating vessel, an exploit for which their rescuers were each rewarded from the Mercantile Marine Fund. Mean-while, at Ballyhalbert, six miles to the south, another Belfast collier, the brig *Eunice*, and the *Emma* of Wigtown, were ashore and being battered by wind and sea. Three men were lost and two saved from each coaster, the rescue of the survivors of the *Emma* being effected by the *Mary Ann*, a small Ballyhalbert boat crewed by six local men, James Curran, James Cully, William Blakely, Hugh McMaster and David and John McVay. Three men of the *Emma* had given up their numb hold on the rigging by the time the *Mary Ann* approached at great risk and snatched to safety the skipper and sole remaining crew member. Again, the rescuers were awarded cash sums from the Mercantile Marine Fund.

The Long Rock, off Ballywalter, marks the commencement of a series of off-shore rocks, steep on the seaward side, which stretches to the Ship Rock, three miles to the north. The number of wrecks in this menacing area, and on the Skullmartin, south-east of Ballywalter, finally prompted the establishment of a lifeboat station in the village in 1866. The night of 1 − 2 January 1867 was a wild one, blowing force nine from the east and snowing heavily. In the bleak light of dawn, the trained eyes of Robert Boyd, the lifeboat coxswain, noticed wreckage on the Long Rock, and, alerting his men, they set out in the lifeboat *Admiral Henry Meynell* to investigate. Four sodden and weak men were found clinging to spars and rigging, all that remained of the brigantine *General Williams*, a collier bound from Maryport to Belfast, which had struck at 2 a.m. and become a total wreck in ten minutes. Boyd and his crew brought the exhausted men ashore, and also recovered the body of a young deckhand, Richard Gribben of Ardglass, who had succumbed to exposure shortly before first light. One man's condition gave particular cause for worry, but he was tended at Boyd's house and slowly revived, while his colleagues were looked after by Mr. William Morrison and supplied with new clothing by William Gibson, a local merchant and shipowner. The *General Williams,* built at Shelburne, Nova Scotia, in 1856, was the property of John and James Stewart, coal merchants of Belfast, and Martin Wallace, a brick manufacturer.

The last victims in this grim sequence of collier wrecks met their ends in a howling southerly on 10 December 1868. Five men of the schooner *Myrtle* perished at Burial Island, while about a mile to the south, only one man out of four in the *Liffey*, another schooner, escaped.

While these losses suffered by the collier fleets make the 1860s the worst period on record for the Ards coast, several other notable incidents took place, including a wreck that revived memories of the *Sapphire*. This was the *Grasmere*, and, unlike the other wrecks involving emigrant ships on the Down coast, absolutely no excuse could be offered for her loss. The *Grasmere*, 432 net tons, had been built at Chepstow in 1847 and belonged to P. Henderson and Co. of Glasgow, from whom she had been chartered by H. M. Emigration Commissioners. Conditions aboard many emigrant ships were a disgrace, but the government insisted on certain standards on vessels they employed, such as the *Grasmere*, which were for selected settlers only. Under Captain Charles Turner, the *Grasmere* sailed from Greenock on 14 December 1863 with 114 emigrants destined for New Zealand. Contrary winds detained her in Lamlash Bay, but Turner heaved up again on the morning of Thursday the 17th., and made sail on his southerly course. The day turned out calm and clear, and a fair wind meant that as darkness fell the *Grasmere* was approaching the Copelands, land and lights being clearly visible. However, with what the subsequent inquiry described as 'great negligence', the master brought the *Grasmere* too close to the Ards coast, and at 7 p.m. with the helmsman frantically trying to rectify the error, the vessel crashed on to Ship Rock, off Ballyferis, a mass of milling people emerging on deck, alarmed by the shuddering impact. The luckless emigrants and the crew of twenty-two were taken off by coastguards and ferried to Belfast by the steam tug *Wonder*, but the *Grasmere* broke up five days later. The Board of Trade, finding Captain Turner guilty of careless navigation, suspended his certificate for six months.

Captain William Stokes of the paddle steamer *Earl of Dublin* had more to worry him than Captain Turner as he turned in to his bunk at midnight on 21 March 1867, having left his mate to continue on the course from Glasgow to Dublin, for it was a gloomy night with continual snow squalls and a heavy sea. The *Earl of Dublin*, a new ship on only her third voyage, had on board thirty-three passengers and a general cargo, which included iron stowed on deck, this later being held to have affected the compass. At 2 a.m. she passed the Copelands light, at a distance the mate calculated to be six miles. As the weather worsened until it was blowing a south-easterly gale and the snow was falling without respite, the mate lost sight of the Copelands but failed to pick up the South Rock Light. He roused Captain Stokes, who sent a man aloft to watch for the gleam of the South Rock, but the look-out's first cry was 'Breakers right ahead!' The wheel was spun hard to starboard, the engines rung to stop and then reverse, but the *Earl of Dublin* thudded onto rocks on the mainland to the west of Burial Island. All on board were taken off safely, and the steamer might have been refloated had not a subsequent storm added to the damage. Her wreck was bought by Harland and Wolff, who rebuilt her and sold her back to the original Dublin owners, but the new name *Duke of Edinburgh* brought no change of luck, for she was wrecked on Ailsa Craig in fog on 19 January 1870.

That year of 1867 also witnessed perhaps one of the saddest stories in the annals of local shipwrecks. Captain Knowles, an army officer quartered in Dublin, had been on leave in Scotland and decided to return from Greenock to Kingstown in his big schooner-rigged yacht *Tana*, built on the shores of Belfast Lough at Rockport in 1855. With him he brought his wife, their fifteen-month-old child and a servant, Agnes Murray, while he enlisted three men to crew the *Tana* for him. The *Tana* was beating her way to windward off the Ards coast on the pitch-black night of 11 September when, at 11 p.m., she struck the Skullmartin and sank in little over five minutes. Secured on deck had been a boat, but it was filled with lumber and could not be cleared in time. As confusion reigned, Agnes Murray inadvertently let the child fall into the sea and it was never seen again. Mrs. Knowles and the servant put on lifebelts and floated, tied to a mast, while the Captain, with no lifebelt, clung on beside them. Above, gripping the rigging, were the three crew members. For long, nightmarish hours the little group tried to keep each other's spirits up, but Mrs. Knowles and Agnes Murray, both distraught by the loss of the child, died during the night, as did Captain Knowles just before dawn. At first light the wreck was spotted by coastguards and the survivors brought ashore in the last extremities of exhaustion. All on board could have been saved, declared Ballywalter lifeboat coxswain Robert Boyd, had only distress signals been sent. Mrs. Knowles's body was washed ashore, and at the inquest the jury, returning a verdict of accidental death, recommended that a lighthouse be constructed on the Skullmartin. This was never done, but a lightship was placed off the reef in the 1880s.

The name Skullmartin, like Burial Island, conjures up powerful images of death, but it is in fact a corruption of *Sker Martin*, a name by which it was known in earlier times, *sker* being Norse for an offshore reef — as in The Skerries off Anglesey and off Portrush. Before the establishment of the lightship, three wrecks occurred here in seventeen months, the most serious, the *Loch Sunart*, having attached to it as romantic a story as any attending an Irish wreck.

The first of the trio was the steam coaster *Aberystwith*, Llanelly for Londonderry with coal, which was lost on 27 June 1878. While the crew of the 137 gross ton steamer were vainly trying to lighten and free their ship, on the other side of the world a young seaman was reflecting on the adventure that had earned him global publicity. Tom Pearce had been an apprentice on board the full-rigged ship *Loch Ard* when she was wrecked to the west of Melbourne on 1 June 1878. Pearce was the only crew member to reach the shore, but on hearing cries he swam out to the wreck again and brought to safety a teenage girl, Eva Carmichael, the daughter of a Dublin physician who perished with the six other members of his family. The wreck, and the tale of the young survivors, caused a sensation, the citizens of Australia even hoping the pair would marry, but Eva Carmichael returned to Ireland and Pearce joined the crew of the new iron square-rigger *Loch Sunart* which had just arrived at Sydney from Glasgow on her maiden voyage. The *Loch Sunart*, 1,124 net tons, had been built by A. & J. Inglis on the Clyde for Aitken, Lilburn and Co. of Glasgow, who intended employing her on their monthly Glasgow to Australia service. She began her second voyage on Monday, 6 January 1879, having on board forty-nine passengers and 2,100 tons of cargo, with a crew of thirty-three – including Tom Pearce – commanded by the experienced Captain Gavin Weir. Encountering a south-easterly gale, Weir put into Lamlash Bay, Arran, for two days, and on sailing from this popular anchorage was soon forced to run for Belfast Lough. At 6 p.m. on Saturday 10th, the anchor was weighed, the evening being fine and clear with a slight breeze from the west. Under a full moon, the *Loch Sunart* slowly rounded the Copelands to begin her long trek southwards to the Cape of Good Hope.

Captain Weir was below, examining his chart, the mate was on the fore-castle head and the second mate on the poop with the helmsman when the ship drove on to the Skullmartin. The concerned passengers rushed on deck, their cries for help carrying plainly across the calm water to Ballywalter. The lifeboat was speedily launched, and, helped by local boats and the ship's own boats, was soon busily ferrying passengers ashore. An unsuccessful attempt was made to haul off the stranded ship using a kedge anchor, but the master and crew stayed on board until the following after-noon when, in rain, sleet and a freshening breeze, the lifeboat landed all but a skeleton crew. Whether Tom Pearce came ashore then or later is not clear, but legend has it that the first person he saw on landing at Ballywalter was Eva Carmichael! This is stretching credulity a little far, of course, and the story probably originated in the over-fertile imagination of a journalist. Although Pearce was barely twenty, this was his third shipwreck, for he had been on a vessel named *Helen Ramsay* before the *Loch Ard*; far from being deterred from his chosen career, however, he eventually became a master in Royal Mail Lines, dying young in 1908. Eva Carmichael survived the man to whom she owed her life by about thirty years.

Strenuous efforts to refloat the *Loch Sunart* failed, and although quite a portion of the cargo was salved, including gunpowder taken to Carrickfergus Castle for storage, subsequent gales sealed her fate. All that remained to do was hold the official inquiry, and this resulted in Captain Weir losing his certificate for nine months — a severe penalty — while that of the mate was suspended for three months.

The next casualty on the Skullmartin, the iron schooner *Ladyland*, also brought repercussions, Captain Ritchie and the second mate both forfeiting their certificates for three months. The *Ladyland*, bound with pitch from Glasgow to Port de Bouc near Marseilles, was wrecked on 13 November 1879. The last total loss on the Skullmartin was the barque *Cuyuni*, which stranded and later went on fire on 30 September 1883, when on passage from Glasgow to Demerara.

Like most of Britain's lifeboats, the Ballywalter station had a distinguished and colourful history. The station was closed in 1906, as the coastguards had withdrawn from the locality, leaving the boat with insufficient men to crew it, but there had never been a regular crew, and volunteers were often enlisted. Twice on difficult services a clergyman was on board. The Reverend Henry R. Wilson, incumbent of Drumbeg near Ballywalter, helped make up the numbers when the boat was launched on the dark evening of 15 December 1876 to aid the schooner *Jenny Lind* of Coleraine, Maryport for Portrush with coal, which had lost her rudder in a southerly gale and been beaten on to the Long Rock. At the third attempt, the lifeboat came alongside the *Jenny Lind* — named after a celebrated Swedish opera singer of the day — and snatched to safety Captain Monaghan and the crew of four. At a meeting of the R.N.L.I. in London the following month, it was agreed to present Rev. Wilson with the thanks of the Institution inscribed in vellum for his role in the rescue feat.

When the square-rigger *Castlemaine* came ashore in Ballyhalbert Bay at 10 p.m. on 3 March 1881, it was blowing so hard from the south-east that the lifeboat could not be launched till 8 a.m., but when the crew began their exhausting row to the scene, among them was Rev. Blackwood, incumbent of Ballywalter. At last, after great toil, they pulled under the lee rail of the *Castlemaine* and took off her crew of twenty-five. Destined for Rangoon, the big deep-sea sailer had left the Clyde two days previously, but became a total loss for her owners, T. Williams and Co. of Liverpool.

Partly owing to the sterling work of the Ballywalter boat, the 1870s saw a considerable reduction in the death toll compared with the 1860s and before, there being only two wrecks with fatalities. The little smack *Boaz* of Carnarvon was lost just north of Ballyhalbert on 9 April 1877, two men drowning, while later that year, on 5 December, the schooner *Diligent*, Bridgwater for Belfast with bricks, took the ground off Cloughey and went to pieces, drowning with her Captain Edwards of Barmouth, her master and owner, and the two crew members. The *Admiral Henry Meynell* earned further plaudits for her services during probably the worst gale of the 1880s, a fierce southerly on 6 — 7 February 1883 that bore three vessels on to the Ards coast. The Ballywalter boat saved six men from the brigantine *Euphemia Fullerton*, Maryport for Londonderry with coal, which was lying on the Long Rock. She had sailed from the Cumberland harbour in company with the *Clara*, a schooner belonging to the prominent Belfast coal merchant William M. Barkley, which was also driven aground in the gale, on the McCammon Rock, just north of Portavogie. James McDowell, the cook, was the sole survivor of the crew of six, the rest of whom were washed away as he hung on to the rigging. The third and largest wreck was that of the steam coaster *Strathyre*, Troon for Dublin with coal, at Kearney Point. For four hours the eleven-man crew had to stay on the collier, until, with her deck slowly being submerged, shore boats took them off.

A mile south-east of Kearney Point lies the sunken rock known as Butter Pladdy, the cause of the worst accident to befall any of the ten ore-laden tramp steamers lost on the Down coast. The *Harold*, 1,257 gross tons and the property of Henry Briggs, Sons and Co. of Hull, steamed on to the rock on 17 May 1890, while making for Ayr from Bilbao. Coastguards put out from Kearney, but Captain Smith declined their assistance. The *Harold* floated off on the tide and was soon under way again for Ayr. But the encounter with Butter Pladdy had had its effect, for suddenly, when north-east of the South Rock, the steamer went down, a tremendous explosion taking place as she foundered. Fortunately, the steamer *Telegraphic* was passing and picked up seven dazed survivors, but ten others died. The *Harold* was recently found by a diver, who reported seeing the jagged hole the explosion had opened, and the solidified piles of iron ore still in the holds. Butter Pladdy, scene of only a few wrecks, claimed the Dublin barquentine *Annie Ada*, later that same year.

Although the 1890s at last began to see fewer ships lost on the Ards coast, now and again a bad wreck would occur. Next to the *Harold*, the most serious was the Italian barque *Teresina* of Naples on 13 January 1895. Outward bound for Trieste with coke, the *Teresina* still had her Mersey pilot on board when she was caught by a blizzard off the Skerries and blown northwards, taking water, until she was swept on to the rocks near Quintin Castle. Savaged by the gale, she split in two within minutes of stranding. As the conditions rendered it impossible to launch Cloughey lifeboat, the full responsibility for a rescue bid fell to the local coastguards, and eight men, including Captain Mortola and the pilot, were brought to the shore safely, but three others perished. The survivors, some on the brink of death, were hurried along the coast road to Quintin Castle, at that time the residence of Captain Ancketill.

Several other vessels were lost in the vicinity of Ballyquintin Point, among them the smack *Herald*, Dublin for Donaghadee with manure, 26 March 1897, and the Belfast steamer *John R. Noble,* coal-laden from Irvine for Newry, 7 December 1899. Wrecks of small vessels such as these were so common they tended to pass relatively unnoticed, but the loss of two barques in more dramatic circumstances placed the area in the headlines of local newspapers once more. Patrick Monan, a farmer whose fields overlooked Ballyquintin Point, had been in Portaferry on business on the evening of Friday 25 September 1908. Returning home through wind and rain, with his thoughts largely anticipating a warm fire and his supper, he heard the faint echoes of human voices and discerned the vague bulk of a vessel on the rocks. Monan owned a boat, and, alerting four of his neighbours and urging them to accompany him, he had it drawn by farm horses over a mile to a suitable launching point. When the resourceful farmer and his friends reached the casualty they found it was the Swedish barque *Trientalis*, and that she had been aground for several hours. With the stern under water and two masts collapsed, the crew of eleven were huddled on the foredeck burning their straw palliasses for heat. Two trips were necessary before the grateful men were ferried to safety, but the *Trientalis*, bound from Barbuda, West Indies to Derry with phosphate, was irretrievably damaged.

An horrific error resulted in the loss of the fine steel barque *Surcouf*, belonging to the port of Nantes, early on 25 February 1909. After a good passage from Hobart with nickle ore, the *Surcouf* encountered hazy weather as she made for Glasgow. Captain Trehondart, supposedly misled by outdated charts, mistook the South Rock lightship for the Mull of Galloway light, and the big barque crashed broadside on to the rocks at Tara Point, filling the next day then being gradually submerged.

Connah's Quay, on the estuary of the River Dee, one of the last strong-holds of sailing coasters, saw the launch between 1901 and 1903 of three similar ketches, *Catherine Reney, J. & A. Coppack* and *Sarah Latham*. Arguments flared among the local maritime community about the merits of the ketches for the coasting trade, and the doubts some voiced about their seaworthiness were substantiated when the *Catherine Reney* failed to save herself from a lee shore and was wrecked at Donaghadee on 31 December 1905. Destined for Belfast from Connah's Quay with fireclay goods, the ketch was observed to be in difficulties off Portavogie in a south-south-easterly gale. As night came on, worried coastguards watched for her drifting ashore, and eventually cries were heard coming from the vessel, evidently stranded off the Commons, Donaghadee. Ballywalter lifeboat was towed up the coast road by four horses lent by Lord Dunleath, but launching it proved impossible. The coastguards next fired a rocket line, but the crew could not secure it. Nothing more could be done, and one by one the bodies of four men were washed ashore. For a great many years afterwards, the stones of the foreshore here were interspersed with tiles from the spilled cargo of the *Catherine Reney*. Just a week before this long-remembered tragedy, the Italian tramp *Costanza*, River Plate for Belfast with grain, had steamed in fog on to the McCammon Rock, where she became a total loss.

About 10 p.m. on the night of 17 March 1915, the steam coaster *Upas* of Newry slipped out between Ayr harbour piers, and Captain William McFerran shaped a course southwards, for the *Upas* was bound for Warrenpoint with coal. As the 469 gross ton steamer passed down the Firth of Clyde, the easterly wind freshened until it reached gale force and blinding snow showers continually drove out of the darkness. Mate Samuel Hanna left the bridge at 4 a.m., having just picked up the South Rock light-ship and set the usual course that would leave the lightship to starboard of the collier. However, as the snow blotted out all visibility, Captain McFerran became anxious lest the *Upas* might be standing into danger by steaming inside the 'South Ship', so he hove to, only for the cargo to shift as the deeply-laden collier plunged from crest to trough with steerage way off her. With the *Upas* listing to port at an angle of 45 degrees, Captain McFerran appears to have intended trying to limp up the coast in the direction of Belfast Lough, but he must have known that the end could not be long delayed

Ashore, the people of Portavogie and district were awakened by blasts from the steam whistle of the stricken vessel, and crowds gathered to gaze in awe and concern at the sight of her creeping northwards while lying almost on her beam ends. The eight men aboard the *Upas* could see the people watching them, but grimly realised that no small boat could possibly be launched in the sea that was crashing on to the shore. Although the *Upas* carried two lifeboats and a small dinghy, the list made launching the two on the starboard side impossible. The single boat on the port side was almost in the water already, so several men scrambled in, only for it to be upset by a davit rolling on top of it. The occupants were tipped into the freezing water, but the only two to survive were Samuel Hanna and second mate James McShane, who were hauled from the water by a boat from the Belfast collier *Ailsa Craig*, which had arrived on the scene, and later transferred to the Donaghadee lifeboat after they had witnessed the *Upas* go under. So six men were drowned in the still-remembered tragedy of the *Upas*, including young Joe Hanna, the mate's brother, on his first trip. Captain McFerran was last seen standing high up on the tilting after superstructure beside one of the useless starboard boats.

While the outbreak of war in 1914 brought the new menace of attack by submarine and mine to shipping everywhere, the eternal hazards of wind and sea still claimed victims such as the *Upas* and the steel barque *Inverurie*, wrecked on Ship Rock, Ballyferis, on 15 November 1914. Donaghadee lifeboat, which had been called out to both these incidents, earned further distinction on 12 November 1915, after a frightening incident off the town. The French ketch *Cyrano* was homeward bound to Brest with pig iron and coke from Glasgow when her mainmast fell in a gale, and, dragging beside the wooden hull, battered holes in it. As the *Cyrano* was being overwhelmed, the lifeboat took off her crew of six, a service for which the crew were decorated by the French government. The ketch was later blown ashore on the sands at Millisle.

U-boats marauding in British waters often would not waste torpedoes on small craft, but capture them, order the crews off and despatch them by bombs or gunfire. No fewer than five coasters were sunk by the former method off the Ards coast on 2 May 1917, the steamers *Derrymore, Morion, Saint Mungo* and *Amber*, all off Ballyhalbert, and the sailing vessel *Ernest,* off Portavogie. The story, doubtless apocryphal, is told that the submarine commander jokingly informed the crews of the bus times as they rowed for the mainland! A much less friendly encounter occurred on 30 April 1918, when *UB 85* surfaced off Ballyferis and ordered the steam coaster *Kempock* to surrender, as she was on her way from Belfast to Garston. The *Kempock* had just had a gun mounted at Belfast, and her master, Captain John Roberts of Moelfre, decided to fight it out with the Germans. After exchanging fire for two hours the valiant Captain Roberts had to order his crew to abandon the old ship, which dated from 1866, and they landed unharmed at Donaghadee. But there was a sequel. When the submarine was later sunk, her commander, Krech, stated that they had received so much damage in the duel with the *Kempock* they could offer little resistance. As a result, Captain Roberts was awarded the D.S.C. and he and his crew were granted a monetary reward. The final war loss in these parts was the tramp steamer *Neotsfield*, torpedoed a few miles off Ballyhalbert on 14 September 1918.

In the aftermath of the war, an upsurge in world trade proved lucrative for shipowners, but the brief boom after the years of dislocation was followed by a severe slump in freight rates. Many companies folded, while a few interests turned to illegal means of avoiding ruin. Two men appeared at Swansea assize court in the spring of 1921, William Jones, managing director of the Dorothy Talbot Steamship Co., Swansea, and David John Rees, the company secretary. Jones was charged with inciting a Captain Plummer to deliberately cast away the steamer *Glendalough*, and sending an unseaworthy ship to sea, while Rees and he were jointly charged with conspiring to incite a Captain Hall (Plummer's brother-in-law) to cast away the steamer *Dorothy Talbot*. Behind this lies one of the most bizarre stories involving an Ulster wreck, for the *Glendalough* had been lost at Ballyquintin Point on 25 March 1920. She was a wooden craft of 301 gross tons, a former sailing vessel fitted with an engine in 1919, and was wrecked while on a voyage from London to Belfast with wood blocks for Harland and Wolff. Captain Plummer and the crew of eight, including two Negroes and a Greek, swam to safety and were given shelter by Patrick Monan of *Trientalis* fame and other locals.

In the first hearing, at Swansea Borough Police Court, Plummer had been charged with purposely wrecking the ship, thus abetting Jones' attempt to defraud the insurers, but he stated that the ship's steering had failed as he was bringing her into Strangford Lough for shelter. The charges against Plummer were dropped when it was learnt from the evidence of former masters how bad a craft the *Glendalough* was. Captain Hook declared, 'She was only an old pig which could not move but only crawl along', while Captain Couve recalled, 'My heart fell down to my boots when I saw her!' Evidence was given however, that Jones failed to have necessary repairs carried out, and that he was aware the ship could not survive long. 'Both were vessels of an extremely old and rotten type', said Mr. Wilfred Lewis, Crown prosecutor, of the *Glendalough* and the *Dorothy Talbot*. The accused seemed to have a strong motive for crime, as their company had an overdraft of almost £12,000, and the *Glendalough* was insured for a highly unrealistic £61,800. Jones and Rees were committed to the Assizes for trial, where they were both found guilty and sentenced to two years and nine months hard labour respectively.

There is a link between the submarine victims of the war years and the brigantine *Helgoland*, wrecked at Tara Point on 11 January 1924, for during hostilities, commanded by Lieutenant A. D. Blair R. N. R., she had been a 'Q' ship, luring submarines close then firing concealed guns. The *Helgoland* which was built of iron and steel in Holland in 1895 and later fitted with an auxiliary engine, was bought in December 1923 by Captain Arthur Fielding of Southport. On his first voyage in her, from Wexford to Port Ellen with barley for the Islay distilleries, she dragged her anchors while seeking shelter off the Ards coast, and stranded at Tara Point. Fielding — who had not insured his new command — and his crew of four took to the rigging where they had to remain all night before they could be rescued.

Butter Pladdy not only caused the worst loss of life among the numerous ore-carriers wrecked locally, when the *Harold* sank, it was also the scene of the end of the largest ship to be totally lost on the Ards coast. Shrouded by dense fog, the Spanish *Arantzazu Mendi* scraped on to the sunken rock on 9 May 1939, while on her way from Bougie, Algeria, to Glasgow. A vessel of 6,646 gross tons, she had been built at Sunderland in 1920 and belonged to Cia. Nav. Sota y Aznar, Bilbao. Cloughey lifeboat was soon in attendance, but apart from the mate, who went ashore to telephone the bad news to the ship's agents, the Spanish crew of thirty-five stayed on board. Eventually, however, they were replaced by a salvage crew, who in turn had to be taken off on 18 June when the steamer began breaking up in mountainous seas, their rescue earning Robert Young, coxswain of the lifeboat, a decoration for gallantry. Part of the *Arantzazu Mendi* is exposed at low tide.

Coxswain Young inadvertently found himself at the centre of possibly the most spectacular of all local shipwreck incidents, when in the early hours of 21 January 1942, the lifeboat was called out to the motor coaster *Cairngorm*, ashore off Ballyquintin. It was a foul night, utterly black with a south-easterly gale whipping rain and sleet across a heavy sea. Making her way to the casualty, the lifeboat crew were astonished to find themselves surrounded by large ships! Initially, the reaction was that they had strayed out into the main shipping lanes in the North Channel, but Robert Young quickly declared that he was certain of his whereabouts and that it was the looming shapes around them that were in error. What was happening was this. The *Cairngorm* had fired distress signals, which had been sighted by H. M. S. *Montbretia*, a corvette escorting a convoy northwards from the Mersey. The *Montbretia* approached to investigate without certainty of her whereabouts on this awful night — recalled later by Young as the darkest in his experience — and the convoy followed her blindly. The warship and four freighters, the *Asiatic, Orminster, Bronxville* and *Browning* struck the rocks, and a cheerless dawn revealed a sight that no-one who saw it ever forgot, for between Kearney Point and Ballyquintin Point lay seven ships, the six that had come ashore during the night, plus the coaster *Dorrien Rose*, which had stranded a few days previously.

Meanwhile, Newcastle lifeboat had been launched and arrived on the scene at 10.30 a.m. after a voyage of the utmost difficulty. Most of the ships' crews were in no danger as they were so close to shore, but the coast-guards were taking men off the Lamport and Holt liner *Browning*, stranded further out. The rescuers were forced to retreat by the rising tide, and for an hour the Newcastle boat tried vainly to go alongside. With sterling seamanship, coxswain Patrick Murphy then brought his boat through a narrow channel between the rocks and the bow of the steamer, and into her lee, where thirty-nine men, eleven more than the lifeboat was supposed to carry, were taken on board. The lagoon they were in was so small that Murphy could not turn to go back the same way, so with great daring and supreme skill he chose his moment and guided the heavily-laden boat on a wave across a reef on which lay the ship's stern! The mate of the *Browning* declared that had he known what Murphy intended, he would never have left the wreck. Deservedly, coxswain Murphy was awarded not only the gold medal of the R.N.L.I., but also the British Empire Medal, and the rest of the crew were also decorated.

A large-scale salvage operation was mounted involving the Naval tug *Bustler*, which towed off the *Montbretia*, and a fleet of salvage vessels and coasters. All the ships were refloated, but two the *Asiatic* and the Norwegian motorship *Bronxville*, were very badly damaged. The owners of the former wrote her off, but she was taken over by the Ministry of War Transport and became the *Empire Torridge*, while the *Bronxville,* the steel deck of which was bent up and down in waves, spent six months repairing at Belfast. She sailed for New York, but on the return voyage to Britain was torpedoed and sunk, a flaming pyre, on 31 August 1942, though without loss of life. The *Browning* and *Montbretia* were also submarine victims in November of that year. The salvage work brought its own stories — fifty cases of whiskey were found to be missing from the holds of the *Bronxville* when they came to be officially opened!

Wrecks since that vile night in 1942 have been rare, and only one has involved loss of life, the *Ruth II*, a Danish auxiliary schooner, which drove aground at Ballyvester, south of Donaghadee, on 10 January 1943, the cabin boy drowning. A unique incident occurred on 30 November 1954, when half a ship came ashore off Tara Point! The Greek steam turbine tanker *World Concord*, bound from the Mersey to Banijas in ballast, snapped in half without warning in a hard gale in St. George's Channel on 27 November. Captain Athanassiou and six crew members were in the bridge section, on the forepart, and were gallantly rescued by the Rosslare lifeboat. The after part was towed to safety, but the forepart broke away from the tug taking it to the Clyde and finally drifted on to the Co. Down coast, where it lodged until freed on 17 December. Eventually the estranged halves were re-united and the tanker continued to trade until 1974, when she was scrapped in Taiwan.

Burial Island claimed the Norwegian motorship *Roskva*, a converted corvette, on 21 January 1955 and the Dutch coaster *Willemijn* on 21 August 1958, both in fog; in both cases the ship was badly damaged but refloated. Another Dutch motor coaster, the *Frida Blokzijl*, became a total loss, however, after being blown ashore at Kearney Point on 6 March 1962. Captain Jan Blokzijl and his crew of four were saved by the Cloughey lifeboat, the coxswain, Walter Semple, later being decorated for valour. Despite all modern aids, coasters still go aground on the Ards coast once every two or three years, such as the wooden *Vingafjord*, Peel for Portavogie in May 1973, and the German *Anne Catherina*, whose master initially thought he was on the Scottish coast, near Kearney Point on 5 April 1977. Thankfully, though, it is now well over thirty years since a life was lost, a far cry from the carnage of the 1860s and before.

Headstone at Slanes Graveyard, near Cloughey, to a boy of the 'MALLY'

The Danish Schooner 'RUTH II', wrecked near Donaghadee 1943.

The Norwegian 'ROSKVA', aground Burial Island 1955.

Another Burial Island victim, the Dutch 'WILLEMIJN' 1958.

Liberian Tanker 'WORLD CONCORD', the Forepart of which came ashore at Tara, 1954.

High and Dry — The Dutch 'FRIDA BLOKZIJL', Kearney Point, 1962.

The 'BRONXVILLE' sits aground after the Convoy incident, 1942.

The 'BROWNING', another member of the Convoy to go ashore.

Chapter Six

THE COPELAND ISLANDS
AND BELFAST LOUGH

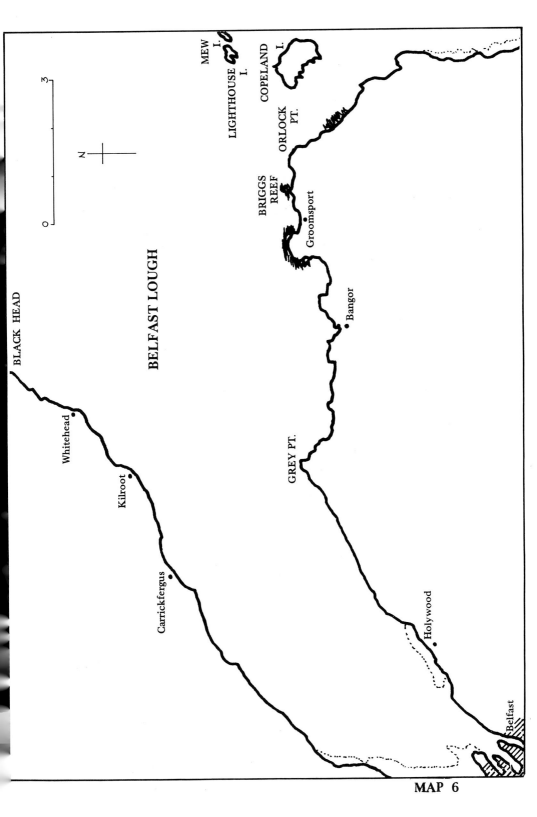

BLACK HEAD

Whitehead

Kilroot

Carrickfergus

BELFAST LOUGH

MEW
I.
LIGHTHOUSE
I.

COPELAND
I.

ORLOCK
PT.

BRIGGS
REEF

Groomsport

Bangor

GREY PT.

Holywood

Belfast

N

0   3

MAP 6

Belfast Lough, curving beneath the hills of Down and Antrim is an arm of the sea some thirteen miles long, gradually narrowing from about seven miles in width at the mouth to less than two miles as Belfast harbour is approached. The lough was for long known as Knockfergus or Carrickfergus Bay, a memory of the times before Belfast was the chief settlement of the region. While most of the present-day shipping is bound to and from the modern port of Belfast, Carrickfergus harbour, dominated by the massive Norman castle, is still busy. Vessels exporting salt from Kilroot jetty or bringing coal to the resort of Bangor complete the lough's traffic now, though in the past quays at Cultra, Holywood and Whiteabbey and the now-derelict White Harbour near Whitehead all handled vessels.

While there has traditionally been a considerable trade between Belfast Lough and the Clyde, the majority of ships have always approached the lough from the south, from the Cumberland coal ports, the Mersey and farther afield. After the rugged Ards coast has been passed, the Copeland Islands, lying on the southern side of the entrance, are the last hazard before the relative safety of Belfast Lough can be gained. Although the collective name for the three islands is usually taken as coming from a Norman family named Copeland who settled on the adjacent coast in the twelfth century, early maps, such as that of Johan Blaeu in 1654, term them the Copman Islands, probably from the Norse 'Merchants' Islands'. The group comprises the Copeland Island, a mile off-shore and formerly inhabited, Old Lighthouse Island, a mile north-east of the main island, and Mew Island, a few hundred yards east of Old Lighthouse Island, on which is situated the present lighthouse, dating from 1884. This replaced the lighthouse of 1816 on the neighbouring island, which in turn had succeeded the Copelands' first light, a coal-burning beacon tower erected in 1714. Alas, records of shipwrecks on the island do not go back as far as details of the lights, but it was obviously felt absolutely vital to maintain a warning fire here, for coal had to be specially imported from Ayrshire and unloaded in a little creek on the east side of Lighthouse Island.

One of the earliest recorded casualties was a Donaghadee to Portpatrick ferry named *Westmoreland*; her salvage is mentioned in a letter dated 28 June 1795 from James Arbuckle, Collector of H.M. Customs, and Edward Hull, Surveyor, to the Marquis of Downshire, who was Lord Lieutenant of Down and patron of the port of Donaghadee. The following October a further epistle records an accident to a 'Guineaman', this doubtless being a vessel engaged in the notorious slave trade, in which lucrative triangular voyages were made from Britain with goods for barter on the coast of Guinea in Africa, thence to the Caribbean with the wretched slaves confined below, and finally home — which was usually Liverpool — with tropical produce and a profit of up to £25,000. This pernicious trade was abolished by a bill of 1807, but not before the Copelands had seen the demise of one of Liverpool's leading slavers. The *Enterprise*, under Captain John Heron, was near journey's end on the stormy evening of Tuesday, 25 March 1803. Fitted to carry 363 slaves, the holds which had echoed to the groans and laments of the uprooted negroes were now full of sugar and fruit from Havana, and, it is said, £40,000 in silver dollars, but the ship's owners, J. Leyland and Co. were to be cheated of their rewards, for the *Enterprise* crashed on to the rocks of Mew Island and fell over on her beam ends. Of the crew of eighteen, nine drowned, while two of those who scrambled on to the bleak, windswept island succumbed to exposure, including a negro who had somehow been enlisted into the slaver's crew.

As might be expected, the wreck, which became known locally as the 'Dollarman', engendered colourful legends, such as the story that the drowned crew members had crammed their pockets with silver as they abandoned ship. Divers visited the wreck site in 1833, and, it is thought, recovered at least some of the treasure.

Following this spectacular incident, the islands continued for long to be fed their more mundane diet of sailing coasters. Just after Christmas 1814, Captain Campbell and the crew of the *Betsey* lost their lives when their ship was wrecked on the main island on passage from Greenock to Newry, while the following decade was notable for the losses on Mew Island of two vessels named *Henry*, the first, belonging to Rothesay, early in 1837, and her namesake, of Greenock, two years later. February 1824 witnessed a wreck occasioning loss of life on the main island, but the ship's name is unknown.

After the entry of the City of Dublin Steam Packet Co., into the Belfast — Liverpool trade in 1824 to challenge George Langtry, the founder of a regular steamer service, a keen trade war ensued, ending only when an agreement to share the traffic was made. Both owners' paddle steamers henceforth ran in conjunction, on one occasion even grounding close to each other on the same day! In thick fog on 6 July 1847, Langtry's *Sea King*, creeping into Belfast Lough, struck the eastern end of Mew Island, and the island also claimed the Dublin company's *Athlone* that day. The latter was refloated, but the *Sea King*, despite the attentions of a salvage expert summoned from his efforts to refloat the *Great Britain*, toppled over, filled and sank. No loss of life attended these wrecks, but Mew Island was in more vengeful mood in the fearful gale of 30 — 31 March 1850 that accounted for the *Preston* and *Peggy* farther south. The Canadian-built barque *Theresa Jane*, Knight, master, had left her home port of Liverpool for Mauritius with a general cargo valued at £18,000. Mew Island, however, was as far as she got, for, late at night, with the south-easterly gale sweeping rain across an angry sea, the *Theresa Jane* drove on to the rocks and sent seven of her crew of fifteen to their deaths. Dickens mentions the wreck in his magazine 'Household Words'.

Mew Island, set as it is the farthest east of the Copelands, tends to have troubled more ships passing Belfast Lough on their voyages up or down the Irish Sea, in addition to the usual quota of vessels entering or leaving the Lough. Its most famous 'visitor' was Samuel Cunard's wooden paddler *Africa* later in the same year, 1851, that she set up a record trans-Atlantic passage, west to east. Leaving Liverpool for Halifax, her usual destination, at noon on 24 October 1851, Captain Ryrie shaped a course for a northerly rounding of Ireland as the weather seemed clearer to the north. Below, the 132 passengers accustomed themselves to life on the last word in passenger ship design, for the *Africa* had been completed only the previous year at Steele's Glasgow yard. The great paddles beneath their high sponsons churned the calm Irish Sea as the *Africa* passed the Calf of Man at 6 p.m. and the South Rock at 8.40. Within minutes, however, the Cunarder was shrouded in dense fog and her master reduced speed. With all officers on deck, the *Africa* groped her way towards the North Channel, but about 10.20 p.m. came the shock of impact with land. Immediately the engines were reversed and bunker coal jettisoned, but the tide was ebbing and the liner was firmly stuck, they knew not where. Towards midnight a steamer loomed up and informed them they were on Mew Island, not far, as it transpired, from the sunken wreck of the *Sea King*. Captain Ryrie despatched the third officer to the mainland with instructions to summon help from Belfast, and the next day tugs appeared, fifty men from the shore aiding lightening operations. The *Africa* was freed on the mid-morning tide, and, making only a little water, returned to Liverpool, Captain Ryrie never having left the deck from his ship's departure until his arrival back 36 hours later. The spell of thick weather in the Copelands area continued, and early on 26 October the schooner *Ceretica*, Limerick for Liverpool with oats, came ashore on the north side of the main island, two days later sliding below the waves.

As Captain Silly guided his iron paddle steamer *Yorkshireman* out of Morecambe harbour on Wednesday, 4 January 1854, he perhaps reflected on the wisdom of Midland Railway, to whom the brand-new ship was on charter, in ever opening a passenger service to Belfast as they had done in 1851, for the *Yorkshireman* had but a single passenger on board on this cheerless midwinter morning. Before long, however, the master had no time for musing, as a south-south-easterly gale hurried flurries of snow over the ship; he rang down for half speed, preparing for a testing passage. By late evening the paddler was approaching the Down coast, but the snow was not heavy and Captain Silly was relieved to discern a light well to port which he took to be that on Lighthouse Island. Altering course to port, the *Yorkshireman* swung round into Belfast Lough — or so those on board thought. In fact, the Captain had mistaken the lighthouse on Donaghadee pier for the Copelands light, and so, four miles south of her assumed position, the *Yorkshireman* ploughed on to Foreland Point, a rocky ledge pointing from the mainland towards Copeland Island. The crew and the unfortunate passenger took to the boats, but were forced to stay under the shelter of the ship's stern all through a bitterly cold night that saw their vessel break in two forward of the paddle boxes. Eventually, at 7 a.m. the frozen complement landed, and after he had been thawed out, the mate left for Belfast on foot, delivering news of the wreck late that afternoon, having trudged some sixteen miles through deep snow.

This was considered to be the worst blizzard to have affected Ulster since March 1827, and before the bad weather had run its course another wreck had occurred in Donaghadee Sound. The snow had turned to rain, but a south-easterly gale was still blowing when the big new American square-rigger *Mermaid*, of Bath, Maine, laden with goods worth £30,000 consigned to Philadelphia from Liverpool, was wrecked on the south-west side of the Copeland Island. At great risk, a Donaghadee boat and an island boat snatched to safety Captain Robinson, his crew of nineteen and three passengers. The *Mermaid* soon broke up, spilling all manner of valuable cargo into the sea, and a number of prosecutions were later brought as a result of theft from the nearby beaches. Thirteen years then followed before the main island was the scene of a major casualty, but that year of 1867 was a black one, for on 1 January all six crew of the brig *Adeline Cann*, Glasgow for Dublin, died, while the master and a sailor of the schooner *Thomas Whitworth*, another collier, were drowned on 5 December.

Although the Commissioners of Irish Lights reported in 1859 that the light on Lighthouse Island and the attention it received were very efficient, by this date Belfast Harbour Commissioners among other interested parties were of the opinion the light would be better situated on Mew Island. A succession of wrecks on this island in the 1860s and 1870s reinforced the agitation until finally, in 1882, the new lighthouse was begun. Sailing colliers, again, were the chief sufferers on Mew Island: the *Amanda* of Glasgow, for Galway, 24 January 1860, the *Earl*, Workington for Derry, 26 June 1861, and the *Ann Lovitt*, of and for Dublin from Whitehaven, 26 November 1877. It was apples and onions that filled the hold of the little smack *Azur* of Jersey, 34 net tons, as she neared Belfast at the end of a long voyage for a craft of her type from St. Brieuc in Brittany, on 2 December 1868. But, attempting to make the Lough in a north-westerly gale, she was carried on to Mew Island when the master and a member of the crew died. At the inquest on the master, held at Donaghadee, the jury added their voices to those recommending that a light be placed on the island. The *Ann Lovitt*, wrecked in heavy rain and a southerly gale with the loss of one life, was the last Copelands wreck involving a fatality. This was due in part to the new lighthouse, completed in 1884, and also to the general decline in casualties with the gradual supercession of sail by steam and the successive Merchant Shipping Acts.

Steamers, of course, were by no means immune from the perils of the Irish Sea, but when the *Alexandra*, a Spanish trader belonging to Palgrave and Co. of Dublin, was refloated having been aground at Clogher Head, Co. Louth for most of January 1877, it seemed that the large-scale salvage job devoted to her was almost over. Her iron hull temporarily patched, it was now planned to tow her the ninety-odd miles to Belfast, where Harland and Wolff would effect permanent repairs. So, early on 29 January, the battered *Alexandra*, her stern low in the water, set off in tow of the Liverpool tugs *Challenger* and *Kingfisher*, with a small steamer, the *Sea Mew*, being towed after her. Her regular crew having been paid off, on board were two representatives of Lloyd's, Captain Teulon and Captain Morrison, and a salvage crew of over twenty engineers, shipscarpenters, divers and labourers. From the outset pumping was necessary, but as the weather suddenly worsened off Carlingford Lough, the journey began to turn into a nightmare and off the South Rock the *Challenger* let go her tow rope, preparing to stand by the wallowing *Alexandra* should anything go amiss. Completely exposed to what was now an easterly gale, the little convoy laboriously struggled northward, most of the *Alexandra's* crew fully occupied at the pumps. Late in the evening, the lights of Donaghadee were passed to port, but just when the long 90° turn into Belfast Lough was starting, a heavy sea threw the *Alexandra*, already scarcely manageable, on her beam ends. The *Challenger* made repeated efforts to go alongside, eventually coming close enough to permit about a dozen men to leap aboard before the *Alexandra* went down by the stern a mile or so east of Mew Island. Five more survivors, including Captain Teulon and Captain Morrison, were later found in a lifeboat, but in all eight men drowned in a disaster that should never have occurred, for the subsequent inquiry found that the *Alexandra* had not been sufficiently seaworthy to begin her tow.

With a load of grain in her holds, the iron square-rigger *Ulrica* lay hove-to off Dublin Bay in a freshening south-easterly wind on 6 January 1897, at the end of a 137-day passage from San Francisco. Taking such a ship as the big four-master into port was not easy, and the skipper of the *Ulrica's* tug, the *Flying Sprite,* had left her to fetch another tug in Dublin to assist in the manoeuvres. As darkness closed in, the *Ulrica* was blown northwards by the increasing strength of the gale, all Captain John Johnston could do being to steer for the nearest shelter, Belfast Lough, and hope that the fates were with him. The *Ulrica* nearly made it; at 4.30 a.m. on 7 January she lurched on to what, since the building of Mew Island lighthouse, had now become Old Lighthouse Island. Her crew of twenty-eight all landed safely, but within hours it was obvious that the *Ulrica* would be a total loss — the end of a fine ship, built at Barclay, Curle's Glasgow yard in 1884 and owned by J. Rae and Co. of Liverpool, that had once sailed 370 miles in a day on a voyage to Australia.

The heyday of the sailing coaster had passed by 1900 and the schooner *Gipsy Maid*, of and for Padstow with coal from Glasgow, was the Copelands' last traditional victim when she struck the main island on New Year's Day 1911. It was thirty-one years to the day when the Dutch motor coaster *Fredanja*, Maryport for Donaghadee, piled up on the north-east end of the Copeland Island; her engines were put astern, but it appears her crew must hve left hurriedly for the story is that she sailed herself off the rocks before foundering! The *Fredanja*, 277 gross tons, had been one of the evacuation fleet at Dunkirk in May 1940. Less than three weeks later, on 20 January 1942, another of the fleet of Dutch coasters that traded around the British Isles during the occupation of the Netherlands, the *Karanan*, was rounding Mew Island, inward for Belfast with foodstuffs from Liverpool, when she collided with the tanker *British Engineer* and sank with the loss of two of her crew. In more recent years, skilful salvage operations refloated two casualties on the Copeland Island, the bucket dredger *Beaver Chief*, aground from February to May 1962, and the German container ship *Craigavad,* which sailed on at full speed early on 30 August 1972, but was towed off, her back almost broken, eleven days later.

The considerable number of casualties in Belfast Lough can be attributed more to an inevitable consequence of the volume of traffic than to any significant danger to navigation in the Lough. The majority of wrecks have occurred on a six-mile stretch of the Co. Down shore from Orlock Point to Grey Point, a succession of sandy bays and rocky promontories, of which Briggs Reef, covered at high water, has claimed most ships. Shown on the first published map of Belfast Lough, that of Captain Greenville Collins in 1693, as 'the Bride', the reef has also been referred to over the years as 'the Brige' and 'the Bridges', so it seems certain that the title is not derived from a surname. There is a North Briggs Reef on the Antrim shore of the Lough, but no wrecks have been recorded there; in fact relatively few vessels have made the forced acquaintance of this whole regular, sheltered northern shore, although collisions off Carrickfergus and Greenisland were common in the days when this area was a popular anchorage for wind-bound sailing ships.

King William III became one of the Lough's most notable visitors when he arrived at Carrickfergus on 14 June 1690 on his mission to defeat the Jacobite forces. It was in William's reign that there occurred the earliest-known wreck in Belfast Lough, or as it then was, Carrickfergus Bay, a Scottish vessel named *Speedwell* which stranded on a sandbank off Carrickfergus. While hardly any eighteenth-century losses have been remembered — the foreign galliot *Anna Maria* at Bangor in 1782 and the brig *William* near Carrickfergus in 1799 are two of the few — at least the tale of one outstanding ship is on record. During the American War of Independence, privateers preyed on British shipping, and after France and Spain entered the fray there was general expectation of an invasion of Ireland as a prelude to a possible invasion of England. The Ulster people, remembering how they had repulsed Thurot after the French landing at Carrickfergus in 1760, again organized their own defence. The dashing American raider Paul Jones had sailed into Belfast Lough and captured a ship in 1778, and as a result the 14-gun frigate *Amazon* was built. Her only recorded engagement was with a 22-gun Spanish brig off Bangor on 17 September 1779; all through that day they fought until nightfall ended the battle with several of the *Amazon's* crew dead, but with the Spaniard more badly damaged. The master of the *Amazon*, Captain George Colvill, and many of his crew were Bangor men, and thus it is doubly tragic that it should have been in Ballyholme Bay, so close to Bangor, that the *Amazon* ended her brief career. In a fierce northerly gale on 25 February 1780 she was driven ashore, all her crew perishing, as, it seems, did eleven Donaghadee men who had put out to aid the distressed warship. Captain Colvill lies buried in the graveyard of Bangor Abbey, while on the adjacent lawn stands one of his ship's cannon.

As previously stated, Briggs Reef has been the only consistently troublesome spot in Belfast Lough. The last century saw a long succession of vessels ground here, in all types of weather, while sporadic gales accounted for most of the accidents elsewhere in the Lough. The Reef numbered among its victims the Portaferry brig *Andrew Savage* homeward bound with rum from Antigua, 14 August 1815, the *Eleanor*, Dublin for Belfast with tallow and hides, 18 October 1823, and the *Celia*, timber-laden from Quebec, 1 December 1839. The first-named at least was refloated safely, but with her master so anxious to keep the weather shore on a squally day that he did not see the Briggs buoy, the elderly collier brig *Lady Mountstewart*, of and from Workington for Belfast, became another total loss here in January 1853. The dreadful blizzard of 4 March 1827 — by which snowstorms for years to come were judged — flung ashore two Scottish vessels, the *Ann* of Irvine and the *Jennet* of Dundee near the foot of Crawfordsburn Glen, about two miles west of Bangor. The crews of both ships were drowned, and the 1820s also witnessed loss of life on the Antrim side of the Lough, when, on 3 October 1823, the *Thomas*, Troon for Belfast with coal, was thrown on her beam ends by a squall and went down off Carrickfergus with the mate and three passengers — possibly the master's family.

Lying between Ballyholme Bay and Groomsport is Ballymacormick Point, now National Trust property popular with ornithologists and strollers admiring the views up and down the Lough. The charms of this lonely spot so near the bustle of Bangor mask a past that has seen tragedy and heroism. The decade of the 1850s is easily the most eventful on record for Ballymacormick Point, the loss of the *Trafalgar* on 27 January 1851 being the first of four wrecks in eight years. Of and for Fleetwood with railway sleepers and pig iron from Glasgow, the smack was rendered sluggish by deck cargo and struck in pitch darkness and teeming rain, so her owner and skipper William Harrison and his two shipmates were fortunate to survive. Less lucky were the men of the Larne schooner *Martin*, which was relentlessly carried on to the east side of the Point by an absolute hurricane early on 28 September 1856. The *Martin* had a load of Maryport coal for Larne poorhouse, but the weather had given her no chance of making Larne Lough, and she lay for five hours on the rocks near Groomsport with the wind howling round her crew as they clung tenaciously to the rigging. About 9.30 a.m. the *Martin* capsized, tipping the five men into the surf. Of the anxious watchers on shore, quickest to react was Captain Studdert, a Donaghadee coastguard who, nothing daunted by the dreadful conditions, had a boat launched and personally dragged dazed survivors from the wreck. The skipper, Captain Thomas Shannon of Larne and a boy, Thomas Stuart of Belfast, drowned, but three men including the master's brother were rescued by the intrepid Studdert.

Following the loss of the sailing coaster *Splendid* in January 1858, Ballymacormick Point was again the scene of a wreck in 1859, though this time the negligence of Captain McQueen of the paddle steamer *Elk*, rather than any inherent danger in the spot, was to blame. A product of Denny's Dumbarton yard in 1853, the *Elk* belonged to G. and J. Burns of Glasgow, who employed her in their Glasgow to Belfast night service. She was carrying 140 passengers, mail and general cargo when she left the Clyde on the evening of 6 June, for what was a routine crossing until thick fog was encountered at 1.30 a.m. Captain McQueen, doubtless loth to lose time, had neither the *Elk* slowed nor the lead hove, and shortly after 3 a.m. she slid ashore some five miles off course. The passengers and cargo were landed safely, but the *Elk* was written off by her owners and at an auction held in a neighbouring field, her wreck was purchased by a Mr. Madden of Belfast for £1,020. The last chapter in this sorry story was the suspension of the master's certificate for a year by the official inquiry.

The mate of the full-rigged ship *City of Lucknow* bore a large responsibility as she scudded southward in the early hours of 9 February 1861. He was on watch, and aboard were a general cargo worth £112,000 consigned to Calcutta from Glasgow, four passengers and twenty-seven crew. All seemed well, however, for Captain Brown had set a course before retiring, the *City of Lucknow* was bowling along at twelve knots and, though snow had begun to fall, a light that could only be the Copelands was visible well away to starboard. But something was amiss. The light was in fact a shore light at Carrickfergus, which meant that instead of being outside the Copelands, the *City of Lucknow* was careering towards Bangor! The inevitable happened as she smashed onto the rocks beside Seacliff Road with an impact that hurled everyone from their bunks. There was no time for recriminations, and the first priority was to land the passengers, which was successfully achieved by the ship's boat, whereupon all but one of the crew, an aged seaman named Thomas Mason, then reached safety. With such a valuable cargo at risk, salvage was begun as soon as conditions warranted, and a flotilla of small craft helped unload all manner of goods, which were ferried to Belfast by the schooner *Experience*. After temporary repairs, the *City of Lucknow* was pulled off the rocks, but foundered off Rockport, five miles up the Lough, in an abortive attempt to reach Belfast under tow. That was the end of the *City of Lucknow*, 888 net tons, built at Glasgow in 1859 and owned there by George Smith's City Line. What had originally happened? Captain Brown said he had no doubt he was setting a course east of the Copelands, but, in recording the suspension of the certificates of Brown and the mate for a year each, the precis of official inquiries for 1861 states that the accident was due to 'errors of those in charge'. The snowstorm that probably contributed to the wreck also saw the loss of the *Tom Swim* of Fleetwood, outward bound from Bangor, on Briggs Reef.

The first hours of December 1867 heralded a particularly severe north-westerly gale that soon had ships in the Irish Sea running for shelter. Early that evening the Dublin collier brig *Erin* arrived off Crawfordsburn, but her anchorage was an exposed one and within an hour she dragged and came ashore at Swinely Point. Captain Wilkinson and his crew of three clambered up the rigging, but were soon forced down again as the two masts were groaning ominously and threatening to fall. Lashing themselves to the side of the disintegrating *Erin*, the men were incredibly lucky to survive the night and even the coastguards watching from the shore had given them up as lost when at 5.30 a.m. they heard voices and met the mate and two seamen walking up the beach at low water. Captain Wilkinson was too weak to move, but he was hurriedly brought to a nearby house where, happily, he was soon restored. As the coastguards were making their way back to Bangor, their work as they thought, done, they came upon a wreck at Wilson's Point, on the west side of Bangor Bay. It was that of another collier brig, the *Argent* of Newry, and already one seaman had died when the ship's boat was swamped. The mate had reached safely, but four other men were still in the rigging. Groomsport coastguards were on hand with their rocket apparatus but it was only after the Bangor men arrived that a rescue was effected. That turbulent month of December 1867 also marked the sinking of the smack *Ann and Catherine*, Whitehead for Bangor with limestone, off Kilroot, her lone crewman drowning.

The pattern of Belfast Lough wrecks mentioned earlier can be traced right through the nineteenth century — regular strandings on Briggs Reef and intermittent casualties elsewhere. The reef saw the demise of the smack *Cruiser*, Troon for Castletown with coal, and her three crew on 21 October 1864. No further loss of life occurred here until 1886, but the intervening years saw the wrecks of the brig *Hays* of Amble, Berdyansk for Belfast with grain, 20 December 1872, the schooner *Gratitude*, of and for Bangor with coal, 13 August 1874, another collier the Maryport brigantine *Keoka*, 4 March 1875, the iron steamer *Corinth* of Cardiff, Neath for Belfast with coal, 8 April 1878, and a larger iron steamer the *Emily* of Sunderland, 8 February 1884. The loss of the latter was completely unnecessary, for, after sheltering off Bangor on passage from Glasgow to Bordeaux with coal, she proceeded on a clear night but went inside instead of outside the Briggs buoy. There was no chance of the brigantine *Minniehaha* avoiding destruction here on 6 November 1886, however, for she was helpless before a northerly gale encountered on passage from

Ardrossan with coal for J. Kingsberry, the Belfast merchant and the vessel's owner. The first intimation of a wreck came when large amounts of debris were discovered at dawn strewn around the coast, the bodies of Captain William Bell of nearby Donaghadee and his crew drifting ashore over the next few days.

Since that stormy night no lives have been lost here, but added to the remains in this ships' graveyard that now so fascinates sub-aqua enthusiasts were the wrecks of the steamer *Orator*, Greenock for Licata, Sicily, with coal, 21 December 1890, the ketch *Betsy*, Bangor for Ballyhalbert with bricks, 21 November 1893, and the schooner *Caledonia*, of and for Wexford with coal from Ayr, 21 February 1899. At 1,342 gross tons the *Orator*, owned by E. A. Cohen of Liverpool, was the largest total loss on Briggs Reef; Donaldson Lines' passenger steamer *Letitia*, 13,475 gross tons, stranded here in fog on 16 August 1935, but was freed four days later. When their steamer *Davaar* grounded on the Reef in dense fog on 7 June 1895, over 400 bewildered residents of Campbeltown, on an excursion to Belfast, found themselves the objects of a massive rescue operation. With visibility almost nil, Captain Muir was proceeding at 'dead slow' when the *Davaar* inched on to the Reef at high water; when the tide ebbed the 543 gross ton steamer was fortunate not to break her back. She was successfully refloated on 9 June, but not before an assisting tug, the *Ranger*, had run over the wreck of the *Emily* and sunk in half a minute!

Commanding a panoramic view over Belfast Lough, the clubhouse of the Royal Ulster Yacht Club is a stately reminder of the greatest days of yachting. It overlooks the spot where, on 6 November 1890, a splendid yawl and the young aristocrat who owned her were lost. The aristocrat was Lionel Cranfield Sackville, Viscount Cantelupe, and his boat the *Urania*. Having just bought her, he was taking her from the Gare Loch to Southampton with a crew of six, when headwinds off the South Rock forced them back to Belfast Lough. During the night a northerly gale arose, the *Urania* dragged her anchor and drove ashore on Luke's Point, between Bangor Bay and Ballyholme Bay, all but Viscount Cantelupe being saved by breeches buoy before the yacht broke up.

Just before Christmas, 1894, there occurred one of those periodic gales that fix themselves in people's memories, and become points of reference for all future storms. This northerly hurricane left some sixty ships stranded around the British coast, while no fewer than forty-five more went missing without trace. The *Doctor* gale was how it was known for decades to come in the North Down area, for the most serious of the three wrecks here was that of the Barrow-registered schooner *Doctor* on the Groomsport side of Ballymacormick Point. Owned by J. Watts of Watchet, Somerset, the *Doctor* had anchored off Carrickfergus having loaded pitch at Belfast for Swansea, but dragged right across the Lough and was lost with two of her crew. Meanwhile, the barque *Noel,* which had been in company with the schooner off Carrickfergus, also drove ashore at Luke's Point, but Captain Porter, his wife, another female passenger and fourteen crew were all hauled to safety by the rocket apparatus of Groomsport life-saving team. The Nova Scotia-built *Noel*, belonging to Samuel Lawther of Belfast, had left her home port bound for Pensacola, but adverse winds had delayed her at anchor for a fortnight. The final victim of this violent spell was the smack *Pet,* of and from Portaferry with farm produce for the Belfast market; ten minutes after grounding off Holywood on 23 December a few bobbing timbers were all that remained of her, though the master, Wylie, and a companion escaped.

There was nothing comparable to the *Doctor* gale for seven years, until a wild east-north-easterly in November 1901 ravaged all of Britain. At midnight on the 11th, the weather not yet giving cause for concern, the steam collier *Whiteabbey* left Preston on the tide and passed down the Ribble before setting course for Carrickfergus, where she was owned by J. Legg and which was home for Captain Thomas McNeilly and the eight-man crew. The next thing definitely known about the ship was when her lifeboat, parts of hatch covers and a bunk were washed ashore in Ballyholme Bay. As the *Whiteabbey* must have foundered in daylight, it seems extraordinary that no-one saw her go down, but sunk she had, about a mile and a half off Groomsport. The wreck was located, raised and beached in Ballyholme Bay, but the *Whiteabbey,* completed only the previous year at Ardrossan, never seems to have been repaired.

Some other, less serious, losses in Belfast Lough in this era ought to be mentioned: the schooner *Betty*, Maryport for Rostrevor with coal, at Carrickfergus 27 May 1894, the *J. M. K.,* another schooner of and from Dublin for Killough, at Bangor 26 November 1905, and among a plethora of collision victims the Bangor schooner *Slaney* off Carrickfergus, 14 April 1894, the big steam dredger *No. 4* in the Victoria Channel into Belfast docks 25 February 1910 (five lost), and the schooner *James Williamson* of Lancaster off Carrickfergus, 27 December 1913. The latter was run down by the Belfast steam collier *Eveleen,* which had a strange penchant for collisions as she sank another Belfast steamer, the Antrim Iron Ore Co.'s *Parkmore* in the Lough four weeks later, and a larger steamer the *Ravensworth* in the North Channel in September 1917.

Belfast owes a long-forgotten debt to the small Cumberland harbour of Maryport, for colossal amounts of coal were shipped from there to satisfy the needs of the growing industrial city. In a single day in April 1869, twenty-one sailing colliers arrived from Maryport. By the 1920s steam had completely ousted the schooners and brigs, and the fleet of John Kelly Ltd. was foremost in the Belfast coal trade, a position it still holds. Late on 8 November 1923 Kelly's *Castleisland* left Maryport, homeward bound in dirty weather. About 6 a.m. the next morning, she struck the seaward tip of Briggs Reef, holing herself badly. Rockets were launched at once and the steam whistle blown madly until the rising water extinguished the fires. Groomsport lifesaving crew tumbled from their beds, while, four miles away, the Donaghadee lifeboat *William and Laura* set off under coxswain Andrew White, with Lieutenant Vaux, an R.N.L.I. inspector who chanced to be in Donaghadee, on board. With only the bows and superstructure of the collier now above water, her crew of nine, five of them Carrickfergus men, had gathered on the bridge, helpless to save themselves. The ship was 700 yards from the shore, and as the Groomsport men's rocket lines had a range of just 500 yards, everything depended on the *William and Laura*. With consummate skill coxswain White brought the heaving boat alongside the *Castleisland* and one by one the men were taken off, until finally Captain Owens was safe and White — who was always to look back on this service with most satisfaction — turned the *William and Laura* for the fight back to Donaghadee. The *Castleisland*, 315 gross tons, had been completed just a year previously at Hall's Aberdeen yard.

The Glasgow coaster *Appin*, like the *Eveleen*, had an ill-starred career. As Robertson's *Prase* she had stranded at Carnlough in January 1901, while after becoming the *Appin* she had collided with a tanker in the Firth of Clyde. Her apparent death-wish gathered strength in 1933; in October she went ashore at Ramsey, on 8 December she had Portrush lifeboat standing by after she dragged her anchor off Ballycastle, and at last, on 13 December, she dragged again while sheltering off Bangor and drifted aground at Carnalea, her owner, Thomas Dougal, later writing her off as a total loss. At the time she had been on passage from Coleraine to Carlingford in ballast.

In the late afternoon of Saturday, 11 December 1937, the Kelly steamer *Annagher*, 586 gross tons, nosed her way out of Belfast harbour. 'Everything from a needle to an anchor' was how her mate, William Hunter, later described the scrap metal cargo that filled her two hatches. The scrap was destined for Llannelly, so the *Annagher* kept to the Co. Down side of the Lough, a strong following wind promising a lively trip once the Copelands were passed. Off Grey Point a slight list to starboard was noticed, and when it became clear that to venture into the open sea in this condition would be foolhardy, Captain James McCalmont decided to turn back. By this time the *Annagher* was off the Briggs buoy and, having turned broadside to the wind, her list suddenly increased as the unwieldy cargo shifted. There was now nothing for it but to run for the shore; with her starboard deck almost awash and her crew assembled on the bridge, the *Annagher* came ever nearer Ballymacormick Point, blowing her siren and firing rockets as she went. These were seen by Orlock coastguards, and Groomsport life-saving crew were called out as they had been to the *Castleisland* in 1923.

Dashing to Ballymacormick, the Groomsport men saw five rockets soar up, and they scanned the wind-whipped sea anxiously for signs of a ship, but in vain. Then, in faint moonlight, a black object was seen in the water. It was William Hunter, barely alive, the only survivor of the *Annagher*. Donaghadee lifeboat scoured the area for hours, but to no avail, and one by one the bodies of nine drowned sailors were washed ashore. Hunter later told how the steamer 'suddenly went from under us', but could not say why he, a non-swimmer, should have been saved. The wreck was located and buoyed, but salvage attempts failed, and it was eventually dispersed by explosives.

Unhappily, the *Annagher* was not the last Kelly vessel lost near Belfast, for in March 1946 the *Lagan* was cut down and sunk by the steamer *Elmfield* at the mouth of the Lough. This was the last in a long sequence of wrecks that began early in the war, and were independent of enemy action. Donaghadee lifeboat took seven men off the *Coastville*, Bangor for Liverpool, at Ballymacormick Point on 21 November 1940, and followed that by rescuing all nine men of the *Accomac*, Belfast for Silloth, aground beside Seacliff Road, Bangor, on 6 December. A third steam coaster, the *Coombe Dingle*, stranded in Ballyholme Bay on 2 January 1941.

The first of two much larger casualties later in the war was the Danish *Oregon I,* a most interesting vessel, which was wrecked on Wilson's Point on 14 January 1945. A pioneer motorship of 4,774 gross tons, she had been built as the *Oregon* at Copenhagen in 1916. Presumably waiting to join a convoy, she was anchored off Bangor but dragged her anchor in a sudden north-westerly, not being refloated until October 1945, when she was beached for scrapping. Large chunks of the *Oregon I* can still be seen wedged in a gully in the rocks. Only four days after she came ashore, the Pacific Steam Navigation Co.'s *Samanco*, Liverpool for India with 6,550 tons of military equipment and general cargo, joined her a little to the west in what the Chief Officer's log concisely described as 'Whole gale (NNW) with squalls of hurricane force, vessel pounding and grinding on rocks and seas breaking overall. Heavy snowstorms.' Not surprisingly, the *Samanco* suffered very severe bottom damage, but after a painstaking salvage operation that involved refloating her from her bad position, beaching her at a pre-selected spot in Ballyholme Bay, and finally towing her to Belfast, she returned to service.

Enemy operations accounted for just two sinkings in Belfast Lough, but one was a cruel business, for the Ropner tramp *Troutpool* had navigated 6,000 miles of hostile ocean bringing grain from the River Plate only to be mined within sight of her destination, Belfast, eleven crew perishing. This occurred on 20 July 1940, and on 1 November following the Dutch motor coaster *Santa Lucia* was also mined.

Since the sinking of the *Lagan* in 1946 there has been but one total loss in the Lough, the motor coaster *Normanby Hall* of Chester, which foundered off Kilroot in the early hours of 8 October 1965 after a gallant 15 hour effort to tow her to safety. She had grounded in fog at Tara Point on the Ards coast on 6 October while bound from Birkenhead to Belfast, but floated off unaided only to find her steering gear useless. The coastal tanker *Oarsman* took the *Normanby Hall* in tow for Belfast, but she slowly settled in the water, until Donaghadee lifeboatmen finally persuaded her crew to give up their fight. 'We were so near to saving her it was heartbreaking', reflected one later, while Captain Frank Sweet, the coaster's skipper for fifteen years, said 'My feelings are impossible to express' — surely the sentiments of every master who has lost his ship.

Sunk in Belfast Lough — The 'TROUTPOOL' July 1940.

106

The Barque 'NOEL', wrecked at Bangor, 1894.

The Excursion Steamer 'DAVAAR' on Briggs Reef 1895.

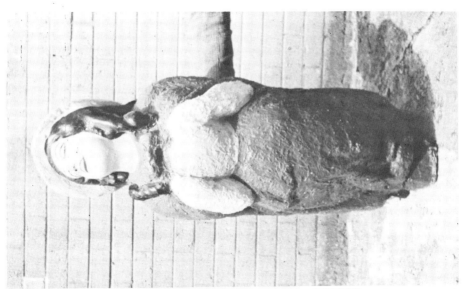

A Cannon from the Privateer 'AMAZON' outside Bangor Abbey

Figurehead of the 'GIPSY MAID', a Copelands Casualty in 1911.

Refloating the Collier 'MANGO', off Kilroot in the 1930s.

The 'ACCOMAC' aground beside Seacliff Road, Bangor 1940.

Seen here in the Mersey, the 'ANNAGHER' sank in Belfast Lough 1937.

The 'COASTVILLE', wrecked on Ballymacormick Point, 1940.

Chapter Seven

THE EAST COAST OF CO. ANTRIM

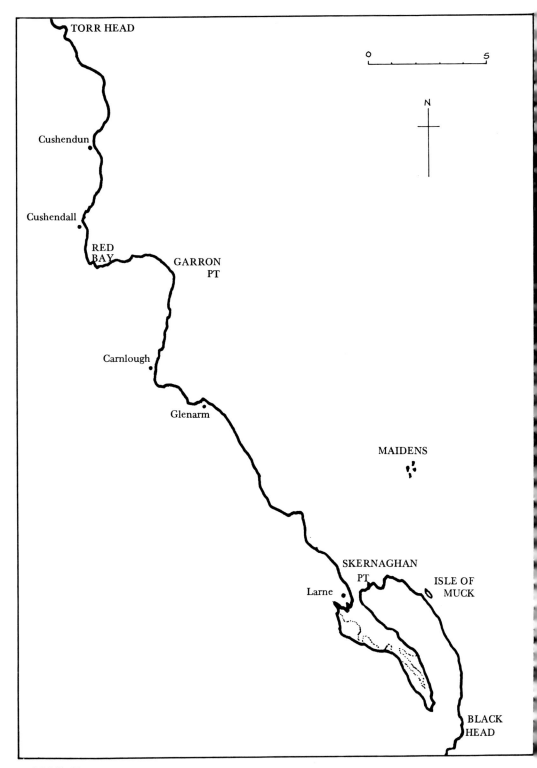

MAP 7

The lighthouse on Black Head, first lit in 1902, dominates the northern entrance to Belfast Lough. North-westward runs the undulating peninsula of Islandmagee, enclosing the shallow Larne Lough, and continuing in this direction the coast lies for some forty miles beneath the heights of the Antrim plateau, chalk topped with basalt. This regular shoreline is punctuated by several bays where the celebrated Glens of Antrim drop down to the North Channel, and in clear visibility the traveller on the coast road has a constant view of the Mull of Kintyre, just eleven miles distant from Torr Head at the north of this unspoiled extent of coast. The Glens men have traditionally maintained links with their Scottish neighbours, in previous centuries through vigorous smuggling traffic and the ferry from Cushendun to Dunaverty near Southend, and more recently in the form of a car ferry link between Red Bay and Campbeltown. The thriving port of Larne at present monopolises all the ferry business, but coasters still berth at Red Bay pier to discharge coal or load limestone. The latter trade is a survival of the period, its heyday in the second half of the last century, when this area was an important quarrying and mining centre. Millions of tons of iron ore and limestone were shipped from Carnlough harbour, a major project of the 1850s closed to cargo vessels a few years ago, Glenarm, the Antrim Iron Ore Co.'s jetty at Ardclinis on Red Bay, and another pier at Fallowvee near Garron Point. The demolition of the latter work, washed away in the great gale of 12 November 1901 that overwhelmed the *Whiteabbey* off Groomsport, is a reminder that while in good weather this is a locality of surpassing beauty, an easterly gale with an icy wind slicing the tops off the breaking waves is the stark winter reality of the Antrim coast which has condemned scores of ships to destruction.

With deep water close inshore, the East Antrim coast is unusually free of offshore hazards. The Hunter Rock off Larne has claimed a few ships, most notably the liner *State of Louisiana* in 1878, but it is the groups of rocks to the north, the Maidens, that are the main black spot. Referred to in seventeenth century manuscripts as the 'Nine Maids', and also as the Whillan or Hulin Rocks in more recent times, they consist of two groups separated by a wide passage. The two largest rocks in the southern group had lighthouses constructed on them in the 1820s; with changing naval design in later decades, they came to resemble from certain angles warships with high 'fighting tops', and it is said that more than one German submarine commander was thus taken in! Now just the more seaward of the lights is maintained.

The extensive smuggling activities between Antrim and Kintyre have already been mentioned. Both coastlines were ideal for the clandestine trade, but the Kintyre smugglers appear to have been involved on much the bigger scale. On 7 November 1781, the *London Chronicle* reports, a large smuggling cutter of Kintyre was wrecked on the Maidens laden with contraband from Gothenburg:

'She had on board 1400 chests of fine tea, 100 ditto silk and 60 ankers of spirits. Out of forty-seven hands, thirty-one were saved. The Captain, Mate and Supercargo are among the number that are lost. The same cutter fought Captain Crawford in the Bay of Blenluce about eight weeks ago'.

This vessel, her name unfortunately lost to us, is described as of 250 tons burthen, and mounted no less than sixteen guns. To assimilate these facts is to realise that here was a ship doubtless engaged in full-time smuggling, bigger than many deep-sea traders of the day, with a very large crew, and formidably armed to repulse H. M. Revenue Cruisers!

Wrecks occurred continually on the Maidens, and at the same point as the smuggler, a large American trader, inward bound, was lost with all hands in March 1798. On the last day of 1821, the sloop *Industry* foundered after striking one of the rocks, and even while the labourers employed by the Ballast Office in Dublin were engaged erecting the lighthouses, the *Alert* stove in her bottom on a rock and had to be towed into Larne. However, the following year, 1827, the workmen on their bleak site were said to be unwittingly responsible for perhaps the most famous of all East Antrim wrecks, one so much hedged around with legend and superstition that it is almost impossible to disentangle fact from fiction. This is the *Enterprise* of Lynn.

What is certain is that of all the hard gales mentioned in this book, the blizzard of early March 1827 was among the three or four most destructive. It wrecked the *Ocean*, with the widow Callaghan aboard, at Ballyferis, left dead seamen and jumbled timbers from the *Ann* and *Jennett* bobbing in the tide at Crawfordsburn, and flung the schooner *President* ashore in Lough Foyle. The brig *Woods* of Maryport was lost on Muck Island off Islandmagee, a similar vessel the *Manilla* of Belfast went to pieces at Glenarm, while a third Antrim victim was the *Barnett* of Workington, at an unspecified location. These were humble vessels with everyday cargoes, soon forgotten, but that the *Enterprise* was special is apparent by the second verse of the ballad 'the Wreck of the *Enterprise*':

'The *Enterprise* of Lynn brave boys it was our good ship's name;
She was loaded with dollars and indigo and from Peru she came;
She crossed the Western Ocean, where the foaming billows roar;
And she left her precious cargo all on the Largy shore.'

The Largy shore runs from Carnlough to Garron Point, but the actual spot the *Enterprise* struck was Ringfad, a patch of black stones a mile and a half north of Carnlough. The *Belfast News Letter* was sparing in its report, describing the vessel as 'a large West Indiaman'. The item continued; 'Eleven of the crew are lost and seven saved. She was chiefly laden with cotton'. Whether from Peru or the Caribbean, and whether or not mainly carrying cotton, the *Enterprise* appears undoubtedly to have included silver coin, and possibly gold, in her holds. Now legend begins to take over. The wreck is said to have occurred at 3 a.m. and the vessel soon began to disintegrate. With first light on 4 March, local people hurried to the scene to effect a rescue, but when it was realised that rich pickings could be had, lifesaving abruptly stopped. Members of a family named McGalliard resisted temptation and continued efforts to bring survivors ashore, and their descendants, the story goes, continued to live in the area with the other family names disappearing owing to varieties of ill-luck — although a different angle on this is that the plunderers were able to quit the indigent Glens for America with their gains!

The newspaper states that Captain J. Bond, his wife and family were among those drowned, but another fragment of legend insists that a baby boy was numbered among the survivors. The dead from the *Enterprise* are said to be interred in the north-west corner of Killycrappin graveyard, in the townland of Nappan.

How, finally, could the lighthouse builders on the Maidens have brought about the wreck of the *Enterprise?* Again, legend claims to know. The labourers had kindled a fire on one of the rocks and Captain Bond mistakenly took its gleam for the coal-burning beacon on Lighthouse Island in the Copelands, twenty-five miles to the south-east. But, on this point and others, the truth is hopelessly elusive.

Badly needed, a light on the Maidens first burned on Monday, 5 January 1829. In 1844, the German writer Kohl published 'Kohl's Travels In Ireland', in which he recounts an intriguing tale. 'A few years ago', as he dates it, a ship was wrecked on a reef off the Maidens. Next day, survivors were seen from one of the lighthouses, in which lived an old man and his daughter. The girl persuaded her initially hesitant father to row to the scene and rescue the men. Kohl continues, 'The whole circumstance is celebrated in a play which has often been acted in London and Dublin', and concludes by regretting to inform his readers that the girl had recently become ill, died, and was buried on the rock. One cannot help thinking, however, that this story is too close in time and detail to the saga, of Grace Darling to be true. Could Kohl have erroneously placed the latter' episode on the Maidens, perhaps through being told, it at Larne? Grace Darling, daughter of a keeper of a lighthouse on the Farne Islands, 'put out with her' father to a steamer's crew in 1838, consequently becoming a national heroine, and died of consumption 1842 - a striking parallel to Kohl's' supposed tale of the Maidens.

The confusing mists of legend begin to clear as the nineteenth century progresses, wrecks are more carefully recorded, and the newspapers improve their coverage. The first steamer loss on the Antrim coast was the wooden paddler *Nottingham*, on a regular Londonderry to Liverpool passenger service, which was condemned after stranding near Larne in September 1833. The rocks between Cushendall and Red Bay had more than their share of victims in the 1840s: the barque *New Zealand*, of and from Greenock for New Orleans, 27 November 1841, the brig *Scotia* of Kirkcaldy, Glasgow for the Mediterranean, 9 February 1842, and the *Helen* of Larne, the Clyde for Glenarm, 29 March 1849. After the *Enterprise* calamity, there was no comparable death toll until the *Taymouth Castle* went down nearly forty years later, but two small coasters to sink with all hands were the *Conductor* of Tobermory, in Larne Lough September 1849, and the *Success*, off Garron Point with a heavy stone cargo that gave her no chance when her seams opened in a force ten. On 19 December 1852, six months after the *Success* foundered, the sloop *Thomas and Mary* of Belfast also sprang a leak off Garron Point and one seaman drowned. There was again one fatality when the brigantine *Stanley* of Glasgow, laden with coal and machinery, was driven ashore near Cushendall on 12 November 1858, but the fact that she touched on the sand instead of rocks saved her from becoming a total loss. The worst wreck between the *Enterprise* and *Taymouth Castle* involved the collier *Darnhall* of Belfast, a schooner of 59 net tons, built at Northwich in Cheshire in 1824. Her crew of four all perished when she broke up on Islandmagee in a force ten south-easterly on 23 December 1859.

The New Year of 1867 arrived with vicious blizzards sweeping across the whole of the British Isles. For fully a week there was scarcely any respite from rampaging south-easterly gales and blinding snow. Between the Mull of Kintyre and Machrihanish, the, Glasgow to Londonderry passenger steamer *Falcon* foundered with many of those aboard, the clipper ship *James Crosfield* broke up on Langness Point, Isle of Man, all hands drowned, part of the harbour of refuge at Portland was washed away, and the main railway line to Holyhead was buried under ten feet of snow. On New Year's Day, a Tuesday, there began the worst succession of wrecks on the Antrim coast since the *Enterprise* gale of 1827, a sequence that was to culminate in another long-remembered calamity. Initial victims were the schooners *Mary Ann*, two miles north of Larne, and *J. E. Hudson* of Drogheda, on Islandmagee, and the brig *Alpha* of Ardrossan, near the *J. E. Hudson*. The inhabitants of the peninsula, turning out from their snug farmhouses to save life, had little time to worry about the number of Islandmagee men away at sea — traditionally large — as a third, bigger sailing vessel took the ground during the night. This was the square-rigger *Berbice,* of and from Greenock for Havana with coal, which was swept into Brown's Bay and broke up several days later. As the harsh weather persisted, coastguard parties patrolled the shoreline. Early on the morning of Wednesday the 2nd., the Cushendun men under a Mr. Phillips spotted a small vessel ashore about two miles south of the village. Two figures were observed in the rigging, and with extreme difficulty Phillips and three of his men launched a boat. Although swamped twice, it was a case of third time lucky, and two seamen, half-dead with exposure, were removed from their refuge. When they had thawed sufficiently, they reported that they were the entire crew of the sloop *Thomas and Eliza* of Dumfries, which had lost her sails in the blizzard while attempting to cross from Irvine to Belfast with bricks and tiles. The selfless deed of Mr. Phillips and his men earned commendation in the press, but they were to have a great deal more work to do before the cessation of this fearsome spell of weather.

While the winds howled, the full-rigged ship *Taymouth Castle* lay safely berthed at the. Broomielaw, Glasgow, loading a general cargo consisting principally of cotton goods and spirits, worth in all £50,000 and destined for Singapore. She was a comparatively new ship, this being only her second outward cargo since her launch at Connell's Clydeside yard in September 1865, for the Glasgow and Asiatic Shipping Co., managing owners T. Skinner and Co. An iron ship of 627 net tons, she was 169 feet in length with a beam of 28 feet, and had recently been joined by a sister, *Huntly Castle*. At last the huge cargo of nearly 3,000 cases and bales, 474 casks and 80 crates was stowed, and tugs took the *Taymouth Castle* downriver to the Tail of the Bank, from which anchorage she slipped away during a brief lull in the conditions. It was Saturday, 5 January 1867.

On the following Tuesday evening, the Austrian brig *Laura* arrived in Lough Foyle and reported that, while three miles south-east of Torr Head on

Sunday, she passed a large vessel under water to her crosstrees, with a seaman lashed high on the mizzen mast, to all appearance dead, and with bales and boxes floating nearby. As the sighting was being telegraphed by Lloyd's agents to the Customs authorities at Coleraine — responsible for this portion of coast — the drifting derelict silently appeared a little offshore, north of Cushendun, but soon even her three mastheads were lost to view. Identification, though, was not long delayed, for the stern of a lifeboat bearing the name *Taymouth Castle* was washed ashore, together with two bodies, all surrounded by an immense quantity of cotton bales mostly bearing the names of Manchester manufacturers. It now fell to Mr. Phillips and his coastguards to keep vigilant watch over the lonely, cliff-backed coast, and a Cushendun correspondent of the *Belfast News Letter* wrote, his letter dated Thursday, 10 January:

' . . . eleven bodies have been recovered, through the exertions of Mr. Phillips, the officer of the coastguards, and his crew. No body yet recovered has a vestige of clothing on it. The cargo continues to wash ashore, and every exertion is being made for its safety by the coastguards. It is thought here this morning that an inquest will be held today on the bodies recovered, but the interment will not take place for a day or so, as some of the relations are expected to identify the bodies. A piece of a linen shirt has been picked up, marked "Wm. Fullerton, no. 9, Ardrossan" — a person who is known to have been on board the ill-fated ship'.

As with the *Enterprise*, tales impossible to verify have been handed down. It is said that the corpse of a negro was taken from the water and put on a cart, and when the word spread that a black man had been found, crowds of onlookers gathered to glimpse this unprecedented sight in their neighbourhood. The bodies of the crew are supposed to have been interred in one grave near Layd, where the covering mound of earth is still visible. Many people in the Glens even today have heard tell of the 'cut and run' wreck, so called because of the actions of looters outwitting the authorities; though this could possibly spring from the Canadian steamer *Lake Champlain*, which stranded for a time in Cushendun Bay in 1886, from the known wholesale spillage of the ship's cargo, it seems the *Taymouth Castle* is much the more likely source.

The *Taymouth Castle* was evidently overwhelmed by exceptional weather, but it was just bad navigation that cast away the *Shamrock* of Whitby near the same spot five years later. This barque, 365 net tons, loaded coal at Ardrossan for St. Jago, Cuba, and passed Ailsa Craig at 8 p.m. on 12 February 1872, the wind fair from the south-east. Her west-north-west course was not altered on passing Sanda Island to starboard, and at 2 a.m. land was seen off the port bow. Now Captain John Storm ordered a north-north-east course but the land was still visible, the *Shamrock* could not tack off and she stranded at Tornamoney. The Board of Trade inquiry ruled that Captain Storm should have altered course on passing Sanda, and withdrew his 'ticket' for three months.

That many sailing coasters, especially in the coal trade, were old, small or unseaworthy - sometimes all three - is amply borne out by several casualties that occurred around this time. The schooner *Susanna and Anna* of Belfast, Troon for Larne, sprang a leak and sank off the Maidens on 13 August 1873, and in the same vicinity six days later the lugger *Ellen* of Strangford, just 25 net tons and belonging to R. Defoy of Portavogie, also went down while bound for Belfast from Ayr. These vessels were forty-six and thirty-eight years old respectively, but it was as far back as 1796 when the brigantine *George* of Workington had been built at Aberystwith. Her lengthy career terminated at Larne on 20 December 1876, during a spate of easterly and south-easterly gales that also accounted for the schooner *Resolution*, of and from Preston, blown away to the north on her voyage to Ramsey, and wrecked in Cushendun Bay.

That year of 1876 is a significant one in the history of the merchant marine, for operators of defective craft were now liable to be penalised by the Merchant Shipping Act - passed largely owing to Samuel Plimsoll, M.P. – which empowered the Board of Trade to detain unsafe or overloaded vessels. This contributed, with the trend to steam and better lighting of the coasts, to a gradual drop in wreck numbers everywhere, but of course the weather ultimately ruled, and no-one could prevent wrecks like the brig *Torrance* of and from Irvine for Belfast with coal, which was driven ashore near Garron Point in a force eight from the south-east on 29 November 1874, three of her five crew members perishing.

A curious little coincidence in the annals of Antrim wrecks concerns two Scottish vessels named *Caledonia*, both lost off Glenarm in somewhat unusual circumstances. The first, a sloop of 33 net tons, built in 1813 and owned by D. McIntyre of Lismore Island, ran for Glenarm in bad weather on 27 April 1878 while bound from Ballachulish to Glasgow with slates. Entering the harbour, she unshipped her rudder on the bottom, but two days later she made sail with no apparent damage, only to start taking water quickly and founder after her crew hastily abandoned her. On 25 November 1880, the schooner *Caledonia*, 69 net tons, lay at anchor off Glenarm awaiting a fair wind that would take her to Irvine with her load of limestone. Captain Kennedy, an Islay man who owned the vessel, and his two crew went ashore but on returning after dark rowed about looking vainly for their schooner! The absconding *Caledonia* was later established to be the vessel seen to founder a few miles offshore by a passing steamer.

Glenarm pier today presents a sorry sight with its seaward end crumbling, but at this time the harbour, together with its neighbours, was bustling with activity. They supplied iron ore and limestone to the iron and steel industries in Scotland and Cumberland, and must have presented an animated picture in the late nineteenth century, especially at Carnlough and Ardclinis with the narrow-gauge railways bringing down cargoes. But not all vessels loading here reached their destination safely. The brigantine *Onda* of Belfast, at 126 net tons sizeable for Carnlough, was irreparably damaged leaving the harbour for Glasgow in July 1874, the schooner *Express* of Dumfries failed to get out of Red Bay after loading for Workington and was lost in an easterly, and a year later in August 1881 Workington was also the destination of the ore cargo on the schooner *Maggie Lorimer*, but she was cast ashore after loading at Glenarm.

The strangest story, though, concerns the steam 'puffer' *Macrae* of Glasgow, whose crew left her after she broke her moorings at Glenarm in December 1895, and watched her drift out to sea. She was next heard of nearly fifty miles to the south-east, a wreck at Port Logan in Wigtownshire!

The more extensive harbour works at Larne also exported limestone, but after the purchase of the harbour by the far-seeing James Chaine in 1866, passenger traffic came more and more to be the chief source of prosperity. Not content with helping to establish the Larne to Stranraer route, the dynamic Chaine induced the State Steamship Co. Ltd., to begin sending their passenger liners to Larne, to facilitate emigration from Ulster to America. The *Pennsylvania* took the first sailing in April 1873, and eventually calls became weekly. On the morning of Christmas Eve, 1878, the *State of Louisiana* was approaching Larne from Glasgow, the British terminus, with seventeen passengers and 2,000 tons of cargo. Unknown to Captain McGowan or his officers, the buoy marking the Hunter Rock off Larne had been displaced, and was about 400 yards from its correct position. The *State of Louisiana*, a three-masted iron vessel of 1869 gross tons built on the Clyde in 1872, wedged on the rock, badly holed. Two tugs from the Clyde and two from Belfast could do nothing apart from take off the crew and passengers and a little of the cargo. Soon fifteen feet of water was swilling about the holds. The *State of Louisiana* was advertised for sale on 13 January 1879, but finally the big steamer, a few inches over 300 feet long, cracked into three parts and disappeared. She lay undisturbed until 1966, when local divers found her remains some eighty feet down. She was positively identified, not by a name plate, bell or builders' plate as is usually the case, but by a chamber pot bearing the company crest!

Five miles north of the Hunter Rock lies the Highlandman, or Highland Rock, marking the outermost extent of the Maidens groups. Two wrecks occurred here in 1882. On 3 July, the Canadian barquentine *Maria* of Pictou, Nova Scotia, stranded while bound for her home port with a load of anchor chains and iron goods from Liverpool. The second casualty that year, though, was much the more memorable, for the new square-rigger *Sumatra* was the largest sailing vessel ever lost on the East Antrim coast. Measuring 1551 net tons, she had been completed at Russell's yard in Port Glasgow earlier that year, P. Denniston of Glasgow being her registered managing owner. She loaded a full cargo of coal under the tips at Greenock and sailed for Rangoon, but abruptly ended her voyage and short career on the Maidens. It was all needless, too, for the master and first officer were judged gravely in error with their navigation in a fresh south-westerly breeze; at the inquiry, Captain J. C. J. Jenss forfeited his certificate for a year, and the mate lost his for three months.

The most impenetrable of fogs smothered the paddle steamer *Islay* as she inched her way forward in the North Channel on 19 December 1890. On her regular run to Islay with general cargo and fourteen passengers, the twin-funnelled paddler was one of David MacBrayne's Western Isles fleet, but under earlier ownership had undertaken an additional call at Portrush, and in fact had stranded in fog on Rathlin after leaving Portrush in 1875. Now completely off course, she edged her way on to rocks below steep cliffs. A couple of crew members landed to ascertain their whereabouts, and were nonplussed to learn from the startled inhabitants of a cottage that they were on the Irish coast! In fact, the *Islay* had struck about two miles north of Cushendun, and at the end of the tricky operation, Captain McNeill, the crew and the unfortunate passengers were landed safely, but the ship was a total loss. The townland of Tornamoney, a little to the south, where the *Shamrock* had been wrecked, was the scene of a second fog casualty on 26 June 1891. Outward for St. John, New Brunswick, with coal from Glasgow, the Swedish barque *Eleanor* came ashore. Again, two sailors prepared to land, but their boat was carried by the ebb tide right round Torr Head and Fair Head until they were off Ballycastle, where they were spotted by locals after a five-hour ordeal.

Thus far in this account of Antrim wrecks, there has been little cause to mention the peninsula of Islandmagee, home of so many seafaring families — the McMurtrys, Kanes, Hills, Arthurs and more. The 1890s saw the beginning of a spate of wrecks, and in fact six steamers were lost between 1891 and 1905. Prior to that there had been a number of casualties since the bad New Year of 1867, but all were small sailing coasters apart from the barque *Tobago,* Captain Robert Crosbie of Bangor, which was making for Belfast for orders as to the port of discharge of her molasses cargo from Trinidad, when she grounded at Skernaghan Point on 7 September 1886. Here, too, at this north point of the peninsula the first in the sequence of steamer wrecks occurred. The *Tuskar* of Liverpool, 397 gross tons, had called at Wick and Islay on her voyage from Dundee to Liverpool with assorted cargo. Finally, she loaded 100 tons of limestone at Glenarm and sailed at 7.20 p.m. on 27 November 1891. Thick fog enveloped her, but Captain Kerr, mistaken in identification of a light to starboard, continued at full speed and the *Tuskar* hit the rocks at 8.40 p.m. Just six weeks later, the *Alcedo* became the first ship on record to be lost on the Ulster coast on her maiden voyage, when she stranded at the Gobbins, two miles north of Black Head, with coal from Glasgow for Carrickfergus her first and only cargo. The *Alcedo,* also the first steel ship wrecked on the Antrim coast, belonged to J. Milne of Montrose.

When the Ayr Shipping Co.'s *Ailsa,* ex-*Rose*, became a write-off a mile north of Muck Island after grounding on 26 February 1892, it was the only possible end for a vessel that was so accident -- prone she seemed to have been built under some kind of malign star. Consider her record: December 1869, struck by Anchor liner *Cambria* and beached at Lamlash; August 1870, Greenock for Portrush, aground near Port Ballintrae; December 1877, collided with and sank schooner *Petrel* of Belfast off Pladda; November 1887, in another collision, sank the schooner *Ann Jones* of Aberystwith at the mouth of Belfast Lough. The *Ailsa*, dating from 1867, was on a regular run from Ayr to Belfast with general cargo and one passenger. For years after the accident her boiler was visible at low water, a fact that was mentioned in press reports of the stranding nearby of the steam collier *The Empress* on 9 January 1903.

Having claimed a brand-new collier in January 1892, the Gobbins, a stretch of cliffs taking their name from the Irish for 'snouted', took a decidedly elderly one on 28 May following. In fact the aptly named *Black Diamond* was a real pioneer in her day, for in 1864, when she was built at Troon, the coal trade to Belfast was the sole preserve of sailing ships. Her wooden hull was also an oddity for a steam vessel of 259 gross tons, but she had a robust two-cylinder steam engine from Coates' works in Belfast. She changed hands among Troon owners until bought by Howden Brothers of Larne in 1888, but plied back and forth to Belfast all her hard-working life. The many Belfast coal merchants who owned vessels kept faith with sail, some into the 1890s. William Barkley had run schooners like the *Clara*, wrecked on the Ards coast in 1883, and after his death the same year his son James took over the business, venturing into steam in 1888 with the purchase of the London-owned *Pembury*, 383 gross tons. Leaving Ardrossan at 3 a.m. on 5 August 1897 with coal for Belfast, the fog she soon encountered became ever more dense. About 10 a.m. she struck heavily on one of the rocks of the southern group of the Maidens. Captain Russell and the ten crew members quickly left her, and the chief engineer had no time to blow off steam. Eight minutes after touching, her boiler exploded with a deafening report. The lifeboat was noticed by local fishermen, who escorted it into Larne, but the *Pembury* was a write-off and Barkley had a replacement collier, *W. M. Barkley,* built. Another Belfast owner of the time was H. J. Scott, whose steamer *Ferric*, 335 gross tons, was sunk in a collision in the Clyde in 1898, and on salvage acquired by the Howden family of Larne. In the fierce south-easterly of 16 January 1905 that drove the *Beechgrove* on the rocks near Newcastle, she battled across with coal from Ayr but failed to make Larne harbour and ended up ashore at the Black Arch, north of Larne, where a tunnel takes the coast road through the jutting cliff. Captain J. McCracken and the crew landed safely, but Howdens later abandoned the *Ferric* as a constructive total loss.

All these steamers were from time to time in company with the coasters of the William Robertson fleet, one of Glasgow's foremost. The carriage of limestone for the blast furnaces of Central Scotland was a constant trade of theirs, and the smaller ships were often in the Antrim ports. This is reflected in the composition of the crew of the *Peridot* when she arrived off Carnlough on 25 November 1905, for seven of the nine men, including Captain Hugh Kane, were from the village, while another's home was in Glenarm. The *Peridot*, popular as a lucky ship that had never had a mishap since her completion at Paisley in 1890, brought coal from Irvine and was due to load limestone outwards, but as an easterly gale was getting up and darkness falling, her skipper was not inclined to risk the narrow harbour entrance, and he ran away south for Larne Lough and shelter.

Overlooking Skernaghan Point lived a Mrs. Montgomery. On looking out the following morning, she discerned what appeared to be a coat and singlet on the rocks. Fearing some kind of boating accident, for it had been a wild night, she told her neighbour Alexander McCalmont, who decided to investigate; horrified, he saw bodies rocking in the tide and what was unmistakably the hull of a ship, just visible and almost broken in two. A mile away was the coastguard station on the hill above Portmuck, but when the coastguards hastened to the scene, there was nothing to be done. The *Peridot* was destroyed and her crew all drowned. The small local communities were no strangers to news of death at sea — memories went back to how the locally-owned schooners *Jane Shearer* and *Jessie McLeod* had both gone missing without trace — but the loss of the 'lucky' *Peridot* was especially keenly felt and the tale of her wreck was preserved in the traditional form of a ballad.

To be the largest wreck on the Maidens was the unwelcome distinction of the *Housatonic*, a steam tanker of over 3500 gross tons, belonging to the Anglo-American Oil Co. Ltd. of London. She left Barrow on the afternoon of Saturday 3 January 1908, bound in ballast for New York. Off Belfast Lough at 10 p.m., with the weather good, Captain J. B. Henry of North Shields set his course and retired below, leaving his first officer in charge, but in little over an hour there was a terrific, grating shock as the *Housatonic* contacted Russell Rock, the most westerly of the northern trio. It was palpably obvious the tanker was greatly injured, for the 'black gang' were forced to swarm up the engine room companionways by an inrush of water on the gashed port side. Captain Henry ordered the crew away in a boat, but the officers, he decided, would stay. Rockets were lit and fired, but with an ironic twist of ill-fate, one fell back on the ship and began a fire. Now all those remaining aboard prepared to quit the tanker, but the sequence of accidents persisted, for Second Engineer Hudson of London misjudged his leap into the lifeboat and drowned between it and the hull. The second lifeboat pulled clear and towards the sweep of the Maidens lighthouse, and thirty minutes later there was a huge explosion and the *Housatonic* slid off the rock and vanished. The crew's boat hailed the lighthouse keepers at 1 a.m., but the officers had continually to bale, and, utterly exhausted, they did not pull alongside until three hours later. Now it was found that Hadris, a fireman from Barrow, was missing, and no-one could recall seeing him after he left his post with the others. The dispirited crew remained on the rock for twenty-four hours until Howden Brothers, local agents of the Shipwrecked Mariners' and Fishermen's Society, could send their steamer *Kilcoan* out from Larne to pick them up.

The war years of 1914 — 18 brought a wide variety of shipping casualties on and off the local coast. Enemy action was responsible for two sinkings. Outward bound from Belfast, the Elders and Fyffes liner *Chirripo*, 4050 gross tons, was mined and sunk about half a mile south-east of Black

Head on 28 December 1917. Her wreck is often visited by divers, but a major 'prize', the screw, was raised and landed at Bangor about 1970. Sub-aqua club members have also descended in much deeper water, about 150 feet, to the Anchor Line's *Tiberia*, which was torpedoed some one and a half miles north-east of Black Head on 26 February 1918. It was probably the work of *UB-19*, whose commander claimed to have sunk a 3000-tonner that day, though the *Tiberia* was somewhat larger at 4880 gross tons. Built in 1913, she passed to the Anchor Line as a replacement for ships already lost; divers examining a nameplate uncovered the original name beneath — *Frimley*.

The German submarines, though, did not have things all their own way in the Irish Sea, and one was shelled and sunk within sight of the Antrim coast. This was *UB-85*, which, it will be remembered from Chapter Five, suffered damage while fighting the steamer *Kempock* off Ballyferis. Later that day, 30 April 1918, she was intercepted by H. M. armed trawler *Coreopsis*, on her first patrol, and sunk by gunfire about nine miles east of Black Head, all on board being saved.

In both wars the Admiralty requisitioned large numbers of trawlers and drifters for various coastal duties. Although the *Grateful* is described in press accounts of her stranding near Torr Head as a trawler, there is good reason to believe she was employed on war service — a fact the newspapers were doubtless constrained from printing. Snow blown before a west-north-west gale made conditions grim when she was driven ashore just 100 yards from Lloyd's signal station late in the evening of 25 March 1916. The station telephoned the Portrush lifeboat secretary but when he called the crew out it became apparent there was a reluctance to attempt to leave the harbour in the high sea running into the West Bay. When the Torr Head coastguards arrived on the scene, they too felt it suicidal to launch their small boat, and at 2.40 a.m. another telephone call was made to Portrush to try to turn out. The harassed secretary eventually rounded up enough men prepared to go, with five volunteers from Portstewart in a crew led by former coxswain Tom Patton, and the Portrush lifeboat eventually arrived at 9 a.m., only to find the nine crew of the *Grateful* had been rescued by the coastguards at 6.20 a.m. As can be imagined, this incident caused quite a furore in Portrush and district, but one point that was made was that when the lifeboat did put out more than six hours after the original call, the swell had moderated somewhat and first light was dawning.

The Torr Head coastguards were in attendance at the Blue Funnel liner *Laertes,* aground in the summer of 1916 and refloated by the Liverpool and

Glasgow Salvage Association with their famous *Ranger,* and at a more dramatic episode on 3 April 1917, when the Norwegian barquentine *Maja* was wrecked at Tor Cor Point, two miles south of Torr Head. Again a blizzard raged, but the crew of four Norwegians, two Danes, two Finns and two Americans were landed, with the master staying aboard until the coast-guards were forced to rescue him. The cosmopolitan crew found accommodation in Ballycastle and later were accompanied to Belfast by Mr. H. A. McAlister, local representative of the Shipwrecked Mariners' and Fishermen's Society, to whose attention the *Coleraine Chronicle* paid generous tribute — attention, in fact, that had been unsparingly given over the years by Consuls, Missions to Seamen officials and others to whom responsibility fell for crews wrecked on the Ulster coast.

The weather that April of 1917 persisted unseasonably cold, and the 11th brought another snowstorm. It was then there occurred, beside the coast road a little to the south of Glenarm, one of the most dramatic and tragic of twentieth-century Ulster wrecks, that of the *Thrush,* a Royal Fleet Auxiliary salvage steamer and former gunboat. A survivor's account of the wreck appeared in the 'Ardclinis and Tickmacrevan Parish Notes' of December 1954. Here, Mr. J. Campbell MacDonald is telling how an Armistice Day service returned his thoughts to the *Thrush* and in particular a shipmate, Willie Bridgewater of Brigg in Lincolnshire:

' . . . I was able to reach safety after many attempts to defeat the conflict between the sea surging on to the rocks and its backwash from the cliffs. When daylight came, Willie and eight others of our shipmates were found dead on the beach. Eventually the rest of the crew were rescued by breeches buoy from the small part still remaining of the ship.

All these memories came back to me as the Bishop of London continued the wireless service, with the prayer "Let light perpetual shine on them". I had heard these same words years before from the Naval Padre who read the burial service for our shipmates in the snow-covered cemetery at Glenarm. The Naval party from Larne had fired the usual volley over the graves and the buglers had sounded "the Last Post". The flag-covered coffins were lowered to their last resting place. The surviving ship's company of the *Thrush ,* those few able to be present, stood at attention quietly and sadly. We were dressed in ill-fitting, some new, some second-hand, fishermen's clothes, provided by the kindly village folk, led by the Earl and Countess of Antrim, who had rallied to our aid.

As the official service finished, one of our seamen, Lofty Evans, stepped forward, removed his cloth cap, and in his fine Welsh tenor voice started singing a music hall ballad popular at the time:

"There's a long, long trail a-winding
Into the land of my dreams . . . "

We all knew the words and we joined in harmony. This simple melody, sweetly sung in tune, spread to the Naval party, and everyone, including the Padre, was singing it before we had finished the chorus. No doubt my shipmates would have preferred to have sung a sacred hymn to their dead comrades, but they did not know the words. Instead they offered this nostalgic song with all due reverence.

So Willie Bridgewater of Brigg rests peacefully in Glenarm in Northern Ireland. As the solemn and impressive Cenotaph service finished, I drove off wondering if Willie is remembered now by anyone in his home town. An Irish mother occasionally puts flowers on his grave in memory of her own son who was lost at sea and had no known grave. Like Willie, he was only seventeen when he gave his life in the service of his country.'

The *Thrush,* which dated from 1889, is reputed to have been commanded for a time by the future King George V, during his Naval service. The same gale that wrecked her drove the Naval auxiliary *Prince Victor* ashore nearby.

A second vessel with Royal associations lost in the war years was the *Clementine*, the former Belgian Royal Yacht, which foundered in Red Bay after striking rocks when in service for the Royal Navy. The wreck of the *Clementine* was dived on by the Murray brothers of Waterfoot, and among much that was recovered was the main shaft, which was sold to the lime works in Glenarm. At this time the Murrays were known far beyond Co. Antrim for the salvage contracts they undertook, but an incident during operations on the *Clementine* led to one of the brothers never again donning a diving suit, for he was attacked by what seems to have been a gigantic conger eel, which he estimated to be at least twenty feet long. Certainly, congers have been spotted lurking here by more recent divers. Another salvage job entrusted to the Murrays was the *Irishman*, a steam coaster of 216 gross tons, wrecked near Torr Head in January 1925.

Through these years and subsequently the Maidens continued to be the greatest natural hazard of shipping. The collier *Dalriada,* Ayr for Larne, was lost on the Allan Rock on 26 April 1910, and another steamer, the *Norseman,* Ayr for Magheramorne, near the lighthouse in December 1916, but this pair were both under 200 gross tons. A much larger victim was the Spanish tramp steamer *Albia* of Santander, 1806 tons, which struck one of the northern rocks in the early hours of 28 September 1929. The Donaghadee lifeboat and the Belfast tug *Audacious* were quickly at hand, but beyond landing the crew nothing could be done, though the *Albia* was to remain intact through the winter and off-loading of her ore cargo for Londonderry was continuing seven months later.

The Saddle Rock, thus dubbed because of its shape, lies in the southern group, and one total loss has been recorded here. The elderly steamer *Overton* lost her way in fog while carrying general cargo from Liverpool to Larne and ran on Saddle Rock on 7 September 1955. Again the Donaghadee lifeboat put out, and again efforts to dislodge the ship failed. Her owners, S. W. Coe and Co. Ltd., Liverpool, sold her to the Belfast salvage contractor and scrap merchant John Lee, but the *Overton,* dating from 1911, seemed to want the last word as to her fate for she disappeared in heavy seas on 12 December 1955. The Coe firm, then as now constantly engaged trading to Irish ports, had written off another vessel on the Antrim coast on 26 January 1940. This was the *Hawthorn*, Captain Hollins, which got out of her course from the Mersey to Coleraine with coal owing to the inexperience of the mate, and ended up on the sand in Cushendun Bay. No-one in the locality wanted for coal for a very long time! The *Hawthorn*, 459 gross tons, was later salvaged for further trading under new ownership.

Young Joseph Murphy had the surprise of his life when he spotted a steamer aground below his father's farmhouse, a couple of miles north of Cushendun, just before dawn on 14 December 1955. The bad weather that had washed the *Overton* off Saddle Rock continued, catching the *Saint Ronaig* on her way from Garston to Westport, Co. Mayo, with coal and salt. Joseph flashed his pocket torch and back came an answering lamp. He alerted his father, who dispatched him to the coastguards and hurried towards the ship himself. However, as soon as the *Saint Ronaig* had struck, Captain Smith had called up Portpatrick Radio and the Portrush lifeboat was on its way, as were the Ballycastle lifesaving team, who, after a difficult operation, landed the complement by 10 a.m. For crew member Thomas Bremner it was his second encounter with the Antrim coast in three weeks, as he had been on the *Saint Enoch*, another J. & A. Gardner and Co. Ltd., steamer, when she grounded inside Muck Island.

Very few ships of any era can have had as chequered a career as the Norwegian motorship *Douglas*, 816 gross tons, which was reported aground in fog on the Russell Rock on 17 July 1956. It soon transpired that here was the same vessel, under a new name, that as the *Roskva* had had a similar accident at Burial Island off the Ards coast in January 1955. She had been built by none other than Harland and Wolff in 1940 as the corvette H. M. S. *Pansy*, spent most of the war as the *Courage* of the U.S. Navy, and been converted to diesel power and mercantile use at Copenhagen in 1951. Now Captain Oftedal decided that his wife and daughter, sailing as passengers with the Chief Engineer's wife, had better leave, and they were taken off by the *Hampton Ferry* on the Larne route. Jettisonning part of the wood pulp cargo freed the ship and she was beached and repaired, but her ultimate fate was apt for a vessel originally a warship — bombed and sunk in the Pacific in 1958 while under the name *Seabird,* carrying arms to Filipino rebels!

Of the few total losses in more recent years, two involved trawlers heading for Icelandic grounds; the French *Berry Bretagne,* from Lorient, sank after hitting rocks near Torr Head on 14 February 1963, and the *Irvana* of Fleetwood grounded in Cushendun Bay on the foggy night of 23 March 1964, later being towed away for scrap. The coaster *Vauban,* Red Bay for Runcorn in ballast, was heavily damaged when she struck off Skernaghan Point in November 1970 and had to be pulled free by the Belfast tug *Coleraine,* but another small motorship, the *Raylight,* sank like the proverbial stone after holing herself on Highland Rock at 7 a.m. on 4 August 1975. Thick fog blanketed the North Channel as she headed south from Dunvegan to Kilroot, where she was to load salt, but within twenty minutes of her 'Mayday' call the crew of four were safe aboard the vehicle ferry *Ulidia.*

The 'HAWTHORN' in the surf at Cushendun, 1940.

The 'OVERTON' aground on Saddle Rock, 1955.

The SAINT RONAIG', north of Cushendun, 1955.

Fast on the rocks

Formerly the 'ROSKVA', the Norwegian 'DOUGLAS' on the Maidens, 1956.

Fleetwood Trawler 'IRVANA', wrecked near Cushendun, 1964.

The 'RAYLIGHT', later a victim of the Maidens, in 1975.

Chapter Eight

**RATHLIN ISLAND
AND THE NORTH ANTRIM COAST**

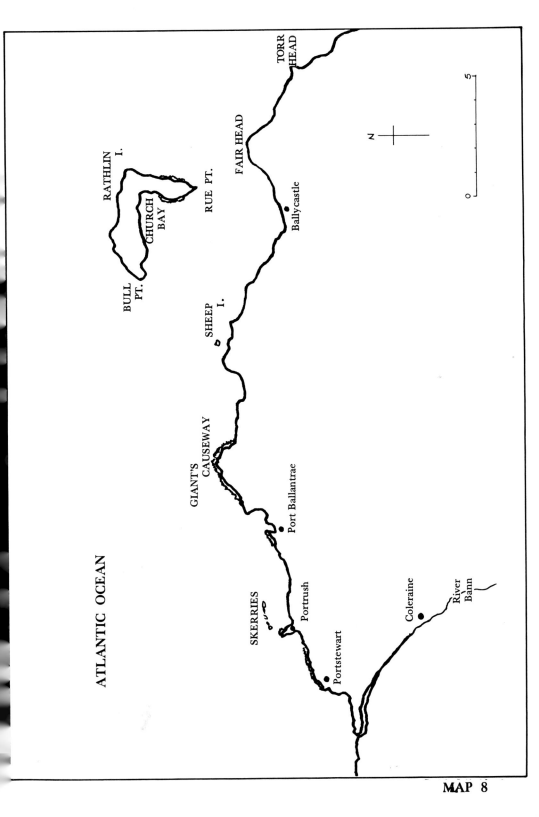

ATLANTIC OCEAN

RATHLIN I.

BULL PT.

CHURCH BAY

RUE PT.

SHEEP I.

FAIR HEAD

TORR HEAD

Ballycastle

GIANT'S CAUSEWAY

Port Ballantrae

SKERRIES

Portrush

Portstewart

Coleraine

River Bann

N

5

0

MAP 8

Rathlin is a mysterious island. Very few people, even from Co. Antrim, have ever ventured closer to it than Ballycastle, and most modern tourists or day-trippers will simply have a mental image of white sunlit cliffs seen across the blue 'Waters of Moyle'. A colourful, often grim history that has witnessed such diverse events as the refuge of Robert the Bruce, the massacre of Sorley Boy MacDonnell's kinsfolk by the English, smugglers pitting their wits against the Revenue cutters and the pioneering work of Marconi has also included numerous shipping victims, since Brecain the Trader perished with his curraghs in 440 A.D. The L-shaped island lies in the course of a ship making a north-about rounding of Ireland, and its obstruction of the powerful tides filling and emptying the northern part of the Irish Sea creates complex and dangerous eddies. Even from the mainland, some five miles distant, Rathlin can be a bleak prospect with a winter gale sweeping across its barren surface and piling surf along the base of the cliffs. In the eighteenth century, some 1200 people resided on Rathlin, but the total has dwindled steadily until now it is less than a tenth of that surprising number. At that time, of course, Rathlin had a lucrative export trade in kelp for use in linen bleaching, but since that trade passed its heyday there has been little commerce apart from the regular supplies from Ballycastle. Steamers did load limestone at a jetty in Church Bay and in recent years small coasters have imported road metal, but all Rathlin's recorded wrecks are of vessels intending to pass it by. The McConaig family owned the brigantines *Annie* and *Flimby* in the 1880s, and at least one trading vessel, the *Industry* of 1791, was built on the island, but it has always been to farming and fishing that the islanders have primarily turned.

Here, as ever, we are bedevilled by lack of sources for wrecks prior to the late eighteenth century. *'Lloyd's list'* occasionally contains tantalisingly brief references to 'Rathlan', and tucked among reports of British vessels taken by French privateers in the issue dated 28 September 1798 is: *'The Two Sisters*, from New York to Belfast, is totally lost on the island of Rathlan'. The strong tides around the island posed a threat to sailing vessels, especially on calm days, relatively rare in these parts. However, 21 June 1815 was such a day, and, with her gear rattling idly, the full-rigged ship *Cumberland*, 340 tons, lay becalmed on a glassy sea, a frustrating conclusion to a voyage from Jamaica to her home port of Greenock. Hour by hour she drifted with the tide close to Rathlin, ultimately striking a sunken rock and wedging, hard aground. Owing to the activities of smugglers, H. M. Revenue Cruisers constantly patrolled the waters between Rathlin and Kintyre, and the *Wickham*, under Captain Fullerton, came alongside the *Cumberland*

and took off the crew, together with nine puncheons of rum, two bags of pimento and three of coffee. Nothing more was saved, as the luckless ship, built at Whitehaven in 1800, broke up the next day. Another vessel bound for her home port which got no nearer than Rathlin was the Norwegian brig *Mercurius* of Trondheim. Having sailed from Derry after putting in for repairs, she went to pieces on the island in January 1816, but Captain Lorenzen and his crew escaped.

Casualties on and off the threatening shores of Rathlin continued at an average of about two per annum at this time, and as often little beyond the ship's name has survived, to catalogue them all would be tedious, but among the number were the brig *Hope*, Liverpool for Oban, 16 December 1820, the *Union*, another brig, Belfast for New Brunswick 17 May 1822, and two more vessels belonging to Greenock, the sloop *Jessie*, 1 March 1825 and the *Jeanie* eight years later. While details of the circumstances of these and other losses may be sketchy, what is not in doubt is the importance of a wreck to the island people. A ship aground was a diversion in the predictable annual routine, an opportunity to have the temporary company of strangers such as Captain Lorenzen and his Norwegians, and not least an illicit though forgivable chance to purloin useful items from the wreckage. Wrecks were not forgotten quickly, and the nameboards displayed in the island's pub at the Church Bay settlement have stimulated recollections of passed-down stories ever since. Two such souvenirs from the 1840s are the names of the *Saracen*, wrecked on 24 July 1847, and the paddle steamer *Her Majesty*, said to have strayed off course in fog and gone aground off the north end, in April 1849. It has been repeated in print that the vessel was a former Royal yacht, but this is definitely untrue; she was built in 1844 for a Fleetwood to Ardrossan passenger service, and in January 1849 inaugurated the Fleetwood — Derry run, the route she was sailing on when wrecked.

Prior to the start of full tabulation of wrecks by the Board of Trade in 1875, one must search a variety of sources for shipping casualties around our coasts. Thus the Minutes of Evidence taken before the Royal Commission on Harbours of Refuge, 1858, are essential, mentioning as they do a dozen or more losses on the north coast of Ireland in connection with a scheme mooted that would have made the Skerry Roads off Portrush a Harbour of Refuge by joining the islands to the mainland. Alexander McAllister, chief boatman, Coast Guard, Portrush, was among those examined:

'Do you know of any life or property that would have been saved by a Harbour or Refuge during the eighteen years you have been on this station?'

'The *Charlotte* was wrecked west side of Rathlin Island, bound to Portrush, wind north-west. If a Harbour of Refuge had been formed here she would have availed herself of it and been saved'.

McAllister tells how the *Charlotte* was unable to enter Portrush owing to the heavy sea, ran along the coast but got embayed and was wrecked off the harbour in Church Bay. Another witness at this hearing held in Portrush, incidentally, was the pilot Alexander Clarke, who thought little of Church Bay as an anchorage for sailing vessels: 'There is one spot of clean sand, but if you miss that your anchor will not hold'.

To the Minutes is appended an absorbing list of all shipping casualties around the British Isles for 1856 and 1857, and if known, the reason for each accident, which in the case of the brig *James Stewart*, wrecked in Arkill Bay, Rathlin, 10 August 1856, were threefold: a strong tide, a force ten easterly and a malfunctioning compass! The *James Stewart*, Greenock for Newfoundland with general cargo, was manned by thirteen men, all being saved.

Belfast Custom House holds an invaluable collection of ships' registers, and pinned into the document relating to the *Lady Mulgrave* is a letter in the handwriting of her owner, Daniel McLaughlin of Cushendall, advising the Registrar that his vessel had become a total loss on Rathlin on the night of 29 November 1853. The *Lady Mulgrave* was a schooner, built at Saltcoats in Ayrshire in 1836.

A west-running tide and a south-easterly gale combined to push the small schooner *Elizabeth* on to the rocks on the east side of the island on 26 February 1874, causing the death of all her crew. Registered in Strangford and owned in Killough, the *Elizabeth* had loaded nitrate of soda an oil cake in Liverpool docks, destination Ayr, but the gale bullied her away to the north. She was observed off Rathlin early on the Thursday morning of a week of awful weather that had seen the passenger and cargo steamer *Myrtle,* Portrush for the Clyde, turn back off Torr Head. Three tiny figures could be discerned trying frantically to claw the schooner off the lee shore, but as the swelling group of islanders watched helplessly, the *Elizabeth* struck and disintegrated. The bodies of the crew were recovered, and Robert Gage J.P., the owner of the island, arranged burial, a large number of locals being present at the funeral.

Another illuminating insight into the hardships of life at sea in the last century is given by the tale of the ill-starred last voyage of the *Arriero*, a victim of Rathlin in 1876. A brigantine of 166 net tons, built at Glasgow in 1862 and the property of Messrs. Harrison and other shareholders of Liverpool, she left the Mersey on 9 February bound for New Calabar. Captain Archibald Russell opted for a south-about rounding of Ireland, but owing to severely adverse weather off the Tuskar Rock, he put back and ran up the Irish Sea. The men 'before the mast' complained now of leaks in their accommodation in the fo'c'stle and Captain Russell put into Campbeltown, where he had the brigantine surveyed and pronounced sea-worthy by the harbour master. Still five hands refused to continue on the passage they had signed articles for, whereupon they were taken before a local court and each jailed for a month! With replacements engaged, the *Arriero* proceeded, rounding the Mull of Kintyre and running before an increasingly fierce south-south-easterly, finally dropping anchor at 8 a.m. on the 25th in Church Bay — sixteen days out from the Mersey! Here she lay for a week but when the wind went round to the south-west she drove ashore and became a total loss. The subsequent inquiry declared that Captain Russell being in an 'unfortunate anchorage', should have taken his first chance to heave up and depart.

Timber-laden from Porsgrunn for Barrow, the Norwegian barque *Hirundo* struck at Bull Point on 30 March 1880. Captain Torjrison and his eight-man crew escaped but the wreck later floated off and was reported, a dangerous derelict, by the tug *Sea King,* which had passed it off Fair Head.

The inexorable tides rather than the anger of the winds accounted for the barque *Girvan* of Ayr, 694 net tons, on 5 July 1884. Having loaded general cargo at Glasgow, she was towed as far as the Mull of Kintyre before dispensing with her tug and commencing her voyage to Adelaide, but on a calm, summery day she failed to make an offing and drifted on to the west end of the island. Within the week she had filled, but much of her cargo was landed safely, including, it is said, whisky that is still buried in forgotten hiding places! Two days after the *Girvan* stranded, the Dominion liner *Sarnia* was inward bound through Rathlin Sound from Quebec for Liverpool, and most of the seventy passengers were on deck enjoying another glorious morning, with the wreck of an unknown barque an added attraction. Suddenly, however, the *Sarnia* was densely veiled by a fog band and steamed on to Rue Point! The tug *Lord Elgin*, assisting the *Girvan*, made for the new casualty when visibility cleared, landing the passengers safely at Ballycastle, whence they were conveyed to Belfast by the 3.30 p.m. train. Quite an operation was required, however, to free the luckless *Sarnia*.

Another sizeable steamer, the *Hungarian* of Dundee, grounded for a time in 1889, and the schooner *Secret* of Portmadoc, Aberdovey for Derry, was an anchor-dragging victim of the poor holding ground in Church Bay in February 1894, but it was not until the dire days of World War One that any further serious shipping casualties occurred round Rathlin. All-out submarine warfare in the later years of the war brought spectacles of huge convoys of up to a hundred ships passing the island, with destroyers darting about and airships overhead to spot U-boats. All manner of debris from ships torpedoed out in the Atlantic was washed up, but on several occasions the reality of war came very much closer, beginning, strangely, with two incidents in one day, 2 October 1917. The steamer *Lugano*, 3810 gross tons, was mined and sunk about two miles south-west of Bull Point, but the second sinking involved Rathlin's most celebrated wreck, and, indeed, the largest on or just off the Ulster coast. H.M.S. *Drake* was a four-funnelled armoured cruiser of over 14,000 tons displacement, built at Pembroke Dockyard in 1902. Rendered obsolete by the advent of fast battle cruisers, the armoured cruisers suffered badly at Coronel — where a sister of the *Drake*, the *Good Hope*, was sunk — and Jutland. The *Drake* herself had spent the entire war on the Atlantic, and was protecting a west-bound convoy when she was torpedoed. The home-waters destroyer escort had just parted from the convoy, returning to keep close company with the stricken giant as Captain S. H. Radcliffe decided to make for Rathlin Island, his command still being navigable. It would appear that he intended to beach the cruiser, but having limped into Church Bay — to the astonishment of the islanders — she soon began to list markedly, turning turtle after her complement of some 900, and the bodies of nineteen men who died when *U-79's* torpedo struck, were taken off. And there the huge hulk has lain ever since, an exciting, though, so the Navy have warned, dangerous dive, a roomy home for conger eels, and a proven hazard for shipping.

In the early months of 1918 the German Admiralty intensified their submarine campaign against shipping passing through the North Channel and there were numerous losses and narrow escapes. Unfortunately in many cases the sources for information for these hectic times are vague and contradictory, but it would appear that four large steamers were torpedoed close to Rathlin: the *Knightsgarth*, having coaled warships in Lough Swilly, five mile west-north-west Bull Point, 5 January 1918; the *Andania*, a Cunarder, two miles north-north-east Bull Point, 27 January; the U.S. tanker *Santa Maria*, Rathlin Sound, 25 February; and the Armed Merchant Cruiser *Calgarian*, position unknown, 1 March. The latter, a former Allan liner of 17,515 gross tons, suffered the worst casualties, although seven men were lost in the *Andania* and two in the *Knightsgarth*. The *Calgarian* had been taken over by the Admiralty as a brand-new ship in 1914 and assigned to the Ninth Cruiser Squadron. Under Captain R. A. Newton, she was zigzagging at twenty knots after handing over a convoy to destroyers when struck by a torpedo at 550 yards range and finished off by two more with the loss of forty-eight lives.

Spars, overturned lifeboats, hatch covers, bales of cargo and all the sombre refuse of war were brought in by the tide throughout the conflict, and here it is worth recording briefly a few of the fine ships that perished further out into the Atlantic: the Armed Merchant Cruisers *Viknor*, 'somewhere off Tory Island' and *Clan Macnaughton*, both with all hands; another Allan liner, the *Carthaginian*, mined off Inishtrahull; and the Government transport *Tuscania*, torpedoed north of Rathlin, forty-four dead out of 2,235 on board.

To survive almost the whole war and then be sunk in a collision with a ship belonging to the same port was the ironic fate of the Glasgow steamer *Diamond*, Cardiff for Derry with steel, which went down after being struck by the *Lily* a mile north of Rathlin on 13 April 1918. Four men escaped, but nine died. Between the sinking of the *Diamond* and one of Rathlin's most notable tales of rescue in 1930, there was a single total loss, the steam coaster *Dingle*, of Belfast and for Portrush in ballast, which stranded on Rue Point on 30 November 1921.

The Board of Trade placed lifesaving apparatus on Rathlin and a volunteer team were always on call for any emergency. Such an eventuality occurred on 1 March 1930, and a highly competent, well co-ordinated rescue was accomplished after the steam trawler *Shackleton* strayed on to a rock off the north of the island in thick fog. She had been fishing off St. Kilda and was returning to her home port of Fleetwood when she grounded about 3 p.m. Her SOS was received by Malin Radio, relayed to the Ballycastle coastguards and in turn to Portrush lifeboat and Rathlin Post Office, where the postmistress began what was to be twenty-four hours continuous duty. Joseph Anderson led his life-saving company, and with a horse pulling their rocket apparatus, they made their way over rough terrain trusting to local knowledge for their whereabouts. Meanwhile, Portrush lifeboat was becoming hopelessly lost among rocks near the Giant's Causeway, so poor was the visibility, and reluctantly turned back.

Aided by the shouts of the trawlermen, the volunteers located the *Shackleton* below a cliff about 7 p.m. and the fifth rocket they fired was attached, fourteen men being hauled ashore with Captain William Wilson the last to leave just before dawn. By this time another trawler was standing by and after the local dwellers had provided food and warm clothing, the crew of the *Shackleton* were ferried out and taken home. The life-saving team were the deserving recipients of the National Life-Saving Shield for their deed, and won this annual award again nineteen years later when the *Pintail* of Fleetwood struck below Bull Point, some of the same men who had gone to the aid of the *Shackleton* being on hand to man the rocket lines and save Captain Stafford and ten others, after clambering down a hundred-foot drop. As Rathlin had been cut off for a fortnight by bad weather, there was a major problem over feeding the unexpected guests, so Portrush lifeboat lay off a sheltered part of the coast and transferred them to the mainland!

World War Two losses around the island were not comparable to the previous conflict, but on 21 January 1942, in atrocious weather, the *Lochgarry*, a Government transport formerly of MacBrayne's Hebrides fleet, struck rocks off the Mull of Kintyre and drifted, crippled, finally going down off the east coast of the island. Twenty-three men were drowned when the lifeboat they were in was dashed against the rocks in Doon Bay. Her remains, like those of the *Drake*, are visited by sub-aqua clubs and although the *Lochgarry* lies in much deeper water relics such as intact china bearing MacBrayne's monogram have been recovered. Another total loss on 17 March 1940 was the Dutch motor coaster *Hinde,* in fog at almost the identical spot as the *Shackleton*. Since the *Pintail* in March 1949 the only large wreck has been a third Fleetwood trawler, the *Ella Hewett* which fouled the *Drake* and sank a day later, on 3 November 1962. Her wreck in turn has brought problems, owing to leakages of bunker fuel polluting Church Bay, and even a full-scale attempt to free and disperse the oil in 1978 caused further acrimony between islanders and officialdom.

There was a curious postscript to the *Pintail* affair in April 1966, when the small fishery protection boat *Impetus*, Port St. Mary for Lough Neagh, drifted on to Rue Point after engine failure, for her skipper, George Barry, had been a deckhand on the *Pintail*, and for a second time was rescued by the Rathlin life-saving team! The Danish coaster *Flemming Scan* was in distress close to the island in a gale in September 1975, but generally in recent decades there has been little to disturb the guillemots, fulmars and kittiwakes that make their homes on the forbidding cliffs of Rathlin Island.

****

The thirty miles of coast from Fair Head to the Bann mouth is surely unparalleled in Ireland, perhaps the British Isles, for scope of interest for the botanist, geologist, archaeologist and historian, as well as for sheer physical grandeur. A succession of headlands juts boldly into the Atlantic, bordering occasional unspoilt strands on which the ocean swell tumbles. Justly famous, the 'Causeway Coast', as it is becoming known, has much more to attract than the Giant's Causeway itself, but however enthralling for the landman, for those engaged in seaborne commerce this stretch of coast has always posed problems. To stand in a cruel northerly gale and see a coaster, five times the size of a counterpart of a century ago, pitch and roll at her anchor in the Skerry Roads, with the spray climbing higher than the Big Skerry, is to wonder why more sailing ships were not lost, as well as understand why many were. The perpetual turbulence of the sea has always handicapped local harbour development, but oddly there were those venturesome enough to build jetties at Carrickmore, east of Fair Head, for coal and later iron ore exports, at Murlough Bay for coal, and east of Ballintoy harbour, for shipping stone. In the eighteenth century Colonel Hugh Boyd, that energetic and admirable landlord, built a fine harbour at Ballycastle to serve the new industries of the town, but for various reasons his scheme never gained success on the grand scale he had envisaged, and the former dock is now the site of the tennis courts. Portrush harbour, begun in 1827 as an improvement on Coleraine for local merchants, became the only lasting success, with passenger services up to 1914, and a variety of imports and exports, one of which, stone, continues, beside being a base for the lifeboat since 1860.

The topic of Ulster shipwrecks is almost limitless in scope. Every one has its story, of death or gallant rescue, of negligence or helplessness before the elements. Some are of special historical importance, however, over and above the intrinsic fascination they hold for those with a specialised interest in ships and maritime history: the slaver in Dundrum Bay, the privateer *Amazon*, the *Amitie* off Ardglass. Historically important as these and others are, the magnitude of the find made by the Belgian diver Robert Stenuit in June 1967 dwarfs them all. After some 600 hours of research, Stenuit and his professional team succeeded in locating the wreck of the Spanish Armada galleass *Girona* at Port na Spaniagh, about half a mile east of the Giant's Causeway. This was a find of the utmost significance as previously only one Armada wreck had been found, by a Donegal man named Boyle in the eighteenth century. Boyle had no interest in preserving the relics he recovered — he melted down the bronze guns — but Stenuit was more than just a diver, he was a marine archaeologist, and we must be forever thankful that the treasures of the *Girona* were not raised piecemeal to be kept as souvenirs by amateurs, but treated with the care their rarity as a collection warranted.

The *Girona* was a most interesting ship. She was not a galleon as is popularly supposed, but a galleass that was propelled by 300 oarsmen and sails too, her oars meaning that she could be manoeuvred whether or not the wind was favourable. She belonged to the squadron of Naples, then a Spanish possession, the capital of the Kingdom of the Two Sicilies, and was a splendid vessel, decorated by carved figures and with stained glass windows in the officers' quarters. Operating on the flanks of the Armada as it sailed up-channel, the galleasses were in the thick of all the action as the speedy warships of Drake, Howard and Hawkins mauled the lumbering galleons. When engaging galleasses, the English tactics were to kill the oarsmen thus compelling the Spaniards to hoist the sails, under which the vessels tended to be sluggish. With sixty of the 130 ships sunk, and 9,000 men lost, the surviving ships ran up the North Sea before a south-westerly gale, fleeing for home via the northern route. The *Girona*, which had emerged from the fighting largely unscathed, put in to Killybegs in Donegal for repairs. Here she was joined by the crews of two other Armada members, the *Sancta Maria Encoronado,* which had been wrecked in Blacksod Bay, and the *Duquesa Santa Ana* which had taken on the latter's men, but which had herself come to grief on the Donegal coast. The master of the *Sancta Maria Encoronado*, who now took charge of the *Girona*, was Don Alonzo Martinez de Leiva, a favourite of Philip II, a flamboyant young cavalier who just lost the vote for commander of the entire expedition to the Duke of Medina Sidonia. Knowing it was madness to attempt to return to Spain, as winter was approaching, de Leiva decided to make for the Catholic west of Scotland. Thus on 26 October 1588 the *Girona* left Killybegs with no fewer than 1300 men aboard, only to lose her rudder and be driven on to Lacada Point shortly before midnight the following night, the black, seaward-probing rocks piercing her hull, out of which spilled men, gold coin, jewellery and every conceivable artifact. The number of survivors is unclear, being variously estimated at between five and thirteen. The dead were buried between the boulders above the high water mark in the cove which hence-forward has been known as Port na Spaniagh — 'the bay of the Spaniards'.

Living in Dunluce Castle, perched on a rock a few miles to the west, was James McDonnell, son of the celebrated Sorley Boy, and no friend of the English. He organized the evacuation of the survivors to the west of Scotland and thence to Spain, some of the men reaching home as early as February 1589, although at least one was at Dunluce a year later. This may have been Adam Mornin; a Port Ballantrae family named Mornin in later centuries claimed descent from a Spaniard of this name who escaped from the *Girona*.

So the *Girona's* remains lay untouched for 380 years. Historians have tended to place her wreck at Bushfoot, two miles to the west of the correct spot, but Stenuit disregarded them and dived at Port na Spaniagh, trusting the accuracy of the old Gaelic name. The relics he salvaged form a splendid, vivid illustration of life in the sixteenth century, not only at sea, for there are such apparently mundane objects as cutlery, candlesticks and even an inkwell lid among the nautical material, not to mention the priceless gold jewellery worn by the many noblemen. Among the more glamorous exhibits in the *Girona* Room of the Ulster Museum in Belfast are several hundred gold and silver coins, a superb gold salamander with a ruby set in its back, and two rings, one possibly belonging to a Jesuit father and the other, most poignant of all the relics, bearing the inscription, 'No tango mas que dar te' — 'I have nothing more to give you', this probably identifying the ring as one given to an officer by his sweetheart before he set out with the Armada, anticipating glory but instead meeting a wretched death on the inhospitable north coast of Antrim.

For more detailed studies of the *Girona* the reader is referred to two excellent, complementary works, Stenuit's own 'Treasures of the Armada', and 'The Armada In Ireland' by Niall Fallon. With a full knowledge of the events of October 1588 it takes little imagination to stand on the narrow path above the precipitous drop to Port na Spaniagh and visualise the crippled man o' war skewered on Lacada Point — a grimly symbolic epitaph to the great plan Philip of Spain conceived 'because such was the mission he had received from God'.

Grandson of the pioneering Colonel Hugh Boyd, Ezekiel Davys Boyd alas failed to maintain the position of Ballycastle as an industrial town. In March 1782, however, the *Belfast News Letter* refers to him in a more creditable context, in their report of the stranding near Ballycastle of the sloop *Nancy*, for Mr. Boyd was instrumental in organising the rescue efforts. The *Nancy* had loaded yarn, beef, butter and hides in Portrush as well as embarking passengers, destination Liverpool. She came ashore in a hard gale and Boyd and a party of the Ulster Volunteers, 'our brave and useful Volunteers' as the newspaper refers to this 'Home Guard' of the day, with difficulty took off Captain James Walters, the crew and passengers from their chilling refuge in the rigging, although one man later died. Ballycastle around this time also had an important salt-making industry, these being the days when vast quantities were utilised for preserving food, and the saltpans were east of the town, near where legend has it the Celtic heroine Deirdre and the Sons of Uisneach made landfall. On 9 June 1790 the sloop *Ann* of Larne was lost off the saltpans with her owner and one of the hands.

The extreme smallness by today's standards of so many trading vessels of the past is apparent throughout this book. In the mid-nineteenth century schooner, brigantine and ketch rigs became more widely adopted, but prior to this sloops and smacks, single-masted craft averaging forty to fifty feet in length operated in thousands round the British Isles. Such references to Causeway coast wrecks as have survived from these times usually mentioned sloops: the *Jane* of Glasgow, Port na Spaniagh, crew drowned, and the *Endeavour* of Arbroath, near Port Ballintrae, both March 1823, the *Abraham and Ann* of Berwick, laden with grain, lost along with her crew near the Causeway, December 1824, and the *Speedwell*, Westport for Dublin with kelp, at Portstewart July 1826 with the loss of a passenger. An early schooner driven from her moorings and wrecked at Portrush was the *William Hoeg*, which in November 1825 anchored at the end of a passage from Trondheim -- a long way for the 67 ton vessel, built at Strangford in 1801 and the property of her master, Captain McKenzie. Continental traders and larger coasters were more likely to be brigs or snows, such as the brig *Psyche*, normally on the coal trade to Belfast, another wreck at Portrush in November 1828.

The catastrophic 'Big Wind' of 6 January 1839 has several times been referred to already. For an age less given to hyperbole than our own, there is no doubt that this hurricane was something extraordinary, tales of its spectacular depradations being handed down by those who experienced it. Records of the host of shipping casualties are patchy, especially regarding the north coast; giving evidence to the Royal Commission on Harbours of Refuge in 1858, a Captain Magowan recalled that six vessels were lost between Inishtrahull and the west end of Rathlin, but names of only two have come to light, the *Mary Ann* of Rothesay lost with all hands in the vicinity of the Bann mouth, and the Revenue Cruiser *Diligence*. The *Diligence* was manned by forty-one crew, and also had aboard a coastguard officer, his wife and family, who were being taken from Glenarm to Donegal where the officer had been posted. Nothing was seen or heard of the vessel after leaving Glenarm, but it was deduced that she must have foundered somewhere off the Giant's Causeway, as items of wreckage 'with the Queen's mark upon them' were washed ashore at Ballycastle.

Another great swathe of wreckage, this time littering the coast between Portrush and the Bann, was the first inkling local residents had of the loss of what later proved to be the *Isabella and Ann* of Stockton, timber laden, in Port Cool Bay October 1846. Day by day bodies began to drift ashore: an old man, tattooed; a young man, ears pierced; a woman, lacking head and arms.

The Minutes of Evidence taken before the Royal Commission on Harbours of Refuge at Portrush and Londonderry in September 1858, run to some 20,000 words and convey a most vivid depiction of weather and tidal conditions, navigational problems and wreck and rescue off the north of Ireland. Mr. Gibbon, Chief Engineer of the Board of Works, Dublin, exhibited his plans for a pier rising to twenty-one feet above high water mark, joining the mainland to the westernmost Skerries. Pilots, master mariners, coastguards and others testified to the need for a sheltered roadstead, as vessels often had to run all the way to Larne Lough or Lamlash in bad weather; Lough Foyle was inaccessible in westerly or north-westerly gales or against an ebb tide, while the Skerry Roads offered excellent holding ground, but suffered from strong tides and a swell, especially in westerly winds, through the west entrance. The witness least enthusiastic towards Mr. Gibbon's plan, Captain Bedford, Admiralty Surveyor, voiced his preference for seeing the islets of the Skerries group joined and the area better lit, but no action on any proposal was taken, the official finding being that a large expenditure for relatively small improvement to the roadstead could not be justified.

It certainly seems as if many masters would have been wary of attempting to enter the Skerry Roads at night or in poor visibility, even if a breakwater had been made, and one would think that Captain Bedford's pleas were both sensible and moderate. So the Skerry Roads was never designated for improvement and the shipping taking refuge here continued to be mostly local traders.

The Minutes of Evidence are studded with references to vessels wrecked in this rugged area in the previous twenty years, such as the brig *Liverpool*, near Portstewart with loss of life, 1841, the barque *Reliance* of Bridgwater at Bushfoot September 1847, and the schooner *Strangford*, on the south pier at Portrush, November 1856. Several witnesses also claimed that the emigrant ship *Exmouth*, Derry for Quebec in October 1847, which was seen off Portrush and was later wrecked on Islay with terrible loss of life, would have availed herself of shelter in the Skerry Roads had it been better known. However, the most locally celebrated wreck mentioned, still part of Portstewart lore, was the *George A. Hopley*, an American square – rigger the demise of which inspired a song, named a sandhill, supplied rum for thirty years and left us one of the earliest known wreck photographs. The 'Hopley' as she is still commemorated by 'Hopley Hill', was a vessel of 549 tons, built in 1846 and belonging to Charleston, South Carolina. She loaded a full and varied general cargo worth £66,000 at Liverpool, and sailed early in

July 1856, homeward bound. Mr. Hutchings, Chief Officer of Coastguard, Portrush, recalled for the Royal Commission:

' . . . she came through Rathlin Sound with a fresh breeze from south-east; the wind suddenly shifted to north-north-west, and blew very hard. I first saw her off Ramore Head, about a mile offshore, with a close-reefed topsail and foresail; she was then on the starboard tack but making great deal of leeway, about three hours afterwards, about half-past eight in the evening she was very close to the Black Rock near Portstewart; the tide caught her there and took her out to sea, but about half-past eleven I received notice she was ashore on Ballyagherton Strand. I took the Captain's deposition, and he said he attempted to wear off the Tuns Bank, but he got so close he had to let go his anchors, and was taken right along the strand at Portstewart . . . she became a total wreck and lies there now.'

The *George A. Hopley* broke up during an autumn gale, and there was a procession of carts night and day to the scene 'liberating' the cargo, which included 100 tons of liquor, and fine quality cloth and china. According to legend, men in Portstewart, Coleraine and district quaffed 'Hopley' rum, sported suits made of 'Hopley' cloth and ate their meals off 'Hopley' delph! The ship's barometer found its way to Laurel Hill House in Coleraine, and numerous other relics are still preserved in the locality.

The Skerry Roads anchorage which the stranger *George A. Hopley* eschewed is blue clay, topped with several inches of sand. The remains of iron rings are still visible on the Big Skerry, these being where warps were made fast to ease the strain on the anchor. Snugly moored here, vessels were usually safe, but during the 1860s in particular the Skerry Roads witnessed exciting scenes as less fortunate craft courted disaster. The new Portrush lifeboat, established in 1860, took off the crew of the local schooner *Margaret Caldwell*, after she had been fouled by the barque *Corioca*, and of the *Clara Brown*, another distressed schooner. Both vessels survived, but several other traders became total wrecks. The smack *Highlander* of Macduff, inadequately equipped with ground tackle, was driven on to Castle Island on 21 February 1862 and later disintegrated. Sub-standard vessels like the *Highlander* seem to have been all too common, and the following year occurred the famous wreck of the *Providence*, a schooner sharply condemned by the *Coleraine Chronicle* as 'the craziest of many crazy craft in the coal trade'. Skippered by Captain Robert Jack of the well-known Carrickfergus seafaring family, and with his son John and nephew George aboard, the *Providence* left Troon for Portrush but had to seek shelter off Lamlash, in Campbeltown Loch and then off Lamlash again. As the grey first light of 3 December 1863 broke, the schooner, a fore-yard and sails missing, was observed attempting to enter the Skerry Roads in a north-westerly gale. She anchored, but being in obvious distress, two boats put out from Portrush; the schooner's crew were unable to jump aboard the rescuing craft as they bobbed and yawed alongside, and by early afternoon the *Providence* had dragged to within 500 yards of the beach. The boat manned by local coastguards cast off again, but capsized in the surf and John Winter, an Englishman, was drowned. Inevitably the battered collier touched the bottom, was rolled over and quickly broken up, drowning three of the five crew including Captain Robert Jack and John Jack.

The second small boat that had put out to the *Providence* was manned by Captain Robb of the schooner *Harmony*, then in Portrush, and four volunteer fishermen, including James Martin. Martin later became mate of the brigantine *Jane*, owned by J. Massey of Portrush, and was the sole survivor of her loss on the Skerries on 8 February 1868. Having just left the harbour with potatoes for Cardiff, she failed to give the islets a wide enough berth and struck heavily on a rock at the north-west, foundering in three minutes. Three men and a boy drowned, James Martin being plucked from the water by his cousin, one of the local fishermen who had put out — as Martin had done in 1863 — on seeing the incident.

Winter sailing in these coasters was very much a case of awaiting a chance to make a passage and then trusting that the weather held. It did not for the *Providence*, nor for the schooner *Energy* of Belfast, Troon for Derry in March 1865, which sprang a leak off Inishtrahull and was buffeted to leeward until she held to an anchor her own length from the breakers off the East Strand, Portrush. The lifeboat *Zelinda* was pulled round by horses from the old lifeboat house — opposite Lansdowne Crescent — but before she could be launched the coastguards had reached the *Energy* and saved Captain Francis McKay, her part owner, and three hands.

The Portrush lifeboat did feature in two almost identical wrecks, which occurred, like the *Providence* and *Energy*, between the town and the White Rocks. The *Vitruvius* of Maryport and the *Amanda* of Coleraine both dragged their anchors and stranded, on 1 December 1867 and 2 October 1872 respectively, but to the appreciation of crowds of onlookers, the lifeboatmen took off both complements. No-one however saw the familiar local trader *James Annand*, Irvine for Portrush with coal for her owner, merchant David Fall, spring a sudden leak and founder off Bengore Head on 24 March 1877, Captain Heraughty and his crew having to row eight miles through choppy seas to Portrush harbour and safety. Also hidden by night, the *Thomas Graham* of Dumfries hit the east end of the Skerries in the gale that destroyed the Tay Bridge, 28 December 1879, and her three crew were marooned till dawn while their schooner drifted ashore, a total loss, at Bushfoot.

The sinking of the ketch *Happy Return* off the Skerries, the distress of a vessel in company with her, and the service to them of the Portrush lifeboat, combine neatly to form a vignette of life under sail a century ago. The *Happy Return*, registered in Padstow, Cornwall, put into the anchorage in an easterly gale encountered on a voyage from Teignmouth to Ballyshannon with clay, and dropped her 'hook' close to the schooner *Ocean Child* of Belfast, Ayr for Lough Swilly with coal. The Skerries not providing security against easterlies, both vessels dragged and hoisted distress signals which soon had the resolute lifeboatmen pulling strenuously towards them, under Coxswain John Hopkins, who had served in every rescue since 1860. Both crews were landed to the accompaniment of rousing cheers, but the condition of Mrs. Harden, wife of the skipper of the ketch, caused concern and she was tended at the nearby Methodist Manse. The following afternoon, 24 August 1882, the two crews returned, but in attempting to tack into the harbour, the *Happy Return* touched on a rock and later foundered in the Roads. The crew of the schooner were also forced to quit her and the two trios of men endured a miserable night out on the Skerries! The *Ocean Child*, dating from 1841, did not survive much longer, sinking off Rathmullen ten weeks later. Having accepted the fact that these small craft were apt to be blown wildly off course, or had on occasions to run great distances for shelter, that she had left Ayr for Ardrossan on her last voyage seems less incredible!

Before leaving the Portrush lifeboat for this chapter, mention must be made of a tragic accident it suffered on 1 November 1889. A schooner was seen to be in difficulty off the White Rocks, but when the *John and Agnes Blair* was on her way, the crew saw the vessel stand out to sea and run away eastwards. Coxswain Hopkins appears to have intended landing at Black Rock Strand, east of Port Ballantrae, but the boat capsized and three men were drowned. The schooner later proved to be the *Dryad* of Beaumaris, Captain Williams only learning of the drama after putting in to Larne for shelter. He was deeply affected by the tragedy and at once initiated a fund for dependants of the deceased.

Next to nothing survives of the wrecks of the wooden sailing coasters, but sub-aqua teams have found substantial remains of two nineteenth-century ships along this coast: the steam coaster *Petrel* and the barque

Nokomis, both iron-built craft. While the latter was a highly dramatic and tragic casualty, the *Petrel* too deserves mention if only for the delight her discovery brought to the New University of Ulster Sub-Aqua Club in May 1976, when this totally forgotten ship was found in just twenty feet of water off the north side of Black Rock, under Runkerry House at the east end of Black Rock Strand. Souvenirs such as steam valves were raised from the *Petrel*, which had lost her way and stranded here one foggy night in January 1882, while bound from Derry to her home port of Glasgow. No remnants were found, however, of the schooner *Emerald*, Sligo for Liverpool with timber, which also hit Black Rock in fog on 8 December 1879.

Strangely, it is off the other Black Rock, situated half a mile east of Portstewart, that the *Nokomis* lies. Belonging to the renowned Derry sailing ship owners Messrs. McCorkell, her net tonnage was 853, length 198 feet and Lloyd's classed her 100A1 after her completion at Stephen's Clydeside yard in February 1876. McCorkell's ships had a steady trade with grain from Baltimore, and it was for the Maryland port the *Nokomis* was bound when she left Derry about 19 January 1884. Making little progress against westerly winds, Captain Murphy ran back to Lough Foyle, coming to anchor off the pilot station at Greencastle. He now wanted a tug to take the barque up to the safest holding ground, but when the *Triumph* was ordered down from the city, her master decided to wait until first light before completing coaling and setting off. When the *Triumph* did arrive, the weather had worsened and she lay at Moville to await an improvement. With the wind now strong from the north-west, Captain Murphy may well have regretted not accepting offers from two other steamers to bring in the barque, but the *Triumph* was the tug regularly employed by his owners and doubtless he felt obliged to wait for her. The night of 26 January came and with it a gale with hurricane-force squalls whipping snow across the sea. The Greencastle coastguards continually flashed a signal lamp to the *Nokomis* as she rode at anchor, but the reassuring gleams of reply ceased about eleven o'clock. Nothing more was known of the barque until dawn revealed her as a total wreck off Black Rock; as was later deduced, she had been forced over the Tuns Bank off Magilligan Point, sustaining damage and probably losing men as she bumped heavily. There were no survivors from the seventeen crew, the Foyle pilot Neal Gillespie also drowning.

The *Nokomis* was the first and most serious of three fatal losses in less than seven years. In 1847 the *Reliance* of Bridgwater had been wrecked at Bushfoot, and forty years later another vessel belonging to this once-flourishing river port in Somerset was destroyed here. The ketch

Royal Standard, 81 net tons, was nearing the Foyle with cement from Newport, Isle of Wight, when she was beaten back, losing sails into t. e December night, and finally grounding 100 yards off the mouth of the River Bush. With a force ten blowing in from the north-west, the four crew launched their boat, but three climbed out again, unwilling to trust their lives to it. Captain Willis was indeed tipped out and given up for dead, but miraculously gained the shore and made his way to the house of a man named McLaughlin. Meanwhile, the crew constructed a makeshift raft by the light of a burning bucket of tar, but a boy named Smart was the only one prepared to risk it, and made the beach successfully as the ketch disintegrated, drowning his colleagues Hobbs and Cready. Smart picked himself up and then he too made for the nearby house, where he was dumb founded to see Captain Willis, whom he had assumed to have drowned.

A mile to the east, towards the Giant's Causeway, the rocky promontory between Portnaboe and Portcoon was the scene of a melancholy wreck in November 1890. Captain Randal Brown of Glynn, near Larne, had recently invested all his savings in the *William and Mary*, a schooner of 60 net tons he had purchased from a Mr. Bie of Whithorn. His first cargo in her was coal from Maryport for Letterkenny, and three times he was forced back to Larne Lough by stress of weather. The schooner was seen leaving once again at dawn on Thursday 7th, and nothing more was seen of her until masts were visible above water twenty-four hours later, and washed-up papers and wreckage identified her. Dead with Captain Brown were his mate, Archibald Thompson of Glynn and a boy, John Craig of nearby Magheramorne.

If the Ballycastle area appears to have been neglected, it is because wrecks here were scarce and fit no discernible pattern: the brig *Perseverance,* Quebec for Larne, December 1841, the smack *Blonde,* Belfast for Rathmullen December 1857, the steamer *Myrtle,* Portrush for Liverpool January 1878 and the barque *Fawcett,* Maryport for Derry, at Carrickmore March 1881. On 6 December 1911, however, the steamer *Templemore* went down in full view of many townsfolk, a tragic finale to a protracted tale of trouble. This six year-old coaster belonged to Henry Lane and Co. of Derry and when off Fair Head on the night of the 4th, bound Ellesmere Port for Derry with coal, she suffered heavy weather damage that obliged Captain Butler to put into Murlough Bay. Two of the crew landed, and helped by local resident Daniel Clarke, contacted the coastguards, and a telegram was sent to the owners who despatched the powerful tug *Earl of Dunraven.* Meanwhile, after the *Templemore* snapped her cables, the Morecambe to Derry passenger steamer *Brier* stood by until the tug arrived.

Charles Maude, a consultant engineer with a Belfast firm, who had happened to be in Derry, was transferred from the tug, while from the shore Joseph McGuinness, a representative of the owners, and John Buchanan, who had driven him from Derry 'in record time', joined the *Templemore*. Her fires were re-lit, steam was got up and she set off for Ballycastle, but with a 5° list which soon increased. As onlookers gave a shout of horror, a swell set the *Templemore* on her beam ends and she went down 1200 yards from land. Three Ballycastle men, John Coyle, William Robinson and Donald Black put out and saved all but Maude and an engineer, John Simms. The latter was last seen in the engine room, but Maude managed to leap overboard and Buchanan recalled later that he had been swimming behind him, 'going strong', it seemed.

Three twentieth century steamer wrecks that today are popular venues for divers are the coaster *Sard* of Glasgow, wrecked between Portrush and Portstewart 22 March 1906, the trawler *City of Bristol* of Fleetwood, aground between Sheep Island and the mainland January 1910, and a smaller coaster, the *Towy*, which sank while in tow for Portrush from Portstewart, where she had grounded while leaving the harbour on 20 June 1930. The *Towy*, owned by Whiteabbey Shipping Co. Ltd., Belfast, seems to have been the last trader to the little harbour at Portstewart, completed in 1887, but a wreck near here a year later is a more significant 'last' in the mammoth catalogue of Ulster shipwrecks. The schooner *Lily* was the last cargo vessel relying on sail° alone to be lost locally when the wind and tide carried her into Stony Port on Sunday 14 June 1931. Captain Jack Orr of Annalong, who had owned the *Lily* since 1912, and his crew were taken off by James Turbitt, the Portstewart harbour master. The *Lily*, just seventy-six feet long, had been built at Portsoy, near Banff, away back in 1878, and in her early days had traded as far as the Baltic to load timber for the east of Scotland. The superb photograph that depicts her forlorn wreck silhouetted against the evening sky has, surely, a profound quality of elegy not just for the subject, but for each and every sailing ship lost on our coasts: the *Rippling Wave* of Fowey, the *United Friends* of Pembrey, the *Elizabeth* of Strangford and so many more.

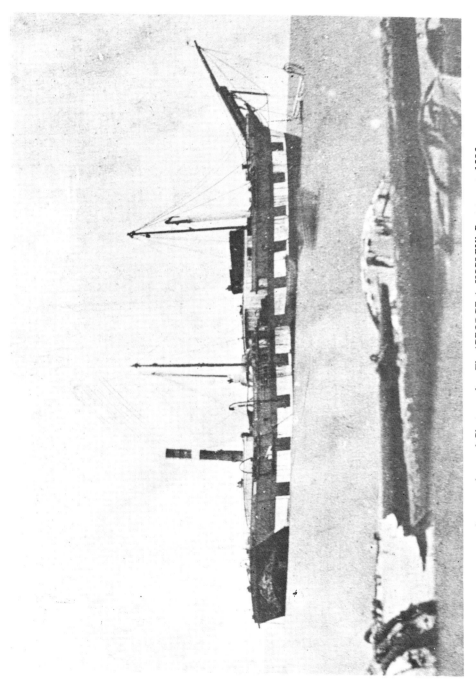

A very early wreck Photograph — The 'GEORGE A. HOPLEY', Portstewart, 1856.

Schooner 'LILY' in an evening setting, Portstewart, 1931.

An Old Portrush Lifeboat, the 'HOPWOOD'.

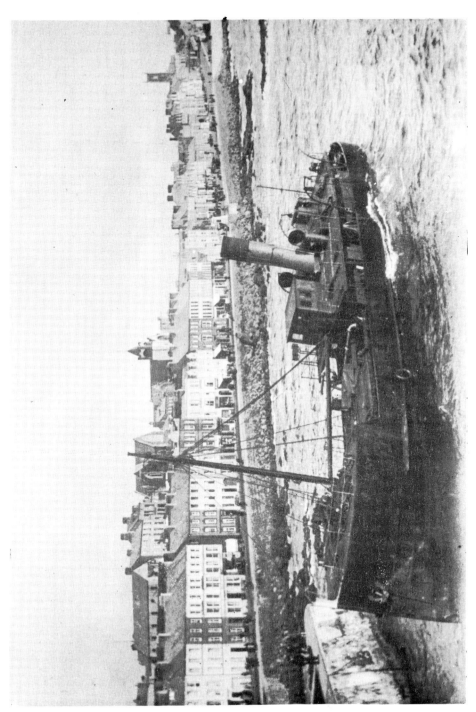

The 'TOWY' aground at Portstewart Harbour, 1930.

The 'REDTHORN' sunk in Portrush Harbour, 1938.

Last resting place of the Glasgow Steamer 'SARD'

Builders' Plate of the 'NOKOMIS', recently raised.

Chapter Nine

THE BANN MOUTH

TO INISHOWEN HEAD

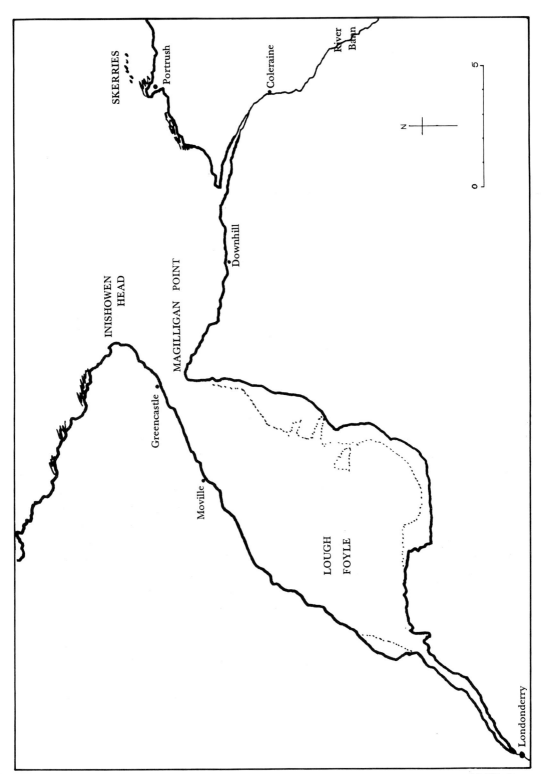

SKERRIES

Portrush

Coleraine

River Bann

5

N

0

Downhill

INISHOWEN HEAD

MAGILLIGAN POINT

Greencastle

Moville

LOUGH FOYLE

Londonderry

MAP 9

' . . . it is a shoal of sand thrown up between the river vent and the sea tide, entirely across the outlet of the Bann. Any vessel which is not skilfully piloted and at the same time favoured by wind and tide will run great risk of touching on this shoal, and if once retained has but a small chance of escaping the breakers which, during the prevalence of certain winds, roll with formidable impetuosity over the bar'.

Thus a report of the 1820s described the mouth of the River Bann and its hazards for shipping bound to and from Coleraine, some five miles upstream. The town rose to prominence after the Plantation of Ulster, when it was developed by the Honourable the Irish Society and received a charter from King James I in 1613 recognizing it as a sea-port and that it should remain so forever. Its present status is as the only important port between Larne and Londonderry, but, largely due to the handicap of the difficult access, progress towards this position has been inconsistent. Pausing for a moment as the morning crowds hurry to work across the town bridge, an observer will be likely to see sizeable coasters discharging coal, chemicals or other cargoes at the quays, but also the biggest boon to the navigation of the Bann in the present century, the port's own dredger *Bar Maid*, leaving for another day's work at the barmouth.

With a river that drains the whole centre of Ulster having an outlet on a north-facing coast, it is inevitable that chaotic conditions will often prevail at the mouth. No improvements will ever allow a vessel to enter the Bann in a northerly gale when an awesome swell clashes with the outgoing fresh water, but this is not the cause of the perennial sand-bar problem. From 1637, when an Irish Society petition to Parliament declared that navigation of the river was 'at most seasons impractical', until a century ago, few vessels larger than smacks and sloops traded to Coleraine, and it is certain that even they must have suffered serious delays in entering or leaving the river. The sloop *Bee* of Dumfries is the earliest known victim of the barmouth. Captured by the Royal Navy as a prize in the Napoleonic Wars, she was a total loss here in 1834. Wreck data is of course scarce for this era and before, but the Bann area is still so infrequently mentioned that this must constitute further evidence of Coleraine's insignificance as a port. A rare reference in *Lloyd's List* records that the *Adventure*, arriving from Liverpool, was wrecked 'near Coleraine' in a severe gale on 21 July 1826, the son of Captain Harris drowning. This wreck may well have occurred on the bar.

The commodious new harbour at Portrush was completed in 1829, and vessels of up to 500 tons could enter at any state of the tide, so until the radical improvements of the 1880s, Coleraine received mostly small sailing coasters; one which was definitely lost on the bar was the *Busy*, of and from Liverpool, 23 April 1850.

With the advent of steam communications by sea and rail, the handicap of the river entrance would have to be overcome or Coleraine could not fulfil its potential as a trading centre in the north-west. Following a report by the engineer Sir John Coode in 1878, two moles of rubble stone were built out from the shore, the plan being to hold back the sand on either side of the river mouth, and also give the Bann a more direct flow that would help scour away the sand bar. With a new quay and a rail link to the harbour also being completed, Coleraine's trade blossomed.

The new moles were still edging seawards when the steamer *Skelligs* of Glasgow grounded at the river mouth on 15 December 1882. One of the first products from the new yard of Workman, Clark in Belfast, where she had been launched just the previous year, the *Skelligs*, belonging to the Clyde Shipping Co., was refloated after the Portrush lifeboat had taken off her sixteen-man crew. This unlucky steamer survived only until May 1884, when she foundered after a collision off the Calf of Man.

At 450 gross tons and 160 feet in length, the *Skelligs* was the shape of things to come, however, and in August 1884 the Laird Line again began a cargo and passenger service to Glasgow, having withdrawn a short-lived attempt in 1865 owing to conditions at the barmouth. The 1880s generally were a period of optimism for the port as the facilities improved and deeper-draughted vessels entered; a report in the *Coleraine Chronicle* dated 12 June 1886 tells how the large brigantine *Storm Nymph* of Belfast arrived safely at the quay with coal, having crossed the bar while drawing fourteen feet four inches.

It was gradually proved, however, that the sand bar problem was recurring and as commerce increased, accidents began to occur almost annually. The depths between the moles, which fluctuated as the sand bar shifted treacherously, the proximity of the moles to the swinging bow or stern of a grounded ship, and the occasional human error of a pilot all contributed to making Coleraine a risky port to trade to.

When the iron twin-screw steamer *Christopher Thomas* of Cardiff arrived off the Bann mouth from Belfast on 5 February 1894, she was drawing a mere six feet, but her master was not happy about attempting to cross the bar and said as much to the pilot, Andrew Logan, when he came out from Portstewart. Confidently, Logan replied that he'd often gone over with such a sea, and took the wheel of this strange old ship, a converted paddler which had been a ferry and excursion vessel on the Severn, but now loaded cargo. Logan lined up the pier ends and steamed in, but a huge wave caught the steamer and carried her bodily to starboard, her screws and rudder tilted out of the water. Narrowly, she escaped colliding with the point of the west pier broadside on, but carried on, brushing the outermost stones and losing a screw before she was cast on the beach close to the pier, on which she knocked a hole in herself on the next tide. One wonders what words were exchanged between Captain Thomas and the pilot, but Logan seems to have been scarcely abashed when explaining to the Coleraine Harbour Board eight days later, 'There have been more vessels this winter than ever before, so there has to be a little point strained to get them in and out'. Against expectations, the *Christopher Thomas* was refloated, continuing her chequered career by being sold to Nigeria for river trading!

A pilot's error also caused the loss of the brigantine *Maria*, Maryport for Coleraine with coal, 14 January 1900. As usual the pilot, in this instance Thomas McLean, boarded from a boat rowed out from Portstewart. He knew the vessel and Captain Robert Shearer of Bangor well, for the *Maria* belonged to F. H. Watt of the old established local coal importers. McLean owned the small tug *Eagle*, but advised Captain Shearer that its aid was not necessary, that there was 'plenty of water', and that he could enter under sail. Disaster quickly followed. The *Maria* struck the bottom between the pier ends and broached to, being pierced by submerged stones off the east pier and beginning to fill. Captain Shearer had the presence of mind to run her ashore lest she block the channel, and she was almost completely submerged soon after all aboard had left. Probably because she was so old, the *Maria*, built at Prince Edward Island in 1863, was not insured and Watt sent men to the scene to save all the sails and rigging they could.

Sailing vessels by now were calling at Coleraine in ever-decreasing numbers, and the last such victim of the bar occurred on 15 March 1901. This was the schooner *George 4th* of Barrow, 99 net tons, which was attempting to cross with a load of manure from Plymouth. The loss of the ship and cargo prompted a columnist in the *Coleraine Chronicle* to write wittily on the Harbour Board in time reaping an abundant harvest of edible seaweed at the barmouth, but it was a sorry end for a fine vessel, built by John and William White on the banks of the Ulverston Canal in Lancashire in 1873 and named, strangely, after a son of William Postlethwaite the owner. Postlethwaite built up a fleet of tough schooners, many from Whites' yard, such as the *Millom Castle*, which can still be seen as a hulk near St. Germans in Cornwall. Their day was ending, however; locally, William Hinde, who owned the *Storm Nymph*, finished with sail about 1890, while Watt's last sailer, the *Essex*, was lost on Arran in 1903. Everywhere, steam began to dominate.

December 1904 saw the *Helen* of Glasgow stick for a time and come off unscathed, but when a similar steamer the *Greenisland*, grounded on the east pier on 16 February 1906, her fate was in the balance for a time after the crew clambered on to the pier. When the *Greenisland* was refloated and docked, the opportunity was taken by owner Charles McFerran Legg of Carrickfergus to have her lengthened by thirteen feet, and she survived until 1955, trading to Coleraine frequently while under John Kelly Ltd. ownership.

The most serious steamer mishap since the *Christopher Thomas* occurred late on the evening of 24 February 1912, when the *Shilbottle* of Aberdeen, outwards for Liverpool with 200 tons of potatoes, was 'dropped' by the swell on to the sand between the pier ends. Unmanageable, she struck the stones at the head of the west mole, and the waves forced her bow right up on to it. Captain Smith, the eight crew and pilot, endured a bad night aboard before the Portrush lifeboat took them off at dawn. In gratitude, the lifeboatmen were presented with the ship's bell, which is still in safe keeping. Lightening, which resulted in potatoes washed up on local beaches, failed to aid refloating attempts and the *Shilbottle*, sold only the previous month by G. Elsmie and Son to G. Couper and Co., became a total loss.

The *Shilbottle* wreck began a sequence of five total losses in a little over ten years, with additional minor accidents — an intolerable situation that gave the port little future unless drastic improvements were made. By 1910, it was known the moles were deteriorating, but the outbreak of war suspended schemes to rectify the position. The Laird Line's popular summer service to Portrush ceased with hostilities, but the year-round Coleraine service was maintained. The *Daisy* was entering the Bann from Greenock on Sunday 23 February 1915 with general cargo and four passengers when a big sea lifted her stern; her bows slanted under and bit into the sand and the ship swung right around, ending up wedged on the east pier, facing seawards. All aboard — apart from the corpse of a woman from the Bushmills area, destined for Coleraine — landed from the ship's boats on the opposite pier, and the crew spent the day in a Castlerock hotel watching the sea break over the *Daisy*, while the passengers eventually reached Coleraine by an unforeseen route!

Dismantling wrecks, especially in wartime with the extra demand for scrap, was a lucrative task, and in September 1915 the Manx salvage contractor Robert Lemon of Peel arrived in his wooden vessel *Diver Lass* to tackle the *Daisy*. Lemon may well have owed his life, as well as his livelihood, to the *Daisy*. He was still at work on 9 April 1916 when the *Corsewall* of Glasgow stranded on the east pier while laden with potatoes for Liverpool. Portrush lifeboat, coxswain Tom Patton, put out against wind and tide but on arrival could not venture close enough to remove the crew. Realising this, Lemon attempted to take a line to the steamer, but the little motor boat he was in was smashed on the stones. Boat and occupant vanished from view, but to the relief of the growing crowd that afternoon, the bold Manxman was seen clambering into the rigging of the wrecked *Daisy*! It was five hours after the accident before a line was attached to the *Corsewall*, and three more before the crew of eight and pilot Doherty were hauled to safety. The *Corsewall*, previously French flag, was written off by her owners, the Kintyre and Galloway Shipping Co. Ltd.

Less than a year had elapsed before the *Craigavad* of Belfast added to the lengthening list of casualties. Having brought coal from Maryport, she missed the tide on 14 March 1917 and anchored overnight in the Skerry Roads, but grounded in mid-channel on entering the following day. Another coaster, the *Wheatberry*, was to follow her in, but her pilot took her to Portrush; her owners, Messrs. Spillers, regularly carried flour to Coleraine, but for a time after the accident sent all their ships to Portrush — an example of how the river entrance was a huge disadvantage to Coleraine's prosperity. The *Craigavad*, 361 gross tons, was managed by Thomas Wilson for Cullen, Allen and Co., and she too never sailed again.

Following the loss of their *Daisy*, the Laird Line were understandably loth to send their larger ships to Coleraine. In November 1922 the newly-constituted Burns and Laird Lines Ltd., discontinued the regular service altogether, but not before the *Taff* had been lost on the bar. On charter from J. Little and Sons of Saltcoats for a run that now extended to Mulroy, but was cargo-only, she struck the west pier on 9 May 1922, her crew landing safely and Portrush lifeboat putting back. Messrs. McCausland of Portaferry undertook fruitless salvage attempts with their steamer *Saint Anthony* and the *Taff*, like her sister *Towy* at nearby Portstewart eight years later, became a wreck. Both vessels were about 200 gross tons and dated from 1914.

Reporting the loss of the *Taff*, the *Coleraine Chronicle* opined that it was especially regrettable as the port had been enjoying record prosperity. But, despite the rarity of accidents in the 1920s, satisfactory depths were not being maintained on the bar, and the long-postponed improvements were put in hand in 1929. The existing moles were extended and raised, and new training banks built inside them a little upstream — in short, the barmouth gradually took on its present appearance. It was a protracted job and during it several steamers and a dredger were wrecked. The Manx *Ben Vooar* of the Ramsey Steamship Co. was carried on to the end of the west pier in June 1936 while inward bound, while the *Redthorn* was also holed here on 21 November 1938. Exemplifying the small margin of error available here, the vessels preceding and following her crossed safely, but the crippled *Redthorn* had to make for Portrush, escorted by the lifeboat, and settled on the bottom there. She belonged to the Liverpool firm of S. W. Coe and Co. Ltd., who had begun their still-continuing association with Coleraine in the 1920s, though she was built as the *Brookside* in 1903 for James Shiels of Belfast; under his ownership she survived a stranding on the Down coast in 1905 while bound for Ardglass, but the 1938 accident finished her as she was raised only to go to Derry for demolition. Coe's fleet, now carrying much of the coal traffic, suffered a second blow only weeks later when the *Briarthorn* was entering on the last day of 1938. She too was pushed on to the west pier by a powerful wave and struck alongside a large blower dredger, which had stranded here and snapped in two a short time before. Thus the *Briarthorn*, 459 gross tons, the *H.G.W. Dredger No. 10* and the *Redthorn* all became total write-offs inside a grim six-week period.

However, the advent of war was to prove that Coleraine could handle the large steamers that the Government utilised to carry army supplies. At the end of the war, with all reconstruction work completed, there was nine feet nine inches available as a minimum depth, compared to a mere five feet six in 1929. Henderson and Nicholl, the contractors, finally left in 1943, the year, neatly enough, that witnessed the last total loss to date. The Coe steamer *Knowl Grove* became a wreck on 21 October in almost identical circumstances to the *Redthorn* and *Briarthorn* — circumstances, really, which had little to do with the actual sand bar. The distance between the pier heads is 500 feet — little enough in a steamer wallowing in the inevitable turbulence where fresh water meets salt, and perhaps slow to respond to the helm. The Harbour Board tendered for the removal of the wreck, accepting a quotation of £3,000 from W. R. Metcalfe of Llandudno, and the *Knowl Grove* was slowly cut up. This ship had once been lost in a different sense, when, sailing northwards, she 'missed' the Shetlands owing to the unfamiliarity of master and crew with the set of the tides!

Despite losing three ships in four years, S. W. Coe and Co. Ltd., were obviously nothing daunted, as they contributed to the unfolding of a welcome period of progress for Coleraine, when cargoes were plentiful and accidents few and minor. Vessels would occasionally 'bump' on the bar, but it was not until the 1960s that serious thought was given to further improvement and if possible a final solution to the sand bar problem. With the trend to larger ships, representing greater capital investment by their owners, and the increasing competition of road transport, the port authorities could not afford to be complacent. The Hydraulics Research Station at Wallingford built a sophisticated model of the river entrance, but could suggest no viable answer to the problem. To add urgency to the search a regular collier, the *Maythorn*, was holed on the east pier on 20 June 1967 and reached Coleraine in a sinking condition. A similar accident befell the timber-laden *Knudsvig* in July 1969, while the *Warlight* of Greenock, from Tarbert, Loch Fyne, with logs, stuck for two hours on 4 May 1970. These accidents and delays to ships of a week or more in entering or leaving the port were just not acceptable in the competitive modern freight world. A custom-built dredger for the special problems of work at the mouth of the Bann was the only resort now, and after much agitation Government aid in the form of a 75% grant was forthcoming. The *Bar Maid*, built at Wivenhoe in Essex, arrived at Coleraine after her delivery voyage on 30 June 1977, and has worked with efficiency and success since. The minimum depth is now an unparalleled fifteen feet, and, buried in the accumulated sand, the dredger's equipment has recently uncovered a veritable junkyard of wreckage from casualties of the past. Her worth could not be better emphasised.

An eight-mile crescent of sand curves westward from the Bann to Magilligan Point at the mouth of Lough Foyle. It is interrupted only by the black cliffs of Downhill, on which stands the desolate ruin of the great mansion of the eccentric Earl of Bristol, also Bishop of Derry, who in 1785 built the adjacent Mussenden Temple; in letters once covered in gold an inscription, lines by Lucretius, reads:

' 'Tis pleasant, safely to behold from shore
The rolling ship and hear the tempest roar.'

The 'rolling ship' continues to give this coast a wide berth as she makes for the Tuns buoy marking the huge sandbank off Magilligan Point, before turning to port and entering Lough Foyle, picking up a pilot and sailing the twenty miles to the quays of Londonderry. The city's heyday for trade was the nineteenth century, when commerce with North America especially thrived, but it was also a vital Naval base in the two World Wars, and remains

Northern Ireland's second port, although many ships now berth at industrial jetties downstream of the city. The port serves a very large hinterland, its imports boosted by the closure of small Donegal ports such as Buncrana and Moville, where the pilot station is situated and off which Atlantic liners used to lie to embark Irish emigrants. Long after the 'packets' ceased to put in to the Foyle one of the channel lights was known as the 'Anchor Line buoy', but the last vestige of the centuries-old trade with North America ended in 1939.

Two Atlantic traders are the earliest-known casualties in this area. In a hard gale on 4 February, 1791, the full-rigged ship *Happy Return* was driven on the sands at Magilligan Point while inward bound to the Foyle from Philadelphia. Three miles to the north, at Inishowen Head, on the Donegal side of the Lough approaches, the *Barclay,* another ship from Philadelphia, was blown aground. Reporting events, the *Belfast News Letter* states the *Happy Return* was feared a total loss, and also mentions a third American trader ashore, the *Wilmington,* for Belfast, in Donegal Bay.

Vagueness in the records over specific locations of wrecks is nowhere more frustrating than in this segment of the Ulster coast: 19 January 1798, the *Three Friends,* Liverpool for Derry, near Coleraine, only Captain Stewart saved; 25 March 1816, the *Shannon,* New York for Drogheda, near Derry and the crew feared drowned; March 1818, the *Ann and Isabella* of Thurso, from Wick, off the Foyle and all aboard lost; 20 November 1826, the brig *Rambler*, Belfast for Derry, near Lough Foyle. Brief facts about these losses are contained in the back numbers of *Lloyd's List*, but the shipping newspaper has a more substantial report of the wreck of the schooner *Gute Hoffnung*, shortly after Christmas, 1814. A schooner bound from Gothenburg to Drogheda, the *Gute Hoffnung* struck heavily on the Tuns Bank, but drifted off again, sinking. The crew jumped into the vessel's longboat but it was engulfed by a breaker and swamped, the master and mate perishing. The remainder of the complement managed to reach the Donegal shore in another small boat, and were fished out of the surf by local cottagers.

Reference has been made to the practice of commemorating shipwrecks shipwrecks in ballads, most notably perhaps in the case of *Enterprise* of Lynn on the Antrim coast. Often these 'come-all-ye's' have little to commend them either as songs or as accurate history, but in an age of widespread illiteracy — and a perhaps enviable ignorance of disasters worldwide — it was necessary to preserve some account of local sensations. Such a ballad, once popular in the Downhill and Magilligan areas, commences:

'Come all ye seamen bold I pray and listen here a while to me,
And landsmen too while thus I do relate to you our sad ditty,
I would melt the heart while I impart and sing this doleful song o'er,
A ship of fame, *Trader* by name, was lately wrecked upon our shore'.

Entitled 'The Captain's Dream' after a doubtless fictitious supernatural ingredient, the ballad is however firmly based on fact. The brig *Trader* of Greenock, owner and master Captain Castle, had weathered Malin Head on her way from Limerick to the Clyde with grain, when her rudder parted company with the stern and she was helplessly buffeted on to the rocks at Downhill. All eight men aboard died, and the bodies were interred a few miles inland at Articlave. Tradition maintains that it was henceforward a customary pilgrimage for Greenock seamen calling at Coleraine to visit the churchyard and pay their respects, while a further item of local lore is that the stocks of many farmers' firearms were shaped from the timbers of the *Trader*, which had been built of oak at Glasgow in 1813. This tragedy occurred in November 1826, and on Christmas Eve following another Scottish vessel, the *Stafford* of Rothesay, was lost off Castlerock with her six-man crew.

Among the chief Derry shipowners of the time, and indeed through the nineteenth century, were the McCorkell family, owners of the illfated *Nokomis* in later years. In his interesting study of Derry shipping 'The Maiden City and the Western Ocean', Sholto Cooke devotes space to the fascinating voyages of William McCorkell's schooner *President*, only 105 net tons yet sent several times to Canada. The March 1827 snowstorms that caused so much havoc around the coasts drove her on to Whitecastle spit in Lough Foyle before she could make port safely with iron from Newport, Mon. Initial salvage efforts were thwarted, but Captain Dugald Mathewson, refusing an offer from local shipbuilder Mr. Hempson to raise her for £70 lashed an empty lighter and puncheons to the hull and lifted her on a tide. The *President* survived and by the autumn of that year was on passage to Riga, eventually being wrecked on the Arklow Bank bound from Alicante to Derry.

The confines of Lough Foyle were by no means totally safe for sailing vessels, especially in southerly or easterly gales. The brig *Donegal*, owner James McCrea of Derry and bound for the Mersey with wheat and oats, was just as lucky to survive as the *President* after she went on the rocks near Greencastle on 31 October 1834. A severe blow on 8 January 1852 wrecked three ships in the Lough, the *Herman,* and *Anna* and the *Arendina,* lost off Redcastle so close to the end of a long voyage from Ibrail on the Danube;

coincidentally, the *Rose*, also for Derry from the nearby Rumanian port of Galatz, was wrecked on Islandmagee in the same month.

About 3.30 a.m. on 23 January 1856 the brig *Kathleen* of Portsmouth arrived off the mouth of the Lough laden with wheat from Alexandria. With squalls from the south-east reaching force nine and visibility hazy, the master realised the pilot, who usually boarded a mile outside the Tuns bank, would not put out. Seeing the light on Inishowen Head, he proceeded in, but the *Kathleen* missed stays; with no room for the crew to wear ship she struck with crippling impact between Inishowen Head and Greencastle, and soon filled. The master and seven hands were hauled ashore by ropes, but the brig, 217 net tons and valued at £900, and the cargo, priced at £1500, were written off.

A little to the north of Inishowen Head the following March the smack *Maclellans,* Troon for Derry with coal, and the schooner *Gwen* of Amlwch, from Liverpool, both stranded, the former later going to pieces. On the opposite side of the Lough entrance, the schooner *Ella*, belonging to Hugh Gilmore of Killyleagh, Co. Down, was a total loss on 26 February 1873, but there appears to have been a fortunate freedom from dramatic shipwrecks until the famous episode of the *Hilding* wreck and rescue in 1878. Captain Bunck of the Prussian *Marie* of Barth frankly admitted his error when the brigantine sailed on to Castlerock strand in fine weather on the night of 11 September 1874. The *Marie* soon parted in two, but the majority of the 1749 barrels of tar she was carrying from Archangel to Cork were recovered.

No navigational error generated the peril the Norwegian brig *Hilding* found herself in on 25 January 1878 as, waterlogged and unmanageable, she was just managing to hold to two anchors off the Tuns bank, signalling her distress to the shore. Destined for the Cuban port of Cardenas with coal, the *Hilding*, 250 net tons, had left Glasgow on the 10th, but after losing her main topmast and much gear in an Atlantic gale, had put about and run for the Foyle. A northerly storm, with violent flurries of snow, and her own deeply-draughted, lumbering condition made a safe entry to the Lough impossible. Now the coastguards summoned the tug *Hotspur*, Captain Fletcher, which towed the lifeboat from Portrush to the wallowing brig. The lifeboat had earned many plaudits for past services, and was to earn more, but for once conditions were apparently too daunting for those on board, and she let go the hawser and came ashore on Magilligan strand. With the afternoon wearing on, the light soon to begin to fail, and his vessel liable to sink under him, Captain Jorgenson now had no real alternative but to slip his cables and let the brig he borne on to the beach, and about 3.30 p.m. she took the ground between Downhill and Magilligan. Conditions were appalling. Backed only by low sandhills, this must be the bleakest strand in Ireland in a northerly gale. Snow mingled with spray drove almost horizontally across the wet sands as the coastguards battled to where the *Hilding* was embedding herself, the wind screaming in her rigging. Captain Jorgenson yelled the shipmaster's last order, 'Every man for himself!', and the mate and he pulled off their seaboots and leapt over the side. No-one saw them even surface. Waves were now breaking over the stern and flooding the decks, and one carried to his death a Swedish A. B. named Sucke, who was attempting to gain a handhold in the rigging. Luckier, however, were two seamen who clung on to a spar and were dragged from the foam alive by the coastguards and a Captain McCandless of Moville. No boats were at the disposal of the coastguards, but the intrepid Captain McCandless procured one, probably sending to Downhill village, and at enormous risk put out as darkness dropped. Huddled in the rigging he found five men, one exhibiting no sign of life, with the *Hilding* disintegrating as she lifted and pounded on the bottom. Incredibly, the apparently lifeless seaman had been merely asleep, and he and his colleagues were snatched from their perch and safely brought ashore. So three men died when it seemed that all would, the survivors comprising five Norwegians, a Dutchman and an Englishman named McDonald.

Meanwhile, in Lough Foyle, five more seamen were at the centre of another drama. Caught in the storm while bound from the Mersey to Sligo, the steamer *Liverpool* of Sligo put into the Lough for refuge. Soon after the anchor was let go, it was realised that the steamer had touched on a bank and was swinging by her stern. The mate and four men lowered a boat to examine the position, but a squall overtook them and blew them away from the ship's side. Rowing before the wind and tide they eventually pulled alongside Derry quay, told their tale and were returned to the *Liverpool* by the local tug *Seagull*. The *Liverpool*, belonging to the Sligo Steam Navigation Co., was freed a few days later.

In close proximity to the scene of the *Hilding* wreck, a second deep-sea sailer stranded in 1880. On 12 December the square-rigger *Quorn* of Liverpool, 1243 net tons, failed to make an offing from the lee shore in a west-north-west gale, while bound from Greenock to New Orleans with coal. The *Quorn* too became a total wreck, but Captain Bernier and his crew of sixteen escaped.

Just two months after the *Hilding* and *Liverpool* incidents, there occurred another steamship accident in Lough Foyle, this time a total loss. With her defective iron hull leaking copiously, the 'puffer' *Lyle* of Port Glasgow anchored on 28 March 1878 while on passage to Ramelton in Lough Swilly with manure, slates and timber. The inrush could not be stemmed and she foundered after Captain Prearty and the three-man crew had rowed clear. Weather conditions played no part here, but that the Lough could in exceptional circumstances be no safe enchorage for stormbound shipping was demonstrated on 1 October, 1882, when a force ten blew from the southwest. The schooner *Fred*, Ardrossan for Killybegs, and the brigantine *Woolton*, the Tyne for Kingstown, both coal-laden, were driven ashore and wrecked at Moville. Captain Boyle of the Rutland Island, Donegal, family who owned the *Fred*, and Captain Foy of Belfast, owner of the *Woolton*, were rescued with their respective crews. The Moville coastguards, opposite whose station these ships came ashore, also helped to safety the crews of the sailing coasters *Copius* of Preston, *Private Note* of Runcorn, and *Marys* of Ardrossan, but this trio were later refloated again. Twelve years later, the ravages of the great northerly gale that caused such widespread destruction to shipping just before Christmas, 1894, caught two steamers at anchor near the Lough entrance and hurled them far up the flat sands opposite Bellarena. The sheer power of the elements that day can be gauged by the fact that when attention was turned to refloating the *Holme Force* of Whitehaven, it was found that at high water she needed another ten feet to float! A channel had to be excavated for her, and the *Holme Force*, which had previously stranded on the Ards coast in March 1892, was eventually freed.

An excursion treat had unforeseen and disastrous consequences for a large party of labourers who set off for a day on the River Foyle on 11 September 1891. The outing was organised by a Mr. Graeme Hunter, who had brought 150 men to work on Derry quays during a strike by the regular dockers, and twenty-three of his men, together with his two children and himself, embarked on the steam launch *Mayflower*, the property of Francis McKeever, a Foyle ferryman. The party had landed downstream at Culmore and were returning up the river when the paddle steamer *Albatross* hove in sight. The *Albatross* combined the duties of tug, liner tender and Derry to Moville passenger boat for many years, and on this occasion was returning empty to Moville for the morning sailing. About 8.10 p.m., some 150 yards from the Boomhall light, the *Mayflower* struck a sponson of the paddler and stove in her bows. Panic gripped her passengers. Hunter just had time to push his elder child Jane into the arms of one William Mearns before the little steamer went down beneath them all, not twelve seconds after the impact. Boats from the *Albatross* plucked only eight survivors from the river, including Hunter and his younger child, but Mearns, a Belfast man, and his brief charge were among the eighteen drowned. At the subsequent inquiry, it was found that the *Albatross* 'was not navigated with proper and seamanlike care'.

The twentieth century was only a week old when the steam collier *Lady Arthur Hill* became a total loss at Inishowen Head while inward bound from Newport, Mon. This did not prove to be an omen, for there then followed a long spell without serious shipping casualties, all the total losses on this section of coast between the *Lady Arthur Hill* and the *Uberus* in 1941 taking place at the Bann mouth. Vessels would from time to time ground in Lough Foyle, such as the steam coaster *Ardachy* of Glasgow, in ballast for Bonawe, which did herself no good at all by stranding on the Middle Bank in April 1922. Her bottom plates were set up and the engine strained, and a tow to the Clyde for permanent repairs had to be arranged.

The *Uberus*, a trawler requisitioned by the Admiralty in 1939 and armed, is officially recorded as wrecked in Lough Foyle on 11 January 1941, but no further details have come to light. If not the circumstances, then at least the whereabouts of loss of the fleet tug H.M.S. *Assurance* are known, for she is frequently visited by the sub-aqua fraternity at her resting place on Bluick Rock, north of Greencastle. Fleet tugs, as opposed to harbour tugs, were fitted out for ocean service and many were employed off the north of Ireland towing merchantmen damaged by torpedo or mine back to port. The *Assurance*, which was wrecked on 18 October 1941, was the first and name ship of a class of twenty-one fleet tugs built by Cochrane and Sons at Selby, being launched in May 1940.

After the war, the graceful passenger ships of the Anchor and Donaldson lines such as the three-funnelled *Caledonia* were no longer to be seen on Lough Foyle, but large ships in the rather less elegant form of tankers with fuel for the Coolkeeragh power station jetty began to become a feature of the contemporary scene. On 22 March 1963, the German *Wilhelmine Essberger* grounded off Redcastle while inward bound carrying 11,000 tons, but later pulled herself off unaided. A small tanker to go ashore here was the *Esso Tenby*, inward from Milford Haven, stuck from 9 to 13 October 1975, but it was a few months earlier that the only significant accident in the Lough Foyle vicinity in recent years occurred. The *Ben Vooar* was a motor coaster of 427 gross tons, a successor in the Ramsey Steamship Co. fleet to the coal-burner of the name wrecked at the ¯ann mouth in 1936. On 2 June 1975 she unloaded coal at Red Bay and received orders to sail for Portrush to pick up a load of stones for the Isle of Man. On arrival off Portrush, a swell made the narrow harbour entrance impassable so the master decided to go and lie in Lough Foyle, but at 2 a.m. on 3 June, she struck rocks a little to the south of Inishowen Head, holing herself and jamming the rudder. Two fishing boats took her in tow and she was beached at Greencastle, later being towed by the tug *Craigdarragh* up to Derry for drydocking. She never traded for the Ramsey firm again, but was sold to a Tyneside concern and renamed *Arran Firth*.

With Inishowen Head reached on this long tour from Carlingford Lough, what really is a continuing story must be concluded. Westwards from Lough Foyle past the lonely, towering headlands of Donegal the wrecks abound, their stories all waiting to be written: the *Trinidad Valencera* of the Spanish Armada, the liner *Cambria*, H.M.S. *Wasp*, the White Star *Laurentic* off Lough Swilly, the *Sydney*, the *Stolwijk* and many, many more. But the story is continuing in another sense; as this book was being completed news came through that Donaghadee lifeboat had taken off most of the crew of the crippled Finnish freighter *Inio*, and that tugs were towing her through bad weather to the safety of Belfast Lough. Progress has lessened the likelihood of shipwrecks around the Irish coast, but the danger of tide and rock, shoal and current are eternal; eternal too, in balance, are the vigilance, selflessness and skill of the men of the rescue services.

Sightseers at the wreck of the 'DAISY', Bann Mouth, 1915.

Two victims of the Bann entrance lie together — 'BRIARTHORN' and 'H. G. W. DREDGER 10', 1938

The Steamer 'BEN VOOAR', aground at the Bann Mouth, 1936.

The Motorship 'BEN VOOAR'
in drydock after her grounding, 1975.

INDEX OF SHIPS' NAMES

Y

BIBLIOGRAPHY

OFFICIAL PUBLICATIONS

Admiralty Wreck Registers 1850 – 1857
Board of Trade Wreck Returns 1874 – 1918.
Parliamentary Sessional Papers, various years, 1837 – 1920.
Report of the Royal Commission on Harbours of Refuge, 1859.

BOOKS
Anderson, R. 'The Port of Coleraine'. (Ballycastle, 1977.)
Beaver, Patk. 'A History of Lighthouses'. (London, 1971.)
Boate, G. 'Ireland's National History'. (1645.)
Cooke, Sholto 'The Maiden City and the Western Ocean'. (Dublin, 1961.)
Crawford, M. G. 'Legendary Stories of the Carlingford Lough District' (1913)
Crawford, W. T. & Trainor, B. (eds.) 'Aspects of Irish Social History 1750 – 1800' (H.M.S.O., Belfast 1969.)
Duckworth, C. L. D. and Langmuir, G. E. 'Clyde and other Coastal Steamers'. (second edition, Prescot, 1977.)
Eames, Aled 'Ships and Seamen of Anglesey' (Llangefni, 1973.)
Fallon, Niall 'The Armada in Ireland'. (London, 1978.)
Harris, W. 'The Ancient and Present State of the County of Down'. (Dublin, 1744.)
Hocking, C. 'Dictionary of Disasters at Sea in the Age of Steam' Volumes 1 and 2 (London, 1969).
Kohl, J. G. 'Kohl's Travels in Ireland' (London, 1844.)
Law, G. 'Rathlin, Island and Parish' (Cookstown, 1961.)
McNeill, D. B. 'Irish Passenger Steamship Services'. Volume 1 (Newton Abbot, 1969.)
Rowland, K. T. 'The Great Britain' (Newton Abbot, 1971).
Stenuit, Robt. 'Treasures of the Armada' (Newton Abbot, 1972.)
Wilson, T. G. 'The Irish Lighthouse Service' (Dublin, 1968).

NEWSPAPERS AND JOURNALS

Belfast News Letter
Belfast Telegraph
Coleraine Chronicle
Down Recorder
Lloyd's List
Mourne Observer
Newry Reporter
Northern Constitution

Journal of the Down and Connor Historical Society 1928.
Sea Breezes.
The Glynns, Journal of the Glens of Antrim Historical Society
Transactions of the Institute of Engineers and Shipbuilders of Scotland, 1938 & 1946 — 7.

MISCELLANEOUS

Irish Coast Pilot (Ninth Edition, 1941)
Lloyd's Register of Shipping

ADDENDUM TO FOURTH EDITION

The enduring interest in 'Shipwrecks of the Ulster Coast' constantly surprises me! First editions have fetched up to £55 on the collectors' market (regrettably, I've barely one for myself!)

New information on the subject inevitably continues to emerge. The creation of a computerised database of all underwater sites by the Environment and Heritage Service, D.O.E.N.I. has accelerated this. The project arose largely out of the 1990 Government White Paper, "This Common Inheritance" on environment and archaeology, following which the Royal Commission on Historic Monuments initiated a survey of all English wreck sites – a mammoth task. My shipwreck records, only 60% of which are mentioned for reasons of space – and readability – have been used as the core of the database by the D.O.E., who of course have developed a similar survey of land sites since the 1970s.

Prior to the 1850s, shipwreck information was not gathered in any systematic annual way. Go back before 1800 and the researcher is like someone trying to shine a beam into a dark vault. There must be plenty to find, but little can be illuminated. Nevertheless, intriguing wrecks originally missed, and clearer details of incidents in two world wars – years still challenging for the researcher – can be mentioned now.

In the Public Record Office, Belfast, (D2015) are the papers of Captain R H Davis, a former deepwater sailing ship man, who was an absolute pioneer in recording local maritime history. The eighteenth and early nineteenth centuries emerge as colourful, rumbustious and very dangerous times to be at sea. Wrecks, looting, French and American privateers prowling, smuggling, heroism, negligence – all around beaches and headlands scarcely changed today. Magilligan Strand saw plenty of hectic action! In April 1794 the large French vessel *Revenge* was wrecked here: " … in 1779, as a privateer, she fought the *Sturdy Beggar* of Greenock and put in to Larne carrying a crew of 229". March 1806 saw a West Indiaman wrecked at Magilligan. This brig was looted, during which three crew and a black drummer were killed, the latter attempting to escape by floating out on his drum. But a few years later, in November 1810, a boat holding thirteen looters was lost during attempts to plunder the American ship *Castor* on the Tuns Bank. Weeks later, the hulk floated off and drifted along to Portrush "where she was taken possession of by Mark Kerr O'Neill Esq." The militia were summoned to the *Castor*, as they were to the Guinea trader *Surprise* when a thousand looters stormed her at Annalong in 1794, while Mr William Montgomery, landlord of Greyabbey, turned out the local Volunteers a few years later and fought those boarding the *Lagan*, a Belfast to London linen ship, ashore on Burial Island off Ballyhalbert. Smuggling in tobacco was rife on the Co. Down coast, so the shore around Cloughey was teeming with "the country people" in April 1744 when the *Freedom* went to pieces on the North Rock in a storm. She was bound for Rotterdam, and some of the crew were lost.

Another "Guineaman" or West African trader was the *Fame* which came ashore on Briggs Reef and then Groomsport on 10 November 1775. Not all wrecks engendered mayhem on the beach (although the poverty then should be borne in mind): when the *Glory* stranded in Bangor Bay on 7 November 1789, landlord Colonel Robert Ward had his pleasure boat manned to put out and save her crew. And not all wrecks by any means involved loss of life, though a serious one caused by the incompetent keeper of the Copelands beacon – "a worthless idle villain" – was the *Lady Loup* of Tarbert, wrecked on Islandmagee on 10 November 1772 with the loss of eight of the eleven crew and passengers. The *Lady Dunbar* was wrecked 400 yards south of Donaghadee harbour on 31 January 1811 with the loss, from twelve aboard, of all but one, a Belfast shoemaker who "providentially reached the beach on a plank."

An important wreck from which the mists have cleared is the *Wolf* (p.70) a warship lost just south of Kearney Point on 30 December 1748 with the loss of 91 of the 106 crew plus Captain Vachell's wife and sister-in-law. Still tantalising, though, is one of the most fascinating, the "Cedar Ship" at Tyrella (p.20). Captain Davis' papers tell how he was shown what appeared to be manacles or slave fetters in a farm out-house nearby! Recent attempts by archaeologists to uncover the site revealed a massively-built ship, but not one old enough to be her. Another historic wreck about which the truth has for long seemed out of reach is the *Amitie* or *Amite* (p.37) But now, as well as more cannon down there, clues have been found in the French archives, suggesting that this may have been the fate of the captured English brig *Friendship*. National Maritime Museum and French sources concur that an armed vessel of this name was taken as a prize in 1795. The bicentenary of 1798 stimulated a rush of new books on the subject, but none shed light on this forgotten, but significant, clandestine affair.

Wreck references can crop up in unlikely places, such as "Irish Whales and Whaling" by James Fairley (Blackstaff Press, 1981). A concern was set up in Derry, but the 400-ton vessel they purchased, the *Neptune*, sank in Ballycastle Bay in 1786. Nearby, in Cushendun Bay, the American ship *St. Tamany* was wrecked on 5 November 1799, one of the passengers bound for Virginia being drowned.

Moving into more modern, but equally dangerous, times, much has emerged on U-boat activities. It is now known that *U-79* which sank H.M.S. *Drake* (p.140) had also laid the mines that sank the *Lugano* and blew H.M.S. *Brisk* in two, one half going down. The same extraordinary day saw the stricken *Drake* collide with the steamer *Mendip Range*, which had to be beached near Ballycastle. The steamer's young apprentice, Potts, took photographs of the sinking cruiser just before the impact. Where are they now? The reminiscences of the commander of *U-19*, Johannes Spiess, reveal that the *Chirripo* (p.125) was torpedoed, not mined as British records state:

> "... the Englishmen at the surface must have thought that they have gone into a mine barricade since they do not try to attack us ... in March 1918 I had my nicest attack. I was blocking the entrance to the North Channel, near Rathlin. The high cliffs with the barns and lighthouses were a nice picture for a painting. Around noon there were six airships in sight, which were flying up and down the cliffs with the wind, just like it was a sport ..."

At 5 p.m. Spiess, forgetting his reverie, sank the *Calgarian* (p.140) two miles north of Rathlin with the loss of 48 lives. Further towards Islay lies the *Tuscania* (p.140) and I discovered that the story of her loss was compiled by a survivor, Leo Zimmerman of Milwaukee, who corresponded with the commander of *U-77*, Meyer, on behalf of the National *Tuscania* Survivors Association. There were over 2,000 survivors, mostly U.S. Army, and they were still meeting 60 years later and probably longer!

Scores of armed trawlers and requisitioned steam yachts guarded the vital North Channel. The "Clementine" (p.128) was actually *Clementina*, wrecked south of Torr Head (not in Red Bay) after collision with a Norwegian steamer on 5 August 1915. Another trawler the *G.M.V.* was mined off Larne on 13 March 1915. Less than an hour after the *Hunsdon* (p.39) was torpedoed, the Royal Fleet Auxiliary *Industry* was sunk by a different U-boat. This has been the most elusive of 20th century shipwrecks, as official sources reveal little. Twenty of the crew of twenty-four were lost, including six from Mersea Island, Essex. The wreck lies about a mile south-east of the South Rock lightship.

Despite – and sometimes because of – modern technology, ships still go aground on the Ulster coast almost annually. The large Russian fish factory ship *Serebryansk*, surprisingly navigating Strangford Lough narrows without a pilot in August 1986, touched a rock and had to summon a fishing fleet support tug for repairs. Within a few months in 1997-8 the coasters *Sea Humber* and *Northumbria Lass*, both bound from Glasgow to Belfast, unaccountably sailed directly aground at Grey Point and Bangor respectively. The last casualty of the century was the Dutch *Bernice*, which was put aground at Cultra on 18 December 1999 after springing a leak – but only a few months later a new millennium saw its initial incident when the German *Koralle* stranded at Killard Point near Strangford Lough entrance on 7 April 2000, at least eight miles west of her northward course.

On 14 January 1900, the *Maria* (p.164) was the first casualty of that new century, entering Coleraine. One wonders what Captain Shearer would think of the coasting trade 100 years on: G.P.S. satellite equipment that can fix a position to five metres; Navtext printers that issue navigation warnings; faxes from owners. Yet he was later well-known for taking his steamer *Montalto* through every possible channel – inside Dalkey Island or, nearer his Portrush home, between the Skerries and Ramore Head. These places and their flowing tides do not change. The barmouth at Coleraine still demands respect. And just as my original final paragraph foresaw, the vigilance of the rescue services is still needed. Portaferry lifeboat *Blue Peter V* was launched to the *Koralle*, and three days later saved the lives of two jet-skiers in the same area. What Captain Shearer would have to say about people careering round the coast on jet-skis is difficult to judge – but not as difficult as his opinion of ships sailing straight up on a beach in fine weather!